DIGNITY, DOGMATISM, AND SAME-SEX RELATIONSHIPS

DIGNITY, DOGMATISM, AND SAME-SEX RELATIONSHIPS:

What Science and Scripture Teach Us

Gilbert O. Rossing

▪ Resource *Publications* ▪

A Division of Wipf and Stock Publishers

DIGNITY, DOGMATISM, AND SAME-SEX RELATIONSHIPS:
What Science and Scripture Teach Us

Resource Publications
A Division of Wipf and Stock Publishers
199 W. 8th Ave., Suite 3
Eugene, OR 97401

www.wipfandstock.com

ISBN: 978-1-55635-999-6

Cataloging-in-Publication data:

Rossing, Gilbert O.

Dignity, Dogmatism, and Same-Sex Relationships.

x + 245 p.; cm. Includes bibliographic references and index.

1. Homosexuality—Religious aspects—Christianity. 2. Bible and homosexuality. 3. Homosexuality—Moral and ethical aspects. 4. Homosexuality—Research—History. 5. Homosexuality—Research—Social aspects. 6. Bible—Criticism, interpretation, etc. I. Title.

Manufactured in the U.S.A.

Contents

Acknowledgements vii

Preface xi

Abbreviations xiii

Chapter 1 Introduction 1

Chapter 2 Sex and Gender 7

      Personal Prologue: No Running Away 7

      Sexual Identity 14

      Sex Definition 22

      Gender Definition 24

      Gender Identification 31

      The Formation of Sexual Identity 39

Chapter 3 Gender Connectivity 43

      Personal Prologue: What You Don't Know 43

      Describing Gender Connectivity 49

      Defining the Attributes of Gender Connectivity .. 53

      Variations of Gender Connectivity 60

      Dissent Regarding Gender Connectivity 73

Chapter 4 Breaking from Traditional Bias 87

      Personal Prologue: Uncertain Certainties 87

      Ambiguity and Analogy 91

      Abolition Controversy Biases: Hierarchism
      and Elitism 100

Cosmology Controversy Bias: Geocentricity 106

Homosexuality Controversy Bias: Procreation .. 110

Problems with the Procreative Bias 120

Scrapping Sexual Reductionism 127

Chapter 5 Same-Sex Relationships and the Bible 135

Personal Prologue: I've Been Bible Thumped ... 135

Old Testament Apostasy and Same-Sex
Behavior 140

New Testament Apostasy and Same-Sex
Behavior 161

Theological Debate on the Homosexuality
Issue 173

Chapter 6 Ethical Principles 179

Personal Prologue: Talking about Sex 179

Grounding Our Ethics 183

The Knowledge of Good and Evil 190

The Image of God 195

It is Not Good to be Alone 199

Intimacy 206

Chapter 7 Conclusion 217

References & For Further Reading 225

Index 233

About the Author 239

Acknowledgements

I owe a great debt of gratitude to four nieces who, while visiting for a 1988 family reunion in Texas, listened to me expound my views about science, religion, and homosexuality. Kristina Lee Carey, an attorney living in the Netherlands, Kristina Wilken Vetter, an attorney in the California Bay area, Stephanie Wilken, an Oregon artist and paralegal, and Ramona Carey, an international affairs specialist in Washington, DC, agreed as one about the importance of what I had just discussed, and that I should develop it into a book. Without their initial challenge, I may never have started this project.

Very early on, when the book's content was little more than summary topics defining possible chapter subjects, I submitted the material for review to Rev. Michael Piazza, then pastor of Cathedral of Hope (in Dallas, Texas), the largest gay and lesbian Christian church in the world. I admired the eloquent lucidity of his preaching and the personal relevance of his theology. He recommended keeping my book personal and affirmed my intent to pursue the project.

Since that time, several supporters kept after me to write my book. Jerry and Nancy Petty, dear friends from Irving, Texas, would not let me abandon the project when I became weary or discouraged. Else Schardt, a supportive sister-in-law, willingly read my book and made helpful editorial corrections.

I am also deeply grateful to the highly qualified, critical readers who took their valuable time to read my manuscript, and who, after reading it, believed it had sufficient value to warrant their constructive criticism and encouragement: James L. Bailey, PhD, Professor Emeritus of New Testament at Wartburg Seminary, Dubuque, IA; Craig Nessan, PhD, Dean, Wartburg Theological Seminary, Dubuque, IA; Donald G. Murphy, PhD, retired Director, Office of Extramural Staff Training, Office of the Director, National Institutes of Health; John C. Bean, PhD, Professor of English and Consulting Professor for Writing and Assessment, Seattle University, Seattle, WA; Rosalie R. Bean, Composition Instructor and Coordinator of the Writing Center, South Seattle Community College, Seattle, WA; Patrick Chapman, PhD, anthropology professor at South Puget Sound Community College, Olympia, WA; Sean McDowell, PhD, Associate Professor, English Department, Seattle University, Seattle, WA; Andrea Rossing McDowell, PhD, Visiting Assistant Professor, English Department, Seattle University, Seattle, WA.; Dayna Fischtein, Project Coordinator, Center for Sexual Health Promotion, Department of Applied Health Science, HPER, Indiana University, Bloomington, IN; J. Bradley Blankenship, Project Coordinator, Center for Sexual Health Promotion, Department of Higher Education Student Affairs, Indiana University, Bloomington, IN.

I am indebted to Seth Goldstein, Rabbi of Temple Beth Hatfiloh, Olympia, Washington, who provided helpful insight into the Hebrew texts I reference in describing ethical principles.

Above all, I am grateful to my immediate family for their support of the project and their patience with me in my endeavor. I particularly cite my sons, Peter and Jonathan, who have the most cause for concern about my writing this book. It is, after all, a book that would never have been written if they were not the dignified, gay men that they are. And so they have been willing to let me write my book even though, quite clearly, their personal lives are highly visible within the text. My very capable daughter Andrea and her likewise capable husband, Sean, both professional academicians, offered advice and counsel in many conversations on how to proceed with this project. When my journey of understanding clashed with the moral values of my oldest daughter, Yvonne, and her husband, Douglas, who unequivocally condemn homosexuality, I felt emotional pain. For this I am also grateful, not for the pain, but for the experience that enabled me to identify with many gay and lesbian persons who suffer similar pain when family members do not accept them.

To my wife Beth, I owe the most gratitude of all. In many ways this book is *our* book. We have walked the journey together. We have talked, thought, and then talked some more about all the issues contained in this book. She read and reread much of the manuscript, and given me invaluable counsel and correction. In other ways, this book is *my* book. At her expense, this book consumed large quantities of my time and energy, which she would have preferred to be spent in more mutual activities. Yet, she remained patient and granted me space in which to think, refine, rewrite, and wrestle with the material through the writing and editing process. And when she became frustrated with what she perceived as the 'obtuseness' of gay-intolerant oppositionists, she ordered me to get busy with the book because, "People need to read it!"

Preface

I am deeply indebted to the hundreds of gay, lesbian, bisexual and transgender individuals I have met over the years, many of whom I'm honored to call friends. I write this book because of them, but not *for* them. My GLBT friends, most of whom possess secure self-understanding, do not need my book or my understanding of homosexuality to help them individuate. Nevertheless, I welcome GLBT readers in the hope that they find something of value to recommend to their straight friends and families.

And so, when I think about the audience for this book, I think broadly of a thoughtful reader in the movable middle of the American culture war over the legal recognition of same-sex relationships. Many readers who fit this description are not religious. Nevertheless, I hope these readers will consider seriously the religious discourse of this book, because anyone involved in the culture war—which includes most of American society—cannot avoid the religious issue. Every person involved in the culture war confronts the religious issue if for no other reason than because the antagonists summon 'traditional moral values' against the legal recognition of same-sex relationships.

'Traditional moral values' have roots that sink deeply into religious moral dogma, even those values that seem more secular than sectarian. Consequently, though many do not participate in organized religion, *nonreligious* people may remain as loyal to traditional moral values as the *religious* person. Therefore, the culture conflict draws a person into a substantially religious domain regardless of personal religiosity. Although this book addresses these religious issues, I intentionally minimize the use of religious code language distinctive of any particular religious group in order to make the religious discussions in this book accessible to the nonreligious reader.

This book most assuredly addresses the religious reader as well; specifically, reflective church laypersons and clergy, counselors, and chaplains whose interest in religious issues extends beyond personal spirituality and church programs.

I also write for students and practitioners in the areas of psychology, sociology, and theology—but not necessarily for professional academics, because I do not offer this book as an academic study grounded within a certain discipline. Nevertheless, I hope that professional scholars will be engaged enough in my discussions to pursue the issues with more exacting scientific and theological expertise.

In particular, I have one specific reader in mind: an earnest and faithful churchgoer, whose interest is more pragmatic than philosophical. This reader remains reserved but open toward the issue of recognizing same-sex relationships, and has not yet decided the extent to which society should grant individual rights to gays and lesbians, not least whether this reader's church should commit to taking an open and affirming stance toward gay or lesbian couples and families.

Wherever readers stand in their attitudes toward same-sex relationships, I hope this book offers sufficient food for thought in order to provide guidance for achieving greater understanding, particularly as readers become increasingly aware of and respectful toward those gay or lesbian persons who may be seated in an office cubicle or a church pew nearby.

Abbreviations

Revised Standard Version   RSV

Hebrew Bible / Old Testament:

Gen	Genesis	Isa	Isaiah
Exod	Exodus	Ezek	Ezekiel
Deut	Deuteronomy	Amos	Amos
Judg	Judges		

New Testament:

Matt	Matthew	1 Cor	First Corinthians
Acts	Acts	2 Pet	Second Peter
Rom	Romans	Jude	Jude

CHAPTER ONE

Introduction

In May 2008, California's State Supreme Court handed down a decision declaring the State's ban on same-sex marriage unconstitutional. Predictable diatribes from those who oppose social acceptance of gay or lesbian relationships railed against the 'tyranny' of 'activist judges,' and decried the decision as one more example of godless liberalism corrupting the nation. That same month, the National Coalition of Anti-Violence Programs released a report showing that in 2007, violent attacks against gay, lesbian, bisexual, and transgender individuals increased 24 percent from the previous year. Part of the increase reflects a growing willingness among GLBT individuals to report such violence. Not coincidentally, however, a significant increase in violence emerged in those areas of the nation where religious groups vehemently opposed campaigns supporting domestic partnership benefits for same-sex couples. Each step forward on behalf of social justice for GLBT people encounters renewed, potentially violent resistance against further progress. With the recent decision of the California Supreme Court, the culture war will likely heat up even more and will also spawn more retaliatory abuse against gays and lesbians.

My personal involvement in the culture conflict over homosexuality began more than twenty years ago, in the early 1980s, when lines increasingly solidified between gay and lesbian activists, and religious and social conservatives. At that time, adversaries against homosexuality felt secure behind their battlements. Societal conditions favored the support of religious and social dogmas against homosexuality. Ahead lay an unprecedented determination within the GLBT community to come out of the closet and claim a rightful place in society. A rightful place no longer meant discretely standing at the fringes of the arts and entertainment, but standing front and center in academia, the military, the corporate office, the classroom, the legislature, the court room, even the pulpit, and in many other places where many heterosexuals remained unaware of a GLBT presence. The legalization of 'gay marriage' in Massachusetts and Canada, and the growing number of American businesses granting health benefits to same-sex couples have further strengthened the influences that battered once-secure lines of defense that social and religious conservatives had raised against homosexual persons. Although interpreted by moral watchdogs as an 'in your face' campaign to force the 'gay agenda' upon American society, the television and movie industry intrepidly presented gay and lesbian characters as normal members of society rather than pathetically comic or malignant perversions.

As time passed, a communication gulf widened even further between proponents and opponents of normalizing homosexuality and gender variants. This breach grew because each side grounded their arguments upon two very different premises. The proponents grounded their argument upon the premise that individual rights and social justice, like same-sex domestic partnership benefits, formed the core issue concerning social acceptance of gays and lesbians. The opponents based their argument upon the inviolability of traditional moral values regarding homosexuality as well as the Judeo-Christian scripture they claimed upheld these values. This divide appeared clearly during the 2007 Washington State Legislative hearings on same-sex domestic partnership legislation. Liberal Democrats stressed the justice of passing domestic partnership legislation while conservative Republicans raised the issue of granting special rights to a class of people identifiable only by their "immoral" behavior. Personally, I was amazed at the extent to which Republican legislators in the Washington State Senate referred to Bible denunciations against same-sex practice and righteously invoked the name of God during highly partisan floor debate preceding passage of the domestic partnership legislation . . . by one vote.

Without a doubt, over the past years of the culture war, the trend of battle favors those who support the GLBT community as a matter of social justice over those who resist the 'gay agenda' as a matter of moral and religious principle. My personal development, however, did not rest upon either premise. My affirmation of GLBT persons did not hinge on social justice, nor would I condemn GLBT persons on the basis of traditional moral values. Rather, I pursued scientific information to discover the nature of homosexuality apart from any prior moral judgments; and I investigated theological issues to establish the life situation the ancient writers of the Bible faced as they addressed same-sex behavior. Science and theology informed the process by which I came to terms with a very personal encounter with homosexuality. As my research progressed, I became more convinced that the cultural conflict cannot be resolved by perpetuating a dichotomy between justice and moral value; between secular and religious points of view. They need not and should not be on opposite sides of an irreconcilable divide. Instead, they represent two dimensions of a common challenge to responsibly bring together what we *can know* and what we *should value* about our shared human condition.

Justice cannot exist without knowledge of fact or of persons, because justice cannot become truly just without the empirical information that exposes our social near-sightedness. We cannot tolerate ignorance of circumstances in which *justice* for *us* imposes *injustice* upon *others*. Neither can justice exist without faith in values. *Justice* needs faith in values that enable equity for every citizen even when no guarantee of equality exists.

In the same manner, moral values cannot exist without knowledge of fact or of persons. In too many episodes throughout human history, poorly formed moral values—warped by ignorance, superstition, and fear—sanctioned the perpetration of terrible cruelty upon other human beings. Moral values cannot exist without faith in a transcendent moral accountability to which every person without exception is responsible. Moral values shaped by vested self-interest—especially vested religious self-interest—risk the formation of laws that sanction the excesses of the elite and truculently reprehend the foibles of ordinary people.

In encouraging a positive, affirming view of same-sex relationships, *Dignity, Dogmatism, and Same-sex Relationships* synthesizes knowledge from primarily two areas: science and religion. Knowledge from science teaches that GLBT people, like heterosexual people, are products of complex biological and environmental factors that shape human sexual identity. Knowledge from Biblical studies teaches that the historical context in which the ancient writers of the Bible lived and their issues with same-sex behaviors have a distinct difference from the contemporary issues with same-sex behavior in our historical context.

The book presents its case in the form of both narrative and discourse. Through narrative, it details my personal journey toward understanding homosexuality. Through discourse, it communicates the intellectual journey that shaped my argument upholding the dignity of those persons whose sexual identity is other than heterosexual.

The narrative begins with the day our oldest son told my wife, Beth, and me that he was gay. At the time, I was pastor of a Lutheran Church (ELCA), a circumstance that made our personal journey rather public. Together, Beth and I journeyed through months of struggling with the new reality in our lives as we sought information about homosexuality in books, journals, and magazines. The journey did not slow even when we learned to accept our son for *who he was*, not merely accept *him* because he was our child. Nor did the journey cease after completely 'outing' ourselves as parents of a gay child. Our journey further expanded when our *second* son told us he also was gay.

The discourse emerges from an intellectual journey toward understanding homosexuality that, like the personal journey, is also continuous and expanding. In the beginning, I cared about information about homosexuality only to help me understand my gay son. But soon, I realized that I needed to reconcile understanding about my son with larger issues raised by traditional religious judgments about homosexuality and by exposure to issues of concern important within the gay community. I therefore revisited Biblical and theological issues about homosexuality that previously I studied superficially; I could not merely accommodate my son's homosexuality by glossing over Church teaching. Also, I sought scientific information that might provide me with a more objective perspective about homosexuality; accepting my gay son must be based on more than subjective, parental love.

Thus I plowed forward into the tangle of scientific evidence, theory, assumptions, and counter-assumptions concerning human sexuality, even though at the time, conflicting opinions existed about the validity of some of the scientific research about homosexuality. Via the reading of books, journals, magazines, and web pages I developed insights into the empirical evidence relative to homosexuality. Via acquaintance and friendship with literally hundreds of gay, lesbian, bisexual, and transgender people I acquired insight into the personal experiences of persons who belong to sexual minorities.

At the beginning of my research, plunging into the theological fray about homosexuality proved more problematic. Living in West Texas in the early 1980s, I could find little theological work written about homosexuality other than traditional judgments against it. One experience that triggered my drive to look beyond traditional moral censure was my personal study of Romans 1:18-32. In that Bible passage, the Apostle Paul identifies idolaters as those ungodly and wicked people who should know the truth about God, but who exchange that truth for a lie. Evidence of the idolaters' wickedness included the practice of dishonoring their bodies with unnatural acts of same-sex behavior.

One day as I pored over the passage, the obvious truth about my son struck me forcibly: though he was someone who practiced same-sex behavior, he was not, *ipso facto*, an idolater. I began to question the kind of logic that concludes that anyone who practices same-sex behavior is ungodly in the same way pagans who practiced same-sex behavior were ungodly. Clearly, given that logic, the terms *Christian* and *homosexual* mutually exclude each other. But I met many devoutly religious people who were indeed Christian *and* homosexual. This disconnect with conventional moral censure compelled me to probe into what the Bible actually does and does not say about the contemporary manifestation of what has come to be called, only in the last 200 years or so, a "homosexual orientation."

Dignity, Dogmatism, and Same-sex Relationships represents the outcome of my personal and intellectual journey. It is not a chronological autobiography of my life experience. Rather, it offers reflections of one who, having completed the most arduous part of my journey, tries to report the overall impact on my life and convictions. The prologues that begin each of the five chapters narrate the personal experiences that ultimately became fodder for intellectual reflection about corresponding issues. After each prologue, the chapter continues with a discourse upon understandings and conclusions that resulted from my excavation of scientific and theological issues. Throughout, I underscore the *dignity* of those engaged in same-sex relationships that the *dogmatism* of Western Religion in particular commonly dismisses, and even now seems unready to respect. In appealing for understanding and respect for GLBT people, I challenge the moralistic insistence of so many religious dogmatists who characterize as "sinful perversions" those who love someone of the same sex, a characterization not consistent with either scientific evidence or with careful reading of Scripture.

CHAPTER TWO

Sex and Gender

Personal Prologue: No Running Away

"Say it!" Discomfort, crawling over my back and legs, scraped my nerves raw with impatience. Even a comfortable bed feels torturous when one sits like bent pipe cleaners for too long: it was two hours and counting. Slumped again into semi-prone position, I hitched myself upright one more time and silently shouted, "Just say it!"

Two hours earlier, our oldest son approached his mother and me in the kitchen. His rigid brow and intensely focused eyes told us he was not about to request an ordinary favor. "I'd like to talk to you," he said. We recognized that his gravity required an immediate response: close our mouths, and open our ears.

After we entered our bedroom, closed the door, and settled on our bed, he paced, he hemmed, he hawed, he stammered and started, sat on the floor, sat on the bed, knelt by the bed, used the toilet: but, whatever compelling distress hammered inside him, he could not speak. Bewildered, we tried to reassure him. "Just start talking, the rest will come." But the unspeakable found no voice.

As we waited, a sense of what he wanted to tell us rose faintly in my mind. Days earlier he came home wearing an earring in one ear, a new fashion for young men at the time. Most of the men, I thought, were gay. But I recalled that some non-gay men also wore earrings, but in the opposite ear so as not to be mistaken for gay. I didn't like the earring, but parental fashion likes or dislikes have little impact upon adult children. The day he showed up at home wearing an earring I simply said to him, "You better wear it in the proper ear or people will think you are gay." He faintly, politely chuckled.

Now, with discomfort and impatience peaking, I wanted the waiting to be over. "Just say it! Say it! You're gay!" But I bit my tongue. Finally, the long hours of inner turmoil and agony broke: He said it, not in those precise words, but with the same meaning: "I have a boyfriend."

That revelation started us on a life-changing journey similar to that of many parents who walked before us and many more who will follow. There is no running away: some parents reject their children while others learn to embrace them, but children's revelation of atypical sexual identity *compels* parents to respond.

Fortunately, the first steps in our journey were *not* to denounce our son, kick him out the door in righteous anger, or induce guilt with pitiful ranting about how much he hurt us. Indeed, there was pain, some anger. There was also guilt—"what did we do wrong?" and shame—"what will people think of us?" and confusion—"what happened to make him do this?"

My initial response to him was, I recall, very parental: no, I confess, I was patronizing. I did not want to run him off with denigration, but I felt I might, at least initially, persuade him to reconsider this immoral dalliance by offering the guidance of my "fatherly wisdom." Having read about human sexuality, I had learned that the hypothalamus is the center of our primitive brain functions, responsible for, among other things, triggering the release of those hormones that prompted sexual urges. I remembered reading an assertion that the primary sex organ of the human body was not the genitals, but the brain, particularly the hypothalamus: part brain control center and part hormone regulator. Being directly connected to the higher brain function as well as the master gland, the pituitary, the hypothalamus acted as the modulator (hormone system) and translator (brain) responsible for critical aspects of primitive sexual function such as sexual arousal and differentiation of male and female mating behaviors.[1]

Armed with this incipient knowledge, I informed him that genitalia, specifically the penis, have no cognitive awareness of their own. Rather, we use the higher brain functions of the *mind* to judge when and how to use genitalia appropriately. Therefore, I told him, "You need to control your mind, the cognitive organizer of your sexual desire, in order to use your genitals for the good purpose for which they were designed" (thus insinuating that proper genital behavior for a male involved phallic penetration in sexual intercourse with the woman he married). He curtly retorted, "It doesn't have to be put in anything."

I didn't catch the nuance in his remonstrance at the time, but I came to understand later that he was telling me that my reduction of his gay identity to the use of his genitals was a gross error. Like many heterosexual persons, I defined homosexuality exclusively as a behavior—specifically a genital behavior—that results from unbridled homoerotic desire. Heterosexual persons almost never reduce their own sexual identity to a genital function, yet they do so to homosexual persons out of the assumption that homosexuality is little more than a behavioral perversion of the heterosexual norm. Our son's retort to my reductionism of his sexuality told me that, at minimum, I had much to learn about homosexuality. Unless we intended to be resolute in our naïve and condemning stand against homosexuality, we needed to learn more about human sexuality in order to understand our son.

Far more intuitively than I, Beth (my wife) immediately understood her need to learn. Her initial response was to inquire, not like a prosecuting attorney who asks questions to win a case, but like a traveler asking directions for getting along in a foreign country. After the night our son "came out," she said to me, "I want to find out more about this. I thought I knew everything, but

---

[1] When researching literature on the nature of homosexuality, I rediscovered information about the role of the hypothalamus in relation to sexual behavior in Mondimore, *A Natural History of Homosexuality*, 108–14.

I really know nothing. I'm going to the library to find books or articles about homosexuality." One of the next days she headed to the public library and returned with three or four books with suggestive title words like 'sex' and 'homosexual' blazing on the covers. With her determination to learn, I joined her, lackadaisically at first, in the first stage of our study of homosexuality.

How much did we study? Both of us soon realized that we faced a circumstance when urgent necessity compelled us to research information about human sexuality with far more than casual gleaning. Our research expanded beyond any previous research we had done on any other subject. Though unable to match that of the scholar, our research was in sufficient depth to, at minimum, learn the geography of the subject reasonably well, at least well enough to become familiar with its highways, though not its byways. Certainly the research was sufficient to produce new perceptions, deeper understanding, modified conclusions, and more passionate interest in continued exploration of sexuality in general and homosexuality in particular.

What I previously knew about human sexuality I started learning early in life. I was about seven years old when I went to the freak show at a carnival that stopped in my town. In addition to the bearded lady and the monkey man, another feature was an infant's cadaver displayed in a sealed jar of formaldehyde. Above the jar was a placard that read 'Baby With Two Sexes.' As a seven-year-old in 1943, I didn't remember encountering the term 'sex' before seeing that sign. I knew there were boys, I knew there were girls, and I knew there were more differences between them than hair length, clothes style, and toy preference. But I didn't know that 'boys,' 'girls,' and much more was subsumed under a single term: 'Sex.' So, I really didn't know what I was supposed to look for in that jar, and besides, I would have been a little embarrassed to gawk between the legs of that baby. When I asked my parents later what 'sex' meant, they quickly brushed off my question by telling me it referred to boys and girls. Well, I already knew about boys and girls, what was I supposed to know about *sex*?

I learned from early Sunday school lessons that God created human beings male and female by simple fiat; in His own image God made them. Of course, beyond the generalities of man or woman, boy or girl, male or female, the particulars of sex were not appropriate for Sunday School lessons.

I also learned along the way that 'male' and 'female' had to do with certain body parts in which fantastically powerful sensations occurred. Because of the power of these body parts, some pretty restrictive taboos applied to boy/girl relations. Dancing was one such taboo because it put those male body parts close enough to a girl to awaken 'inappropriate' sensations. Temptations aroused by dancing led to 'shameful' misuse of those body parts, thereby causing unwanted pregnancy, the socially stigmatized condition of unwed mothers. 'Lust' was the term applied to the drive to have sex: fundamentally, it implied debauchery. Lust was condonable only if channeled within the levee of the marriage bed. Allowed to flow out of its banks into infidelity and perversion, lust generated a terrible gush of sin.

This view of sex, subtly and sometimes not so subtly implied within the Minnesotan, Scandinavian, pietistic Lutheran environment of my childhood, laid out the basic framework in which I and a number of my cultural peers came to understand sex. Infused with a sense that sex was mostly about a natural, human tendency toward depravity, it seemed imperative to define narrow boundaries around sexual feelings and behavior. Sexual restraint was good; sexual licentiousness was bad. Sexual abstinence before marriage was the not-always-attainable ideal.

The sexual revolution of the second half of the twentieth century breached the walls of narrow boundaries. Becoming an adult in the early decades of the revolution brought new exposure to the nature of human sexuality. On the one hand, sexual behavior became more culturally transparent through the "free love" of the counterculture, in art movies, in XXX-rated explicit materials, and via the trumpeting of an unrepressed, sexual freedom in the "Age of Aquarius." On the other hand, church groups responded—with scholarly studies, sex education curriculum for youth and parents, and candid sermons—by examining the issue of human sexuality more responsibly, and by giving a more positive value to sexual pleasure within the boundaries of marriage.

Today, a culture war rages in United States society between those who would return to earlier, more repressive sexual boundaries, and those who want to expand them even farther. On the one hand, our society grows more and more punitive in responding to certain of those out-of-bounds behaviors, while simultaneously extending the boundaries to include behaviors unacceptable to a previous generation. Legal penalties for child molestation are increasingly severe, while social mores, tempered by new and commonly used birth-control methods, extend the acceptability of recreational sex to mutually consenting unmarried couples. Economic independence and reproductive choices for women change the whole landscape of sex and marriage for both men and women: marriage is no longer deemed necessary, child-bearing is a personal option, and sex is an enjoyable amusement requiring no long term commitments.

Homosexuality lies in the middle of this culture war. After centuries of condemnation and castigation of individuals known to be engaging in same-sex behavior, Gay Pride, in the last three decades, eviscerated homosexuality's shame among a large segment of the GLBT community. Public self-affirmation by gays and lesbians also has helped diminish the percentage of the general population that censures same-sex relationships. Instead, we now encounter favorable social recognition of loving, enduring relationships between people of the same gender. The positive, social recognition of same-sex couples lends support for the push toward equal marriage rights. However, even with this cultural moderation, many people continue to see same-sex relationships as an insidious erosion of the stability of Western civilization, and press for legislative initiatives to protect the traditional one man–one woman structure of marriage. When and where the battles will be won or lost is difficult to predict.

Since that unforgettable evening when we learned our son was gay, Beth and I have experienced personally this maelstrom of cultural conflict surrounding homosexuality. As a result, we now feel driven to share the convictions we have formed from our research of human sexuality, particularly homosexuality. Our journey continues amidst this turmoil because we still have so much more to learn, and also because so much more to learn emerges almost daily. The ongoing biological, anthropological, psychological, sociological, historical, and theological investigations into the nature of human sexuality open unimagined insights into the persons we are. It is an exciting and eye-opening adventure to roam the range of current investigations in biogenetics, gender studies, cultural history, neuropsychiatry, and so on.

The fascinating discoveries revealed by our research into human sexuality are *not* of paramount importance to Beth and me in comparison to the invaluable insights we have gained that enable a better understanding of our sons personally and homosexual persons generally. With these insights, we now recognize the importance of reappraising our acquired beliefs, assumptions, and attitudes. This reappraisal is perhaps the most important and demanding aspect of our continuing studies because it represents more than an *intellectual* adjustment to previously unchallenged ideas. Rather, it involves risking the loss of personal relationships with family and friends. It involves finding the fortitude to stand firm under false accusations against our character. In the decade after our son came out as gay, certain relatives and acquaintances subtly and openly averred the perverted, insidiousness of homosexuality. We had to decide whether we would, in silent shame, closet the truth about our son, or boldly, with as much pride as when we speak of our daughters and their husbands, talk about our son and his partner. We also had to come to terms with whether we would assent to those who judged our convictions of faith to be heretical, or would trust with certainty the integrity of our conscience.

Our continuing journey is important to us for another reason. We hope that what we have learned will encourage gay people and their families, who may have internalized the caustic and destructive anathemas of homonegative moral judges, to confidently walk their own journey to discover or affirm their human dignity in the face of condemnatory moral dogmatism. Whether anathemas are blatant denunciations that "God hates fags," or graciously intended assurances that Jesus forgives and restores those who repent of their homosexual lifestyle, anathemas of any kind increase the potential for self-condemnation among homosexual persons who gave themselves totally to God but were not 'cured' of homosexuality, and among parents who thought they'd done everything godly parenting requires to ensure their kids heterosexuality, but "failed."

Sexual Identity

What is sexual identity? The answer seems simple! Every individual is either male or female. Sex and gender are elementary, biological conditions of nature. Equally plain, procreation requires a male and a female. So it seems!

Prerequisite to anything else one might say about sexual identity, we must assert that every human person is a sexual being if for no other reason than that each of us carries in our genetic makeup at least one sex chromosome, though normally two, yet sometimes four or five. The biological fact of life is that not one of us chose to be sexual, regardless of whether we identify as heterosexual, homosexual, bisexual, transgender, or asexual. Being sexual creatures is one of the core biological realities of human nature. *What* we are as human beings is that we are sexual beings; but *who* we are as sexual beings, our sexual identity, is a matter of far greater complexity and richness.

My perception of sexual identity, before I was compelled to reexamine it, was wholly binary: either/or, this or that, one or the other. An individual's sexual identity was male or female, man or woman, masculine or feminine. This binary view organized the mental filing cabinet where I stored orderly folders about gender roles, gender relationships, and good and bad sexual behaviors. To be sure, it was a bit problematic deciding on the right binary folder to hold information about sissies, tomboys, effeminate men, and masculine women. And finally, when it came to my gay son, I was compelled to acknowledge that it was impossible for me to stuff him neatly into my filing cabinet's binary catalog.

I was binary not only in how I perceived the nature of sexual identity, but also in my perception of the underlying cause of sexual identity. In my view, the cause of our sexual identity was biological ('essentialist'/nature), while the cause of particular sexual characteristics and behaviors was environmental ('constructionist'/nurture). According to this binary scheme, I was biologically male, a sexual characteristic essential to my being because it was a result of nature. My love of football, in contrast, was environmentally caused because it was a characteristic constructed through the nurturing childhood experiences of my home and community. Of course football itself, according to the convention, was an appropriate interest of boys because they were biologically adapted to athletics. What was essentially environmental about my love of football, therefore, was only my athletic preference, not my natural masculine athleticism.

I also assumed there was a binary division between male and female sexual feelings and functions that was completely biological. Unfettered by any kind of restraint, we'd all just 'do what comes naturally' like the birds and the bees. The values we are taught and the experiences we have as we grow up construct the moral environment in which an individual's will, mind, and emotion cooperate to form the kinds of behavior we exhibit in company with others of the same sex or of the opposite sex. Therefore, conditioned by influences or temptations toward promiscuous or indecent behaviors, certain kinds of male/female behavior were therefore environmentally caused.

These "simple," binary assumptions about sexual identity became personally devastating to us in 1987, the year our son came out to us. If sexual behavior is the outcome of environmental conditioning, consequently then I must have been responsible for creating the major part of the environment in which our son developed his interest in homosexual behavior. Scientific psychiatric studies widely touted by censorious voices in the 1970s and 1980s identified a typical home environment for producing homosexuality: a household characterized by a strong, dominant mother and a weak, emotionally absent father. A boy nurtured in such an environment proved at risk of an arrested transference of affection. As an infant, the baby's affection focused upon the mother object, the feminine figure that nursed, cradled, and nurtured the infant. In normal development, a child should necessarily extend its affection to include the other parent, the masculine figure. The male affection object, however, if not adequately filled by the father during the vital years of early childhood development, becomes an anxious void in the child's psyche that later, in the critical stages of adolescent sexual development, may be filled by the affections of another available male. The logical implication of having a homosexual son, therefore, was that we were dysfunctional parents: the constructors of an environment that nurtured homosexuality in our son.

Confronted by this disturbing assertion, we analyzed and reflected on who we were and the way we nurtured our children. Something did not fit. We were not the stereotypical at-fault-pair comprised of a strong, dominant mother and a weak, absent father. Oddly, given the environment in which I developed, it seemed to me that *I*, rather than my son, should have been more likely to stray toward homosexual behavior. In reflecting on my own upbringing, I recalled my mother as highly dominant and strong, and my father, because of his work, as both physically and emotionally absent.

The disconnect between the conventional view about the cause of homosexuality and my own personal circumstances, together with the insights that emerged from my research, eroded the authenticity of my binary perception of sexual identity—both its nature and its causes. I began to see that biological *and* environmental factors influence the characteristics of each person's sexual identity through and through. By 'biological' I include genetic and hormonal factors, as well as physical processes like growth and digestion, etc. By 'environment' I include not only our social environment (among whom we live), but also our physical environment (where we live.) In other words, our family nurturing (social environment) may be impacted by the stress of urban living or the isolation of rural life, as well as by the compromised air quality of the city or the exposure to agricultural chemicals on the farm (physical environment). Our environment influences characteristics of human sexual identity that seem to be most determined by nature. Conversely, nurturing factors that appear most to influence characteristics of our sexual identity involve the simultaneous influence of biological factors.

In short, the entirety of sexual identity is biologically *and* environmentally determined. What remains not merely ambiguous but perhaps not even provable is the precise allocation between biological and environmental influences upon any given characteristic of sexual identity, and how much or little intervention applies to each one. Clinical observation cites probable sources of biological and/or environmental influence upon these enigmatic characteristics of our sexual identity. It seems less able to define categorically what determined the development of certain distinct attributes, or to prove empirically the cause of this or that characteristic over the time that a person's sexual identity develops.

Sexual identity, therefore, is a set of characteristics for which the sources interlink and intertwine much like the plane of a Möbius strip.[2] It is not always clear at just what point the source of a particular characteristic crosses over from biologically determined to environmentally determined, and vice versa.

---

[2] A Möbius strip is a one sided surface formed by twisting one end of a rectangular strip through 180 degrees about the longitudinal axis of the strip and attaching this end to the other. http://www.dictionary.com (accessed June 9, 2008). Holding a pencil tip to the surface while pulling the strip forward, a line will be drawn on both sides of the strip without lifting the pencil.

The complexity of sexual identity is given unwitting assent by the way we reference various characteristics observed in ordinary experience. On the surface, identifying sex or gender is quite simple, as when casually we acknowledge that "he is a man" or "she is a woman." But if we say that a boy is a 'sissy' or that a girl is a 'tomboy,' we already introduce descriptions indicating more than that a person is completely and categorically a male or female. We use the terms variably as when we say, "I thought she was a man" or "he looks like a woman," or when we compliment a man for the 'feminine' trait of caring or tell a woman that she needs to develop a 'masculine' toughness to achieve success in a male-dominated, business environment. 'Male' and 'female' *seem* clear and simple terms to assign; yet in reality they become fuzzy and complicated when we try to describe masculine or feminine gender attributes precisely. In this verbal 'fuzziness' about what it means to be male or female, we disclose a basic, even if unacknowledged recognition of the complex ambiguity about sexual identity. We imply that although we perceive a person to be either male or female, that person might also manifest gender characteristics typically associated with a gender other than what we expect. Such common but ambiguous terminology indicates we know more intuitively than we think just how much more complex human sexuality is than a simple binary division between male and female.

The complex, wide scope of sexual identity, implicit in this "fuzziness," provides the proper context in which to consider homosexuality.[3] During the process of my study, this fascinating complexity enabled me to situate the question "What did we do wrong?" within the *whole* context of sexual identity, rather than

---

[3] I begin using the terms 'homosexual' and 'heterosexual' as though they are binary opposites because we are involved in a culture war in which the terms 'homosexual' and 'heterosexual' are standard coinage. Later I will address the complexity of sexual identity development that makes such binary language inadequate.

simply considering homosexuality an aberrant 'behavior' isolated from the full scope of sexual identity.

I believe we must concede that at present, while a biological cause for homosexuality has much well-documented evidence, the precise biological cause is still debatable. At the same time, no complete evidence can categorically prove exact environmental causes of homosexuality. Nevertheless, from the weight of evidence on both sides, both biological and environmental factors clearly influence the way sexual identity develops in an individual's life experience. A complex interaction of causal factors defies making a simple delineation of reasons why one person is homosexual and another heterosexual. The basic factors that determine the development of homosexuality are apparently no more nor less complex than those determining the development of heterosexuality. Understanding the enigma of homosexual sexual identity, therefore, *must* be placed within this expanded context of sexual identity.

Describing the entire scope of human sexual identity, including the determination of categories that encompass its various attributes, constitutes a major task within the academies of biology, sociology, psychology, philosophy, anthropology, feminist and gender studies, etc. Some scholars of human sexuality take a constructionist view of human sexual identity, thereby emphasizing the interaction between individuals and their social/cultural environment that defines sexual identity. Biologist and social activist, Anne Fausto-Sterling claims that sexual identity, defined by the labels 'man' or 'woman,' is a social decision: science has a limited role only in making gender decisions because only our beliefs about gender can define our sex.[4] Sandra Lipsitz Bem, Professor of Psychology and Women's studies at Cornell University, argues on behalf of an ideal society in which polarizing concepts like masculine, feminine, heterosexual, homosexual, or bisexual would be absent from our cultural consciousness in the same way that a concept of male or female eye-color, or

---

[4] Fausto-Sterling, *Sexing the Body*, 3.

hetero-eye-color or homo-eye-color is absent.[5] Recognizing that such an ideal is highly utopian, she recommends that instead of eliminating male and female gender categorization, we greatly expand the number of categories we use to identify the broad spectrum of what gender means.

Other scholars take an essentialist point of view of human sexuality, emphasizing the biological causations of sexual identity. David Buss, Professor of Psychology at the University of Texas and head of the Individual Differences and Evolutionary Psychology Area, supports the notion of sexual differences between men and women as being evolutionary adaptations of sexual selection. One theory of human sexuality—Sexual Strategies Theory—identifies innate desire and the consequences of desire to be the foundation of all sexuality and human mating. Sexual attraction tactics, competition for mating selection, conflict between the sexes, conjugal success or failure, mate retention and mate harmony are organic mechanisms produced only by evolutionary selection within a species.[6] Louanne Brizendine, M.D., Neuropsychiatrist at the University of California–San Francisco, and founder of the Women's and Teen Girl's Mood and Hormone Clinic, claims that biological differences between the male and the female brain lead to differences in the social behavior of men and women. The behavior is controlled by two neurohormones made in the pituitary and the hypothalamus: vasopressin and oxytocin. The male brain uses vasopressin, the female primarily oxytocin and estrogen.[7]

Another approach to the study of human sexuality is the behaviorist approach. Noting the diversity of human sexual behavior, and the difference in phenomenon depending on location and social contexts in a wide range of specific activities,

---

[5] Bem, *Dismantling Gender Polarization and Compulsory Heterosexuality*, 329.

[6] Buss, "Sexual Strategies Theory," 23.

[7] Brizendine, *The Female Brain*, 71.

proponents of this approach conclude that all or even most of the questions asked about sexual behavior will not be answered by the tools and concepts from any single scientific discipline. Through a comprehensive representative survey of sexual behavior in the general adult population of the United States, a social scientific study of sexual practices showed that "human sexual behavior is only partly determined by factors originating within the individual. In addition, a person's socialization into a particular culture, his or her interaction with sex partners, and the constraints imposed on him or her become extremely important in determining his or her sexual activity."[8] Social science identifies and quantifies the various sexual practices in a society, and uses statistical analysis to interpret the evidence about sexual practices in our culture so that we may have reliable information upon which to base our understanding of sexual practice in our society and its impact upon public policy.

For my purpose, in place of the technical description of sexual identity variously expressed among disciplines, I suggest a simple description that increasingly made sense to me as my research progressed. Briefly, I assert that sexual identity is comprised of the attributes and characteristics belonging to four distinct categories. The first category, 'sex definition' is identified by the composition of an individual's sex chromosomes established at conception. The second, 'gender definition,' refers to external and internal sex organs that develop during the prenatal growth of each person. Third, 'gender identification' pertains to attributes, other than the physical gender markers of gender definition, culturally or individually ascribed to or associated along a scale from masculinity to femininity, and grounded in physiological, psychological, and sociological conditions or influences. The final category, 'gender connectivity,' consists of interactions and connections between gendered individuals that variously express some degree of one or all three attributes of *arousal*, *attraction*, and *attachment*.

---

[8] Lauman et al., *The Social Organization of Sexuality*, 3–4.

For the remainder of Chapter 2: *Sex and Gender,* I illustrate the complexity of sexual identity in three of the four categories of sexual identity: sex definition, gender definition, and gender identification. In Chapter 3, I will illustrate more of the complexity of sexual identity through an examination of the fourth category of sexual identity: *gender connectivity.*

Sex Definition

Sex is biologically defined at the instant when fertilization creates a zygote, thereby inaugurating the process of cell division that, during nine months of gestation, develops into a new person. At the moment of conception, chromosomal combinations form to define the sex of the emerging person. When conception occurs, the zygote normally receives exactly twenty-three pairs of chromosomes, including the sex chromosome pair: half come from the father's spermatozoon and half from the mother's ovum. The new sex chromosome pair is normally either an XX combination defining a female, or an XY combination defining a male. The sex chromosome also determines a person's procreative role. The female, having an XX chromosome combination, dictates that she will contribute the egg to procreation; and the male, having an XY chromosome combination, dictates that he will contribute the sperm. Somewhere in the fourth and fifth weeks of gestation, the hypothalamus, pituitary, and other glands kick in the hormones (testosterone, estrogen, etc.) that promote the development of the organs producing either the egg or sperm, and also the organs that deliver the egg or sperm for procreation.

During the time that a newly developing life is in its primitive, embryonic state, before significant organ development of any kind is apparent, the sex can be determined by laboratory analysis of this sex-chromosome combination from an embryo's DNA sample. We might logically conclude, therefore, that the cause of our sex definition is determined solely by biological agency, an inviolable biological event that cannot be modified. Once established, we cannot substitute the sex chromosomes that we received at conception with those of another sex. Granted, persons might camouflage their sex so as to appear to be something other than their defined sex, or mask their defined sex with an overlay of other gender characteristics. Yet, beneath the overlays, the chromosomal sex definition is unalterable.

The scientific accuracy of Genesis, that God created human beings male and female, seems apparently confirmed. Or, as the popular maxim goes, "God created Adam and Eve, not Adam and Steve." The curious fact remains, however, that the story of Genesis, though rich in religious meaning, does not correspond to scientific evidence. It turns out there are more possibilities than two defined human sexes in the created order; there are at least *four* (even more depending on the way one describes the biological condition). Hence, sex definition is not strictly binary after all; that is to say, human beings are not always either male (XY) or female (XX). In addition to the male and female sexes, 'inter-sexes' exist that are neither strictly male nor female. Occasionally, something occurs at conception that causes the sex chromosomes to form differently than the typical two chromosome pair. In some cases, an embryo forms with a single X sex chromosome rather than a chromosome pair. In other cases, an embryo forms with three chromosomes, two X chromosomes and one Y chromosome. Instances even occur in which an embryo is formed with four or even five sex chromosomes. What sex are *these* embryos?

Given this atypical variance in sex definition, we might too easily jump to the conclusion that the variance is due to an exclusively biological cause, some elusive biological incident that formed one individual differently than the usual distinctively male or female. If so, have we successfully isolated the exact causal preconditions or precipitating triggers that result in the conception of an inter-sex child? In other words, can we conclusively identify the Ur cause (that is, the original causal factor preceding any subsequent or consequential causal factors) that set in motion a chain of events in the life cycle of either the sperm or the egg of the parent that results in a male, a female, or an inter-sex embryo? Can we be sure no gene-altering toxins or radiation ions existed in the physical environment of the father or mother, or that no critically affective stress factor upon father, mother, or both existed at the time of conception to upset the electrolytic balance of fluids inside the egg when the sperm penetrated the egg's exterior membrane? Can any existing scientific precision provide an empirically accurate answer as to the cause of an inter-sex embryo, and to measure the extent to which the source was biological and to what extent environmental? Even if we could answer the question *how*, would that answer the question *why*? And whether or not we can answer the question 'Why?', does it change the condition or lessen the responsibility of people involved in that child's life to respond to the inter-sex child with healthy, affirming, and loving receptivity?

Gender Definition

Gender definition, as distinct from sex definition, refers to a second set of characteristics of sexual identity that we recognize by examining genital anatomy after a child is born, or by ultra-sound imaging during pregnancy. When we look at a baby's genitals, we assume we can say definitively "this is a boy" or "this is a girl." Gender definition, apparently tied to sex definition, seems easy to determine. The corollary to chromosome structure is genital equipment to handle the procreative role determined by sex definition. Each person will have a gender definition, with genitals to provide eggs or sperm consistent with their sex def-inition. However, this binary condition is not necessarily the case for every individual.

Although sex is already defined at conception, gender defin-ition does not begin until later in gestation: not until about or after the fifth week. Before this time, according to Edward Stein, there exist in the embryo both male and female biological ductile mate-rials, one set that, in the sixth week of gestation, has the potential to develop into the female oviducts, the uterus, the cervix, and the upper vagina, the other to develop into the male vas deferens, the epididymis, the seminal vesicles, and the ejaculatory ducts. Normally one set of internal genitalia continues to develop into mature organs while the other set atrophies, becoming inconspicuous bits of tissue. In addition to the two sets of ducts, there is initially one, undifferentiated, typically-female organ that, at about the eighth week of development, forms either into a penis and scrotum, or a clitoris, labia, and the lower part of the vagina. And normally, if the sex chromosomes are XY, the embryo synthesizes a protein (the testis determining factor protein) that typically causes the organ to begin to develop into testes, and the testes produce hormones causing the male ductile materials to develop.[9]

Amazingly, each human being starts out physiologically with *both* male and female internal organs and with one external, undifferentiated organ that may become *either* male *or* female. A baby's external genitals that commonly cause us to exclaim, "It's a girl!" or "It's a boy!" do not begin to develop until over a month of life, and they develop from a *single* set of genital materials in the genital tubercle!

A critical period occurs in embryonic development, driven predominantly by hormones and enzymes, when the development of the precursor tissues along one or the other pathway reaches a point of no return. Furthermore, the brain is also affected by these change factors. The same protein and hormonal changes in the embryo that cause differentiation of one's physiological gender also change the way the brain, primarily the hypothalamus, functions in determining the kind of erotic responses that will occur eventually and what basic kinds of masculine/feminine self perceptions will emerge.

In the most basic sense, it seems *gender* definition is in no way acquired in response to adaptive preferences or to influences present in the environment but only by inexorable biological development. The development of characteristics defining the

---

[9] Stein, *The Mismeasure of Desire*, 26–27.

gender of sexual identity arising out of the existence of both male and female biological material suggests, however, that perhaps a certain risk factor exists regarding whether the genital material that develops will be consistent with the sex definition.

Indeed, during that time of gestation when the hypothalamus and associated glands kick in the hormones that cause one of the two sets of genitalia to develop, something occasionally occurs in a pregnancy to cause atypical development of the genitals throughout the remainder of gestation.[10] In some embryos, neither male nor female genitals develop, and in others both sets develop to one extent or another, and still in others, the genitals are poorly formed, for example: external genitals form but not internal, or

---

[10] Mondimore, *A Natural History*, 104ff. Examples of atypical genital development:

1. "Androgen insensitivity syndrome" — Testosterone has no effect on target tissues. Individual develops female genitalia, is raised as female, but in adolescence fails to menstruate and is infertile. They are anatomically female but genetically male. These "women" are generally attracted to men.

2. "Congenital adrenal hyperplasia" (CAH) — Adrenal glands located above the kidneys produce testosterone in both males and females (a much smaller amount.) If high levels of testosterone circulate during the critical moment in a female's development, they develop masculinized genitalia from enlarged clitoris to a full sized penis and scrotum that sometimes makes gender identification very ambiguous.

3. "5-alpha-reductase deficiency" — Males lack an enzyme that converts testosterone to a different form for the normal development of male genitalia. They appear at birth to be female, but have internal testes that at puberty begin secreting the usual levels of testosterone that cause development of typically male voice change and musculature change and the enlargement of the "clitoris" into an organ the size of a penis. Although raised as females, they tend to develop a male self-identity and develop erotic interests in girls.

vice versa, or the external genitals develop as one gender but the internal genitals develop as the opposite gender.

Just as in the case of sex definition, when an inter-sex child is conceived, no clear scientific explanation may be evident for the Ur cause of atypical gender definition. What was happening in the uterus that caused cell division and cell differentiation to develop differently in the gender undefined fetus than the fetus that developed the genitalia appropriate to its sex definition? What was happening in the uterus and/or fetus that caused hormonal or enzyme imbalances at critical moments of sexual differentiation? Answers may exist as to what caused each sequence in the chain of events during gestation, but the original condition that started the cascading sequence may remain a mystery. The original causal factor may have been biological, but it also may have been caused by either physical or social environmental factors.

Just as in the case of atypical sex definition, I'm struck by the wondrous mystery of sexual development in gender definition, and I am also impressed by the ethical responsibility incumbent upon those obliged to respond to the person with atypical gender definition. Until more recent decades, a society such as our sophisticated Western society was comparatively sex and gender primitive. Even a large contingent within the medical community applied such labels as 'freakish' or 'queer' to anyone not strictly gender conforming.[11] In a society that places a radically negative value on conditions divergent from the sexual norm, the names

---

[11] In *Sexing the Body*, Fausto-Sterling states that "they never questioned the fundamental assumption that there are only two sexes because their goal in studying intersexuals was to find out more about "normal" development. Intersexuality, in Money's view, resulted from fundamentally abnormal processes. Their patients required medical treatment because they 'ought' to have become either a male or a female. The goal of treatment was to assure proper psychosexual development by assigning the young mixed-sex child to the proper gender and then doing whatever was necessary to assure that the child and h/her parents believed in the sex assignment" (46).

Congenital Adrenal Hyperplasia, Androgen Insensitivity Syndrome, Gonadal Dysgenesis, Hypospadias, Turner Syndrome, and Klinefelter Syndrome all sound like frightening medical terms implying terrible affliction.[12]

Parents of a child with atypical genital definitions face a profound dilemma regarding the rearing of that child. Is it appropriate to modify, through surgery and hormone treatments, the physiological gender of a child during early childhood, or is it best to counsel such children to adapt to their atypical definition as they move through childhood, adolescence, and into adulthood? Instances of early-age gender modification have sometimes resulted in conforming a child to a physiological gender ultimately incongruent with the emotional gender experience that a child develops during maturation. The 'corrected' gender assigned earlier by surgical and hormonal treatment thus conflicts with the gender they perceive for themselves. This situation obviously raises the question whether early gender correction is ever appropriate. And if appropriate, who should make the decision about which gender to ascribe artificially to the child?

Asking these ethical questions exposes inherent problems in the ethical legacy acquired from the tremendous growth in biological and medical sciences in the nineteenth century, and from the traditional attitudes of religious groups. In that era, instances of atypical sex and gender definition were considered mistakes of nature that science was capable of correcting. What previous centuries viewed as freakish and unnatural, science was now able to explain as extraordinary deviations from the norm. Using increased medical knowledge, such atypical bodies that caused awe and wonder were redefined as curable, pathological

---

[12] Many organizations provide information, support groups, personal stories, and resources designed to help intersexual persons and their families take personal control over their lives and make their own decisions about their sexual identity and what measures they want to apply to their personal situation. Some can be found on line by entering any of the above medical terms into an Internet web search engine.

conditions. According to Fausto-Sterling, "scientific understanding was used as a tool to obliterate precisely the wonders it illuminated. By the middle of the twentieth century, medical technology had *advanced* to a point where it could make bodies that had once been objects of awe and astonishment disappear from view, all in the name of *correcting nature's mistakes.*"[13]

Of course, a long history exists in Western culture, dominantly influenced by Judeo-Christian and Aristotelian values, of associating abnormalities with pathology without couching them in the medical terminology of healthy or unhealthy conditions. More often people described abnormalities using the moral terminology of sin, depravity, or deviation from the ideal. A question comparable in intent to "Who did sin, this man, or his parents, that he was born blind?"[14] is still a question frequently applied today to assign fault to someone or something when radical deviations from the sexual norm occur in human experience.

Very often, however, the moral indictment of sin is not imputed to the individual, but to a general human condition identified in Christian theology as "The Fall." Rooted in the Genesis story of creation in which Adam and Eve are driven from the ideal Garden of Eden because they ate fruit from the forbidden Tree of the Knowledge of Good and Evil, the concept supports the idea that the earth was originally formed in a perfect state where all things were in balance. Human history began in a Garden of Eden where no earthquake, flood, sickness, injury, or death intruded upon the paradisiacal environment of human existence. But the disobedience of Adam and Eve to God's command, under temptation from the Serpent, caused a seismic event destroying nature's perfection and throwing nature down a cosmic descent into chaos that forever disrupted its perfect balance. Therefore, although an occurrence of an inter-sex or Androgen Insensitivity Syndrome fetus may not be cited as evidence of the child's or the parent's

---

[13] Fausto-Sterling, *Sexing the Body*, 37.

[14] The Holy Bible: The King James Version. John 9.2.

moral culpability, it is, nevertheless, often explained as happening to a child and parents because of "The Fall." The medical notion of pathology fits well with this theological view.

From an empirical point of view, such notions problematically define atypical sex and gender definition as unnatural, and from a theological point of view, as something evil. As a result, the primary concern too easily focuses not on what is best for the child, but what can be done to correct nature and/or eradicate the evil. Interestingly, the same concept of "it's an abnormality that must be cured" that was applied to inter-sexuality beginning in the nineteenth-century medical community and continuing through recent decades was also applied to homosexuality. Although the nature of the 'cure' for homosexuality has been psychotherapy or spiritual therapy, whereas inter-sexuality has been 'cured' via corrective surgery and hormone therapy, the same fundamental view prevails—only 'male' and 'female' have clearly defined gender roles designed for sexual compatibility. Anything other than this normalcy is anomalous, an aberration that must be corrected, or an evil to be exorcised. This point of view has potential for a destructive effect on the lives of those whose sexual identity is atypical, as well as upon the lives of members of their families.

Recognition of the close biological and environmental factors that lie beside each other when speaking about sources that shape our sexual identity is an important element in framing ethical viewpoints. When confronted with persons whose sexual identities do not fit the norm, an ethical issue of right or wrong has no bearing on the biological reality of a child's atypical sex or gender definition In contrast, ethical questions and answers prove highly appropriate when contemplating what is in the *best interest* of a child with atypical sex and gender definition, particularly as the child develops. It is most assuredly an ethical issue whether society and the family closet the person with atypical sex and gender definition within walls of embarrassment and perceived disfigurement, or whether they embrace and nurture that person toward a full and satisfying life.

Gender Identification

The third set of complex sexual identity characteristics that I illustrate belong to gender identification. The characteristics are generally subsumed under the broad terms 'masculine' and 'feminine.' They are norms used to define or ascribe those attributes we typically associate with a man and those we typically associate with a woman. Cultural expectations and socially defined roles shape a vast number of these attributes. A good number, however, are intrinsic to the individual person. Whereas male/female *genitalia* identifies gender definition, gender *identification* refers to anatomical, psychosocial, and behavioral attributes typically identified with a specific gender but which may, in fact, also be reflected 'atypically' in the other gender. Some of these 'typical' gender attributes we consider to be inherent, identified by such attributes as general body size and musculature differences between men and women. Others are identified as non-inherent attributes, including personal and/or cultural expectations such as difference in fashion apparel between men and women. Inherent gender attributes we assume to have roots in biological sources. Personal and culturally defined gender attributes we assume to have roots in environmental sources.

When we discuss gender identification in common conversation, we generally talk about it in bipolar rather than binary terms. That is, we tend to talk about these attributes more along a *continuum* between a masculine ideal at one end and a feminine ideal at the other. Because of the more fluid nature of attributes along the masculine/feminine continuum, we need to acknowledge the role of stereotypes. Stereotypes, by nature incomplete, are not necessarily incorrect. They can be useful tags in discussion of gender identification as long as we keep in mind that they are incomplete. Everything from the old adage "boys will be boys" to the recently faddish *"Men are from Mars, Women are from Venus"* point to stereotypical gender distinctions that are real, though inadequate, within the culture that recognizes them. At worst, cultural gender wars popularly employ such stereotypes to sustain gross prejudice and injustice.

Gender stereotypes generally involve characteristics attributable to biological factors, involving observable physical gender characteristics such as: the consistently larger size of males than females; males' stronger musculature and larger lungs, heart, jaws, etc. They also may include male/female differences in the brain's size and functionality, in the way we play, learn, and relate to people; differences between gender in level of activity, gestational lung development, percent of body fat, bone mass, sensitivity to smells, heart rate, and baseline body temperatures.[15]

Gender differentiation becomes clearer when we observe non-human mammals. In nature, for example, a male lion has a mane that the female does not. A bull buffalo's massive size distinguishes it from the smaller cow. The coloration of a male peacock is far brighter than that of a female.

These gender characteristics in other animals appear to most of us who have no zoological background to be extremely simple, rudimentary, and predictable in contrast to human beings. An overwhelming 'sameness' seems to exist from one animal to another of the same sex. To the untrained, unpracticed eye, individual cows in a herd of Black Angus cattle cannot be differentiated one from another: a cow is a cow is a cow.

But variations do exist. In spite of the apparent sameness of gender identification among some other mammals, the physiological and behavioral generalizations about gender identity do not always prove consistent. In laboratory experiments, the injection of testosterone in pregnant rats has resulted in female offspring that develop into larger than ordinary females and that demonstrate male behaviors such as mounting other rats. In this instance, an environmental interruption (the testosterone injection) causes a biological side effect. These experiments illustrate

---

[15] Rosen, "The Gender Divide," 82–86.

the potential of interacting relationships between biological and environmental causation of gender identity.

In a highly populated area in the Dallas/Fort Worth, Texas area, the human waste that winds up in the water from women taking estrogen supplements is believed to contribute to the increasing incidence of male fish in nearby streams acquiring female characteristics.[16]

In the human species, variations in physical gender identity are far greater than among other mammals and present many, commonly recognized departures from the stereotypical masculine/feminine norm. The boy who is short of stature and unusually fine in feature, or the girl who is tall and built like a fullback, together with the infinite gradations between these ends of the spectrum, are examples that illustrate the impossibility of setting down physical characteristics of gender identity unique only to one gender or the other. One can stereotypically claim that boys are larger than girls, but clearly one cannot claim that largeness is an exclusively male gender characteristic or that smallness is an exclusively female gender characteristic. Except from their stereotypical usage, it is difficult to define attributes of gender identity as being gender specific characteristics at all.

In addition to the physical characteristics of gender identity that we ascribe to biological influences, social and behavioral characteristics develop from biological influences, although we tend to ascribe their cause more to the influence of the social or cultural environment.

Behavioral gender identity characteristics are, as in the case of physical characteristics of gender identity, more conspicuous among non-human mammals. Among many species, the male animal is typically more independent and aggressive, while the female is more nurturing and group oriented. In a pride of lions, for example, male social behavior is more independent. Male lions strive to take domination of groups and consequently compete

---

[16] Miller, "Something Fishy," *Fort Worth Star–Telegram*, May 19, 2003, A1.

among themselves to be the dominant male. Females tend to group together with other females and are more adapted to watching after the young. There comes a time in development that male and female cubs who played together from the time they were kittens begin to separate according to gender and begin to reflect the same gender-specific characteristics as the adult lions. One might argue that these behaviors are really influenced by a consistent social environment from generation to generation rather than by biological influence. On the other hand, if that is so, one has to wonder why in generation after generation, no members of the species try to break from the environmental mold

Just as variations in physical gender identity are far more diverse in humans than other mammals and depart frequently from the stereotypical masculine/feminine norm, social behaviors attributable to biological influences also vary widely among human beings. Indeed, humans have stereotypically distinctive gender behaviors. Boys are more likely to play soldier (or some variation) and *become* soldiers than women. They are prone to be more independent than women, particularly regarding family responsibilities. In technically advanced societies, boys tend to play with mechanical things and aspire to be policemen and firemen, whereas girls tend to play with dolls and dresses and aspire to more domestic activities.

That is not to say that the activity *per se* is uniquely masculine or feminine. Rather, the gravitation of one gender more than the other toward engagement in these activities indicates a more biologically rooted social behavior. Some persons, disagreeing in part, believe that much of the gravitation toward gendered activities is culturally guided. They would say children are treated differently right from the start—girls are called "princess," boys are called "champ." From the earliest age, social scripting guides children into socially preferred roles. Boys are taught independence, girls are taught dependence, etc.

I counter this argument by considering children who fit none of the proscribed scripts; they are called "sissy" or "girly boys," not "champs"; "butch" or "tomboy," not "princess." The fair young boy who is sensitive and un-aggressive is not treated like a jock, nor is an athletic girl who is rough and aggressive treated like a demure maiden. Yet they still recognize their self to be the 'normal' gender not because it is socially preferred but because they naturally know themselves for what they are. How does that fair, fine featured, slight of build, un-athletic, non-aggressive child, who recognizes he is innately masculine, come to that self-awareness when he grows up in a family and social community of jocks? He may recognize that he is not a 'typical' male, but he does not recognize himself as being other than male.

I accept that cultural scripts powerfully influence the gender development of a child. But my argument is that the biological formation of gender *identification* is a real influence, along with the reality of physical and social environmental influences, thereby creating a complex mix of influences interplaying with the individual's unique personal makeup to effect the differentiation of gender identification.[17]

A seemingly significant reason for the wide variation in gender identification among humans, and the difficulty in differentiating between biological and environmental sources related to this variety, relates to the fact that human brain functions are far more complex than those of other mammals. Many characteristics of human gender identification, it is believed, form in the more complex regions of higher brain functions. In spite of the strong environmental factor in the development of 'male' or

---

[17] Mondimore, *A Natural History*, 104–21. The amygdala (an almond-sized collection of cells that forms complex connections between the hypothalamus and the cerebral cortex called the "limbic system") is thought to be the center of emotional response because damage to it results in loss of emotional responsiveness and sexual interest. Damage also apparently has a disorganizing effect upon the distinctive emotional characteristics associated with male or female, thereby raising the question whether gender discordant behavior (girl "tomboy" and boy "sissy") may be related to hormonal abnormalities in the critical moment of embryo development affecting this region of the brain.

'female' skills, a body of evidence indicates that gender differentiation is also a matter of brain function controlled by cerebral
hemispheres. For example, the cerebrum, which manages all the
higher levels of brain function, is divided into two halves connected in the center by a solid textured mass of fibers called the
corpus callosum. Certain body functions (speech, for example) are
controlled mainly by one or the other brain hemisphere, not
equally both together. This so-called lateralization is stronger in
men than in women and may suggest that women's ostensibly
superior verbal skills result from a greater sharing of speech
function between the cerebral hemispheres through the corpus
callosum of a female brain than of a male brain. It has been observed, also, that women's speech centers are less affected by
strokes than men's, indicating that women have more bilateral
speech function between the cerebral hemispheres than do men.[18]

Even if one may identify gender-specific brain function, can
one conclude that because *one* gender demonstrates a certain
heightened brain function, the other gender lacks completely that
same function? Does that necessarily reduce the degree of variation that may occur among the larger population of a particular
gender any more than the variations in physical size? And should
gender-specific brain function preclude persons identified one
way from access to occupations and social spheres that have
stereotypically been assigned to another gender?

These questions illustrate that in addition to the characteristics
of gender identification that emerge from biological sources,
characteristics emerge from the interaction of individuals with
their environment. The characteristics of gender that emerge from
that interaction may be characteristics an individual embraces as a

---

[18] Mondimore, *A Natural History*, 122–33. In males, the same high levels
of testosterone that masculinize the external genitalia, the hypothalamus,
and other body structures seemingly cause an earlier maturing of the
right hemisphere. This process is thought to solidify in some way the
circuitry responsible for visuo-spatial functioning and other "masculine"
talents."

matter of choice or preference, or they may be imposed characteristics of gender that the social environment expects from or enforces upon its members. Which characteristics an individual personally embraces and which are demanded of the individual regardless of preference will depend, to a large extent, upon how strictly a society or culture codifies gender identity into its system of public and private laws, and social mores.

An individually embraced characteristic of gender identity is something a person claims for him/her self whether or not it is typically identified with the gender expectations of a culture. Once upon a time, it was unheard of in Western culture for a woman to appear in public dressed in anything but a traditional female skirt or dress attire. At some point, women determined that wearing pants and jeans was not for men only.

In a 1928 photograph of the dedication of the Washington state capitol building in Olympia, only one woman appears in the picture among all the legislative, administrative, and judiciary dignitaries. In the 2005 photograph of the rededication of the same capitol building, the governor is a woman, more than a third of the legislature is made up of women, and there are woman judiciaries. Community clubs like the Kiwanis and Lions were once men only organizations whose members came from the city's professional and business establishment. Now the membership includes women from the city's professional and business establishment. Women challenged the barriers created by gender identity stereotypes that prevented them from entering the professions and occupations that had been the bastions of male privilege and power. They refused to submit to the notion that their gender identity should be restricted to domesticity. In our free Western society, a breakdown, though not complete, has occurred in gender discriminating notions, such as denying women access to work or athletic activities reserved for strong males, or impugning men who choose professions previously reserved for women.

Many social conditions in our culture cause a person to adapt to or succumb to a characteristic of gender identity because cultural influence enforces conformity. For example, adolescent boys in our culture are inclined to identify their masculinity with the gender perception that "boys don't cry." However badly boys hurt emotionally or physically, a common social script tells them merely to "suck it up" and prove how tough they are, to be "all guy!" Our culture encourages girls to be soft and 'feminine', and to readily assume the role of the 'adored and submissive woman' who needs male protection. In some cases the role of submissive wife is politicized, as for example the case of governmental trends toward dismantling social welfare and education support for indigent children and single parent mothers. Arguments have been made in Congress to the effect that such support should be dismantled, not only to reduce the costs of government, but also to affirm our expectation that individuals in a free society should be self-reliant. What it propagates in effect is the imposition of the gender-identity stereotype of female nurturer and domestic partner upon poor females, while prosperous females, predominantly white, are emancipated from stereotypical economic dependence upon men.

As to the basic characteristics of typical and non-typical gender identification, contemporary gender studies seek to explore more fully *how* and *why* atypical characteristics develop. The fact that varying characteristics of gender identity exist is not in dispute; but categorically identifying what characteristics are caused by cultural, environmental influences as opposed to biological frequently proves ambiguous.[19] More importantly, however, is the ethical consideration of how we relate to variations in gender identity. To cite one issue, a serious moral problem occurs in the tendency of a society to make voluptuous sexiness a feminine ideal, and athleticism and personal assertiveness a masculine ideal. The equally egregious corollary is society's common tendency to devalue women or men who conspicuously deviate from those "ideals."

---

[19] Carter, *Current Conceptions of Sex Roles and Sex Typing*, 8–24.

A subject related to the issue of gender identification, but which lies beyond the scope of this book, is the matter of transgender persons. Transgender persons are men who from childhood have experienced themselves as female, or women who have experienced themselves as male. In spite of the fact that their sex definition and gender definition are typically male or female, they experience life emotionally, socially, and psychologically as something *other* than their defined gender—for as long as they can remember and throughout the entire process of their gender identity development. They have never been able to identify themselves with their defined gender, or been able to choose an identity consistent with their defined gender. Their self-identification has been, instead, an inexorable reality that could be attributed only to profoundly rooted biological influences.

Transgender persons are further evidence of the complex and enigmatic nature of sexual identity that demands that we shed some of the traditional assumptions about human sexuality in light of improved scientific understanding. We should especially shed those assumptions that devalue and dehumanize those persons who do not conform to the heterosexual or binary male/female norm.

The Formation of Sexual Identity

Thus far, I have illustrated the complexity that prevails in the formation of human sexual identity in the categories of sex definition, gender definition, and gender identification. As we consider the matter of homosexuality, it is vitally important to recognize this complexity, as well as the variations of individual sexual identity that exist. I believe society feels conflicted in its attitude toward homosexuality partly because it does not sufficiently recognize or appreciate the complexity and varieties in the other categories of sexual identity. In place of appreciation for the complexity of sexual identity, an oversimplified, binary view of human sexuality pervades our culture.

Binary oversimplification consistently crops up in private and public discourse, as in a separate opinion concurring in judgment only with the Washington State Supreme Court's 2006 decision to uphold the ban on same-sex marriage. Justice James M. Johnson wrote, "The binary character of marriage exists first because there are two sexes" (Concur No. 75934–1 J.M. JOHNSON, J. at 30). Johnson makes this comment in the context of his argument that procreation, which he presumes is a core feature of marriage, can occur only between a binary sexual union of male and female. Nonetheless, the categorical assertion "there are two sexes" exposes Johnson's unfamiliarity with the complexity of human sexual definition. True, successful procreation requires that one person must have the capacity to ejaculate to provide sperm, and another person have the capacity to ovulate to provide an egg, and that these capacities must be linked either through coitus, artificial insemination, or fertilized egg implantation. That there are two sexes, however, is false. Consequently, his argument that the *character* of marriage is binary, i.e., between a man and a woman, is based upon a false premise.

One must recognize, therefore, that binary distinctions regarding human sexual identity, such as male/female and nature/nurture, prove inadequate for understanding homosexuality. Within our physical/social environment, during either our pre-natal or post-natal development, and at any given moment within our constantly changing environment, the force of both biological and environmental determinants works to shape our sexual identity. They lie at the center of the dispute regarding the nature of homosexual sexual identity.

A large body of opinion categorically declares that homosexuality is caused only by social environmental determinants. Some define homosexuality purely in terms of behavior resulting from sinful life choices that produce or exacerbate deeply imbedded sexual desires and habits within the personality. According to this view, homosexuality can and must be reversed through psychological, moral, and spiritual means. The role of biological determinants in the development of a homosexual sexual identity are either minimized or flatly denied. In fact, supporters of such a view commonly deny that a homosexual sexual identity even exists. Homosexuality becomes unequivocally defined as an aberration, a perversion of normal sexual identity, rooted in a person's lack of moral will to respond appropriately to influences in the environment, thereby tempting them to choose immoral behavior. Some conservative psychologists claim that psychological pathology is intrinsic to homosexuality.

Emerging from such reductionism, a simple, dogmatic definition of homosexuality *cannot* encompass the enormous complexity and ambiguity of sexual identity in the categories of sex definition, gender definition, and gender identification. We thus must distill from the complex tangle of biological and environmental influences an understanding of how these complex influences play significant roles in the development of *all* characteristics of sexual identity, including homosexuality. A simplistic notion effectively orphans homosexuality from all other characteristics of sexual identity, if we reduce homosexuality to a behavior caused only by bad personal choices, bad influences in a sinful environment, or to a psychological pathology. Such a notion implies that homosexuality is the sole characteristic of sexual identity whose occurrence can be attributed purely to non-biological sources.

The perpetuation of this reductionism can only harm youth whose emerging recognition of their sexual identity, confusing to any adolescent, becomes confounded by their awareness of divergence from the heterosexual norm. It can do only harm to these young people's parents, who must struggle with the shame and self-recrimination that the implication of this reductionism heaps upon them when they discover their child does not 'behave' heterosexually. Consequently, the tragic outcome of this unwarranted shame and self-recrimination often results in estrangement, if not outright rejection of a gay or lesbian child. I will address the issue of homosexuality's place in the complex and enigmatic nature of sexual identity more fully in Chapter 3, which outlines the set of sexual identity characteristics belonging to *gender connectivity*.

CHAPTER THREE

Gender Connectivity

Personal Prologue: What You Don't Know

I "knew" homosexuality was a behavior—until the evening my son poured out his heartache to me. He had just broken up with the young man he dated for some time, the young man he struggled so hard to tell his mother and me about on the night he came out to us. I was home alone the night he came through the door, his eyes swollen red with tears, his face reflecting a combination of despair and rage. I don't remember having to ask what was wrong. I remember only the pain, disappointment, unrequited love, anger, abandonment, and betrayal he expressed because his boyfriend told him he no longer wanted to date him.

I remember thinking, "I recognize this story!" I proposed marriage to a freshman girl my senior year of college, but I was neither emotionally nor intellectually mature enough to appreciate the second thoughts a freshman girl might entertain a year later living 200 miles from her beau. I felt the rejected suitor's insufferable anguish when, at Christmas time after my college graduation, she told me she no longer wanted to marry me. Other college boys were courting her.

After days of pining over a lost love, my father and mother had had enough of my melancholy. My dad took me aside, and advised me that hurting a little while now was better than hurting for a long time in an unhappy marriage. "You'll love again," he told me. And I did. Now as my son poured out his anguish, I heard myself repeat my father's advice. "You'll love again," I said. And he did. And I began to better comprehend what it might be like to be a homosexual man.

A broken heart is not grief over a lost sex-partner. It certainly wasn't for me; and neither was it for my son! I felt a profound void over the loss of an intense personal relationship with a young woman whom I deeply cared about. He felt the void for a young man whom *he* deeply cared about. My son's broken heart differed in no way from mine. I began to understand that reducing my son's homosexuality to a behavior proved as invalid as reducing my own heterosexuality to a behavior. Far more factors than the activities stirring and satisfying sexual arousal define homosexuality and heterosexuality. Both consist of all those subtle and not so subtle dimensions of human appearance and character that invoke personal attraction. And both consist of the social, emotional, and intellectual dynamics that cause two human beings to want to share lives closely attached to one another.

A time came when my wife and I experienced more of the homosexual community than we encountered through our son and a few of his friends. By means of that encounter, we recognized more fully that, like our heterosexuality, homosexuality reflected far more than simple behavior. Our exposure to the larger homosexual community increased tremendously when we attended a Sunday service at a church in Dallas, Texas, that ministered primarily to gays and lesbians. As a middle-aged, conspicuously heterosexual couple, we were an anxious minority getting out of our car in the church parking lot. We held hands for support as we entered a sanctuary filled with nearly a thousand gay and lesbian worshippers. As we tightly grasped each other's hands, we noticed numerous male couples filing into church holding hands. It occurred to us that not too long ago, oblivious to our duplicity, we would have judged such male hand-holding as peculiarly inappropriate.

The remarkable gusto of the predominantly male congregants singing the hymns and service music made this church service unusually inspirational. Otherwise, the service did not differ from the worship we experienced in congregations of heterosexual people. After numerous visits, we decided formally to join the 3000-member church, where for several years we participated actively—two of a few dozen heterosexual people among thousands of Christian gays and lesbians.

Within this congregation (part of the United Church of Christ denomination), we became acquainted with, were welcomed by, and formed close friendships with literally hundreds of gay, lesbian, bisexual, and transgender persons. The experience was profoundly eye-opening. Our years of participation in that faith community gave us exposure to the conversations, jocular banter, life testimonies, spiritual confessions, family struggles, and personal biographies that disclose the stuff of *human* experience, common to straight *and* gay people alike.

Although our sexual identity, whether homosexual or heterosexual, encompasses far more than physical behavior (and certainly proves broader than *genital* experiences alone), physical experiences nonetheless represent pronounced markers of the broader context of sexual identity for everyone. I was struck by how the individual life anecdotes of gays and lesbians, particularly the more emotional/physical aspects of sexual identity development, were in essence very much like my own. Although gay anecdotes described attraction toward and fantasies about men, while mine correspondingly focused on women, the underlying story of sexual development was the same. The similarity prompted me to reflect more carefully upon my own sexual development, and to recognize the personal incidents occurring within successive stages of my maturation that caused me to recognize my innate heterosexual identity. In that reflection, I learned to appreciate homosexual development as I recognized its congruity with my own heterosexual development.

My earliest "sexual" memory stems from an incident when I was five. I went with my family to a Sunday School Christmas program at a little church in a neighboring village. The children filed in, sat down in their seats, and a young woman took her place at the lectern in front of the church to welcome everyone to the program. The moment I saw her, I could scarcely take my eyes away from her. I was so attracted to her that my attention was fixed upon her the entire evening.

I recall the first girl I kissed, also the first girl I asked to marry me. It happened in kindergarten. I still remember her name, and every once in a while I wonder what became of the girl who answered 'Yes' when I proposed to her, and who now might be a 70-plus-year-old grandmother.

During the intermediate years of childhood, before puberty, I discovered the fascinating game of "Doctor and Nurse." This game of sexual discovery, opportunity, and mutual curiosity supplied occasion to see and feel differences between a girl and boy. I was about nine when I thought I'd like to penetrate my "nurse." She quickly said, "No!" because "that was how babies are made."

I never had any interest in the nakedness of other boys during this pre-puberty period, but I had a great deal of curiosity about naked girls. One summer evening, when our parents were out, two or three of my male cousins and I enthusiastically decided to raid my sister's and female cousin's bedroom to pull off their pajamas to see their budding breasts. I also recall being most interested by two specific sections of the Sears Roebuck and Montgomery Ward catalogs: toys and women's lingerie.

I must have been about thirteen when attraction to a girl took the form of a crush. She was a pretty, athletic girl in my church Sunday School class. I wanted to be with her, talk to her, have her like me as much as I liked her; but by this time, I was altogether too shy and too frightened by my own sexual emotions to relate to her. I also remember developing a teenage crush on movie star Debra Paget after seeing the film, "Bird of Paradise." At the end of the movie, Paget—the Island princess—offers herself as a human sacrifice to the god of the volcano, who threatens to annihilate her tribe with rivers of molten lava. With one last, pensive gaze backward down the volcano's slopes, the exquisitely beautiful girl jumps into the volcano's caldron without a scream, and disappears into the inferno. The god is satisfied, the volcano quiets, but for weeks afterward, my heart continued to erupt in anguish.

More crushes and more dating followed as I moved into my college years. With these experiences came greater maturity, marked by interest in a girl for *more* than physical attractiveness. I did not marry the first girl to whom I seriously proposed marriage; and I experienced the rejected suitor's insufferable anguish mentioned earlier. But a few years later I met Beth. We dated, became engaged, married, had children—and as life partners, we shared joys and sorrows, hurts and healings. For nearly fifty years now, I've shared life with a woman I've come to know and to love increasingly over time.

The basic characteristics of sexual identity that developed throughout my childhood continue in my adulthood, and persistently affirm my fundamental heterosexuality. Not long ago, in fact, I stood on a low platform a step above a beautiful, sun-bronzed woman wearing a white summer dress with a low-cut bodice. She lifted her hands, and as I looked down, the unavoidable angle of vision opened sight lines deep into her ample cleavage. Imperceptible to others, but certainly noticeable to me, I caught my breath in an involuntary reaction to the visual stimuli of female beauty.

I share these brief but memorable scenes from my sexual development in order to encourage others to reflect on those highlighted moments in the process of their own sexual development. What one learns about oneself through this specific reflection helps to clarify issues of sexuality too often left unexamined, and too casually experienced without any *conscious* awareness of their higher purpose in human relationships. I suspect that most heterosexual men and women rarely reflect upon an experience to ask what it is about it that triggered arousal, or what dynamics may be involved in sexual attraction. In other words, I suspect that for those who identify as heterosexual, an unconscious mind-set of heterosexism—a bias about sexuality based upon one's personal heterosexual experience—causes great difficulty when trying to understanding those who are by nature something *other* than heterosexual. Thus, many people whose sexual connections are predominantly expressed through relationships with members of the other sex have difficulty appreciating the seemingly vastly different experience of someone with same-sex connections. Acquiring such an understanding or appreciation becomes even more difficult when a popular majority who experience sexual connections in ways like our own reinforces our experience.

No wonder, then, that heterosexism pervades Western culture and plays a substantial role in causing heterosexuals often to marginalize and censure non-heterosexual persons. Many heterosexuals remain as oblivious to their heterosexual privilege in society, just as most white people remain oblivious to the privilege of their race. They do not recognize that the privileges taken for granted as members of the majority are not as accessible to minorities, nor do they understand that indifference toward sexual minorities further deprives them of the basic respect and privileges to which everyone should be entitled.

Therefore, those in the heterosexual majority should ponder the question, "What would it be like if *what* I am is not what peers, parental figures, and cultural stereotypes tell me I should be?" Countless men and women with same-sex gender connectivity struggle with this dilemma from as early in childhood as they can remember; and they continue to struggle with it until they embrace the fact that within their particular sexual identity only same-sex connections are natural. Regarding the biological nature of sexual identity, can one identify a *fundamental* difference between a boy with sexual feelings toward girls, and another boy who says, "Other boys talk about the girls that turn them on, but I'd rather gossip with the girls about the boy that turns me on"? And within the same context, can one identify the *fundamental* difference between a girl who is attracted to boys and another who says, "My friends giggle and glance at cute boys, but I think one of these giggling girls is cute"? The *focus* of attractions and erotic feelings differs, but the fundamental *nature* of sexual identity remains alike.

Unlike individuals attracted to persons of the same sex, I never had the kind of sexual feelings that caused me to question why I felt different from the sexual feelings other boys described, or had to fear revealing that I did feel different, or had to justify my sexual feelings within a sexual majority who felt differently. On the other hand, I share with those who experience same-sex interest and attraction the realization that my sexual identity was never a matter of choice. Without a doubt, I am an innately heterosexual male, and many of those who identify as homosexual have the same certainty about their identity: it was not chosen.

Consequently, I have a great concern when heterosexual men and women, without reflecting upon their own sexual identity, speak so authoritatively about the sexual identity of homosexual persons. I am concerned about the presumption of heterosexual men and women who cannot remember choosing to be hetero-sexual, but are certain gays and lesbians chose to be homosexual. I'm concerned with uninformed heterosexuals who superficially and facilely acknowledge great diversity among heterosexual relationships, but reduce homosexuality to a single "lifestyle."

Describing Gender Connectivity

The sexual development I illustrated regarding the way I relate to females expresses a category of sexual identity that I call *gender connectivity*. The term 'connectivity' implies that sexual, gendered individuals relate to one another, or make connections with other human beings within a wide range of affections, behaviors, and relationships. A biological component to gender connectivity exists just as within the categories of sex definition, gender defini-tion, and gender identification. Likewise, environmental influ-ences factor into gender connectivity just as they do for the other categories of sexual identity. Nevertheless, I emphasize the biological influence particularly to address a predominant assumption, expressed by so many opponents of homosexuality, that same-sex relationships reflect purely a matter of "lifestyle," a life pattern resulting from choices individuals make in response to social influences in their personal lives.

The characteristics and relationships of gender connectivity can be grouped under one of three attributes: *arousal, attraction,* and *attachment.* Among these attributes, the biological factors determining *arousal* prove more recognizable, while those determining *attachment* remain the most obscure. Each attribute of gender connectivity has complexities of its own and all reveal biological *and* environmental constituents, which appear clearly by examining gender connectivity in non-human species.

Gender connectivity among non-human animals may be physical for purposes of copulation, play, or fighting; social for purposes of selecting a mating partner, cooperating in food gathering, or defending the pack; and/or pragmatic for the purpose of protecting the young or identifying friend or foe. *Arousal* primes genital organs or promotes sexual receptivity for the functions of copulation and impregnation. *Attraction* determines the selection process by which one, or some, of the available partners of the species become candidates for copulation or fertilization. Where survival depends, the mating pair or group will connect together in some form of *attachment* to satisfy the need to feed, nurture, and protect offspring until they can survive on their own.

Regardless of the variety of ways gender connectivity manifests across species, its expression within a single species appears to be relatively simple, generations old, and demonstrates a consistent expression of the biological conformation of that species. The gender connectivity patterns among animals that are unique to specific species usually have a highly functional purpose related to survival of the species. Red deer stags, for example, spend long hours during breeding season roaring in a long, low rumble, at least twice a minute all day and all night— that's nearly three thousand roars every twenty-four hours, not counting extra roars the stag makes to intimidate any competing stags. Research has revealed that these stag roars serve as an aphrodisiac to does: those exposed to the roaring come into heat sooner than other females. Subsequently, female red deer who conceive early in the breeding season give birth earlier the following spring, and as a result, their calves prove more likely to survive.[20] This common pattern of gender connection among all red deer provides a clue to the biological component involved.

Arousal for some species is simply a condition of estrus response and the opportunity for copulation. Among bovines, for example, the female in estrus emits pheromones that both attract and arouse the male. The male has greater success penetrating a female in estrus because she is more receptive to male mounting and penetration during that time. Normally, the cow moves away from a mounting male, but not so commonly while in estrus. When raising prime cattle, breeders rely on this consistently pre-dictable biological indicator. They plant a non-breeding-stock bull into a herd of prime cows, and watch for the cow that stands still when the bull tries to mount her. At first sign that the cow does not intend to move away, the rancher chases off the bull and places the cow into a separate pen holding the specially bred mating bull he wants to use for propagating his herd.

Among other species, arousal seems only a periodic episode of procreative emission conditioned by maturation rather than neurological stimulation; like the end of life migration of salmon to spawn in the waters of origin in which they were fingerlings.

Attraction is a fundamental selection process that, like *arousal*, is the same for every member of a species and has been con-sistently the same for thousands of generations. It determines how a member of a species engages in a selection process that links it to a member of the other sex for mating and for any collateral purpose of *attachment* necessary to ensure offspring survival. In some species, attraction is a visual acuity to color, in others, attraction is an auditory response to sounds, and among still others, attraction is an olfactory sensitivity to scents.

---

[20] Judson, *Dr. Tatiana's Sex Advice to All Creation*, 135.

When a female gelado monkey is in estrus, a heart-shaped bare patch of skin on her chest turns red. The visual *attraction* of the reddened patch brings bachelor males to the harem, where they hover in hopes of fending off the group male and capturing one or more of the females. Winning the female is not so simple, however, because the female(s) have their own *attraction* characteristics, which ultimately determine whether an aggressive male is promoted to group male. Before securing this promotion, the male candidate must prove his ability to protect the harem females and their offspring, show prowess in male games of chase and posturing, and demonstrate competence in grooming the females. After experiencing attraction to a male gelado and agreeing which male should be promoted, the harem selects one male out of the band of bachelors. Only then is a new male established within the group, with the corresponding privileges of copulation and procreation.

Attachment does not appear to be a strong component of gender connectivity among most non-human animals. Within some species, no attachments form at all. Among other species, attachments take the form of 'prostitution,' promiscuity, polygyny, or polyandry. A few exceptions of long-term attachments forming life bonds exist among some apes and other primates. Gibbons form nuclear family groups where the male and female establish a lifetime bond; some orangutan 'couples' have lived together as mates for more than twenty years. Individuals of other species, with some exception, seem to establish attachments between mates only for the time it takes to complete copulation.

We generalize about the *attachment* of other species, for example, that they are more typically attached to a herd, covey, hive, pride, pack, or flock, etc., rather than being individually attached as durable couples. However momentary or functional its nature, *attachment* for members of other species reflects a biologically determined pattern of survival, wherein members of each species attach themselves to a larger group, as well as, to some extent, to one another.

Turning to the human species we observe that the overall character of gender connectivity reflects not simplicity, but complexity. A single stimulus alone, pheromones for example, does not trigger human arousal, although it plays a more significant role than once thought. *Attraction* is not confined to primarily physical characteristics resulting in *arousal* to engage in copulation. *Attachment* among humans proves far more complex than mating alliances within a larger group connection, like a herd or flock. Perhaps because human gender connectivity characteristics remain so diffuse and varied, we tend to place much more emphasis on environmental factors that form them. As a result, the biological dimension of gender connectivity compels us to look more closely at each aspect of gender connectivity.

Defining the Attributes of Human Gender Connectivity

Arousal

Human *arousal*, like that of many other mammals, is a function that engages the hypothalamus, the primitive brain positioned below the thalamus and just above the brain stem near the base of the skull. The hypothalamus marshals the stimulation of human *arousal* in two directions. One direction relates to glands such as the pituitary that emit hormone neuro-chemicals into the system to generate the physiological characteristics of *arousal*. This direction appears more primitive, in that the effect upon the system basically compares to many other mammals. And because sexual stimulation for humans is not limited to pheromone triggers or a time of estrus, arousal need not depend upon an external trigger other than the physical manipulation of the penis or the clitoris. Solely from a physiological standpoint, human physical arousal needs no 'other' to achieve completion ending in orgasm.

Because of this 'mechanical' dimension of human physiological arousal, any kind of erotic stimulation, including sexually erotic fantasies, can excite a genital arousal that may be initiated by hetero-erotic, homoerotic, or autoerotic triggers. Heterosexual individuals can achieve orgasm with a same-sex partner, and homosexual individuals can achieve orgasm with a partner of another sex. Arousal leading to orgasm may be masturbatory, with or without sex toys, or may be effected by any external stimulation. Orgasmic *arousal*, therefore, proves irrelevant in determining homosexual or heterosexual 'orientation.'

Because 'orientation' does *not* depend on orgasmic arousal, various same-sex, orgasmic behaviors identified in Ancient times, as well as those traditionally condemned throughout Western history, cannot be directly compared with modern categories of homosexual or heterosexual identity. No concept of sexual orientation existed in Greco-Roman culture: only the sex act itself, not the gender of one's partner, was important. Instead, significance lay in whether an individual assumed an active or passive role in sexual engagement, and whether the active individual possessed dominant or subservient social status. Therefore, the common practice of aristocratic males engaging in sex with both men and women did not trouble people of that era, provided the aristocrat took the active role, and his partner represented a socially inferior status. An aristocratic man assuming the passive role in sex with a social inferior, however, was morally repugnant. In our era, people may label someone who has sex with both men and woman 'bisexual,' or perhaps may try to determine whether the individual is, in fact, homosexual. More than likely, many would consider that the practice of having sex with a man as well as with a woman proves the point that homosexuality reflects only a perverted behavioral deviation from the heterosexual norm. Such reasoning, however, considers orgasmic arousal as the sole factor determining 'sexual orientation' and consequently demonstrates a failure to understand the nature of gender connectivity.

The hypothalamus also marshals the stimulation of human *arousal* in another direction: the interaction and interplay with the higher mental-emotional functions of the brain cortex. This direction involves the uniquely human, higher mental powers of will, imagination, reflection, and care that help make *arousal* a mutually shared enhancement of interpersonal human relationship.

Human *arousal*, therefore, albeit a biological construct of the human brain, incorporates higher-level mental and emotional components expressed in some manageable mode of expression within the context of the biological construct. Like our animal cousins, we possess automatic sexual responses of *arousal*, but with these automatic responses come an equally biological emotional and rational capacity to manage and direct those responses. Ideally the expression of the psycho-emotional-social component of *arousal* will be characterized by respect, care, and responsibility toward oneself and others. Unfortunately, it is often expressed in self-gratification, exploitation, and abuse.

In heterosexual sexual relationships, for example, most people believe male *arousal* should lead to more than an animalistic "slam, bang, thank you ma'am" behavior. A general ethical expectation holds that sex-partners ought to have respect, understanding, and care for one another. The innateness of this ethical expectation is apparent even in the hypocritical double standard of the macho male who messes with someone else's woman but doesn't want any one else messing with his. Women commonly testify to the difficulty of experiencing arousal with a partner who lacks respect or appreciation for their personal worth. This tendency to associate personal responsibility with sexual arousal points to the psychological, emotional, and social components that are biologically constituent elements built into the brain structure of the human species.

This biological function of the hypothalamus to stimulate both the hormonal emission of glands and the higher mental-emotional functions of the brain cortex suggests why humans associate so much guilt with sex or, if not guilt, ascribe some very specific taboos to sex. It also reveals the grounds for society's abhorrence toward acts of sexual abuse, rape, molestation, and incest, which evince a disconnection of physiological aspects of *arousal* from the higher mental functions, or at least distort the higher mental functions. The link within human *arousal* to higher mental, emotional, and social function illustrates the innately biological dimension of human *arousal* and points to *arousal* being much more than purely physiological response to physical stimulus.

Attraction

We tend to think of *attraction* as purely an environmentally conditioned preference for this person or that, for one physical attribute or some other, that develops one way or another depending upon the stimuli to which we have been exposed during key developmental phases of childhood, puberty, and/or adolescence. Nevertheless, the adage that "sex sells" ought to give some clue to the biological foundations of human *attraction*. This common advertising strategy plays on a universally true human characteristic: *attraction* is as profoundly and obviously biological for human beings as for other species.

Nevertheless, human *attraction* encompasses more than simple physical attraction, including also *attraction* to another person's intellect, humor, spirituality, etc. Perhaps because the complexity of human attraction involves more social, emotional, psychological, and rational factors than the bio-physical attraction of simpler species, humans tend to conceptualize *attraction* as making conscious choices based on personal preferences. This conclusion seems natural, given that *attraction*, aside from a prelude to mating, takes on other forms like the asexual, passionate, humanitarian *attraction* to the poor or oppressed, accompanied by an altruistic effort to mitigate their impoverishment or injustice. It might also assume a form like the mixed social–sexual *attraction* teen groupies have toward pop celebrities.

In its diversity we recognize that human *attraction* is not an inevitable corollary of *arousal*. To be sure, *attraction* may relate directly to physical *arousal*, but it may also relate to appealing attributes of human personality without any physical *arousal* involved at all. A person may wish to have sex with someone because of an attraction to that person's provocative attire or sexy demeanor; but a person may also merely seek meaningful conversation because of someone's fascinating intellect, character, or personality. This diversity may point to environmentally conditioned choices made by individuals, but its diverse nature itself provides evidence of a biological constituent of *attraction*.

Earlier, in the discussion about *arousal*, I pointed out that humans associate personal responsibility with *arousal*. We make a similar association with *attraction*. Many individuals sense responsibility toward persons to whom they are attracted, and from persons attracted to themselves. They sense the appropriateness of tact regarding the what, when, and how of *attraction*. They tend to manifest discretion regarding the conditions, the timing, and the process of *attraction* between bio-physically attractive and attracted persons in a way reflective of evolutionary development seen in the instinctual courtship rituals common among many birds and mammals. The plethora of books on how to meet and attract the perfect date, as well as the popularity of online matchmaking, reflects the innate sense of propriety we have regarding the manner in which our attractions should be expressed. The degree to which individuals sense responsibility regarding *attraction* may differ from one person to the next depending on the extent to which external religious or social norms shape how *attraction* is expressed. But the fact that the sense of responsibility exists at all demonstrates that it is essentially, biologically rooted in human nature.

While valuing the innateness of discretion concerning persons to whom we are attracted, we should not make this sense of discretion work against *attraction* itself. A sense of responsibility regarding *attraction* works against it when repressive social mores, traditions, cultural expectations, and religion engender negative ideas about *attraction* per se. A common denigration equates *attraction* with lecherous cravings or with *lust* that inevitably turns into *arousal* leading to immoral sexual behavior. Occasionally parents with this denigrating view of attraction try to protect their children by narrowly sheltering them from associations with "suspect" individuals and persistently warning them about compromising relationships. The end result of this sheltering, however, may produce neurotic fears of sex, or puerile shyness around other people. Repression of attraction that is viewed as carnal desire carries the risk of producing the sexually promiscuous and abusive behaviors that repression is meant to prevent. Rather than engendering negative ideas about *attraction,* the sense of responsibility innate within *attraction* should be valued as a basic discretion that naturally guides someone in the direction of respect and appreciation for a potential mate, comparable to the simple discretions found among some primates. Religion and society should therefore encourage this natural discretion and counsel individuals in ways that enable them to become increasingly respectful of those to whom they are attracted. Hopefully, a broader and more positive awareness of the biological constructs of human *attraction* would effect such an application of religious and social counsel.

Attachment

A greater tendency exists to discount biological factors associated with the attribute of *attachment* than with *attraction.* Quite often *attachment* is seen as a matter of choice isolated from biological determinates. We assume that our associations with certain persons reflect personal selection expressed within an individual's social environment.

Unlike the attachments among other species, we tend to think of human mating *attachment* in dominantly individual, interpersonal, and durable terms epitomized in the twentieth-century phenomenon of the idealized nuclear family of father, mother, and children. *Attachment,* so perceived, appears to be the exception among most non-human species: "In humans, complex interpersonal bondings take place which have absolutely no counterpart in the animal world."[21]

---

[21] Mondimore, *A Natural History,* 154–55.

Attachment occurs in wide variety among humans. Perhaps the first form of *attachment* that comes to mind is 'family.' But 'family' also comes in a wide variety of shapes and forms. Biological families may be nuclear, extended, or communal; one parent or two parent families with children; adult siblings living together, etc. Historically some societies have prized monogamy, others polygamy, others kinship groups, and still others pantagamy (group families in which several males and females share conjugal privileges among themselves).

Non-sexual *attachments* of numerous kinds also exist, sometimes referred to as "families of choice." These might be intimate friendships, or a supportive community like a church or club, or some form of 'neighborhood' that may or may not be geographical. Attachments might be a commitment to celibacy in a monastic community of service and prayer, or an intense—even same-sex, friendship of individuals such as the celebrated Old Testament story of David and Jonathan, whose love for each other "surpassed that of a man for a woman." The kind of relationships formed in business, sports, religion, culture, politics, etc., adds another dimension to *attachment* among humans, one largely absent among other species.

If *attachments* indicate a matter of non-biological choice and preference among members of the human species, then given our intelligence and past experience, we should prove more successful in making and keeping *attachments*, in finding alternative arrangements to eliminate the immense problems we have with them. For example, one might expect the failure rate of marriages, the stifling dullness of many marriages that "stay together," and the extent of spouse abuse in society would cause us to avoid entirely this *attachment* thing we call marriage. But that doesn't work for humans. Regardless of the risks of marriage or cohabitation, or the violence experienced within so many families, people march down the aisle again and again promising to love "'till death do us part." The pledge of enduring love demonstrates that, typically, humans hold a basic ideal that *attachment* should be for a long period of time, "to live happily ever after," as our Western tradition puts it. Even when *attachments* invert into hateful obsessions, it seems people feel compelled to form new ones.

These repeated behaviors based on firmly held beliefs reveal the need for human beings to attach to another human being—not merely a fundamental need, but a biological determinant that causes us to form personal *attachments* (healthy or defective) despite the risks. We cannot escape this component of our biological constitution.

Varieties of Gender Connectivity

Just as variations occur within *sex definition, gender definition,* and *gender identity,* variations also exist for *gender connectivity.* They occur among non-human species as well as among humans. The Noah's ark view, that all non-human species come in male/female pairs, proves inconsistent with the wide range of genders and sexualities found in the animal world. Bruce Bagemihl notes this variety when he writes, "Animals with females that become males, animals with no males at all, animals that are both male and female simultaneously, animals where males resemble females, animals where females court other females and males court other males—Noah's ark was never quite like this!"[22]

Clearly the incidence of same-sex gender connectivity among non-human species demonstrates that biological determinants create variety. Same-sex gender connectivity among non-human species proves more diverse than the simple observation that animals often interact sexually with each other. In spite of a common denial that same-sex gender connectivity exists among animals, it does, in fact, represent a vast and diverse range of activities.[23] Among the many varieties of same-sex activity that Bagemihl identifies include: Silver Gulls, among which females form stable, long-lasting lesbian pair-bonds and raise families,

[22] Bagemihl, *Biological Exuberance,* 36.

[23] Bagemihl, *Biological Exuberance,* 12.

while males participate in promiscuous same-sex activity; Black Swans, among which only males form long-term same-sex couples and raise offspring, and Sage Grouse, where only females engage in group "orgies" of same-sex activity.[24]

Same-sex arousal and attraction among animals clearly indicates that a biological rather than volitional component forms same-sex gender connectivity. The will to choose "immoral" behavior hardly applies to non-human species. No known evidence supports that an animal can be tempted to choose an *immoral* option, or be influenced to choose a *wrong* direction toward same-sex arousal or attraction. Although homonegative individuals attribute the cause of human same-sex arousal and attraction to misdirected eroticism, animals do not make the moral decisions that make same-sex arousal and attraction a supposedly *mis*directed eroticism.

"Eroticism" inherently implies the subjective ability to discriminate the difference between identical conditions in different circumstances (i.e., the erotic significance of exposed genitals in a clinic examination room as opposed to exposed genitals in a strip joint). We have no way to interview animals about their erotic experience. Struts, roars, and plumage apparently excite animals, but why one individual may be more exciting to an animal than another is something they cannot tell us, nor can they tell us why a group of animals will have no erotic interest in a pair in their midst actively engaged in copulation.

The biological dimensions of gender connectivity among non-human species serve as useful indicators of the biological variations of human *gender connectivity*. We share a "sexual plasticity" with non-human species that indicates a biological influence upon our sexual identity relative to *gender connectivity*.[25] Therefore it remains implausible that human *gender connectivity* can be exempt from biological influences causing such variety among the rest of

---

[24] Bagemihl, *Biological Exuberance,* 29–30.

[25] Bagemihl, *Biological Exuberance,* 45.

creation. In the same way that fundamentally biological determinants play a part in shaping variations in all other aspects of human and animal sexual identity, one might also reasonably expect that biological determinants produce variations in human *gender connectivity* upon all three of its attributes: *arousal, attraction,* and *attachment.*

Another clue to a biological component forming same-sex gender connectivity can be found in those cultures where anthropological studies find same-sex behaviors structurally integrated into the social order. The clues to same-sex gender connectivity that we find in those cultures, however, will not reflect conspicuous same-sex behavior, but rather more discreet same-sex gender connections. For example, some parts of New Guinea and Melanesian islands require male transgenerational fellatio of all young boys as they transition into adult manhood.

Ten to twenty percent of New Guinea[26] cultures and parts of island Melanesia institutionalized same-sex behavior.[27] Male children, from birth to early adolescence, lived with their mothers in women's quarters, where a child was physically nourished with breastmilk and nurtured in social development by the women. At about age seven, male children moved from the women's quarters to the men's quarters to be mentored by the men in adult social skills. Within the male-exclusive environment they were subjected to various initiation and purification rites to cleanse them from the female contamination of their childhood. At puberty onset and through adolescence, until he became an adult, a boy was required to perform fellatio with young adult males who had not yet fathered a child. By this means, a child acquired *jerungdu,* a

---

[26] New Guinea, the second largest island in the world, situated north of Australia, was politically divided in 1975 into Western New Guinea, incorporated into Indonesia, and the East half of the island, the independent country of Papua New Guinea.

[27] Greenberg, *The Construction of Homosexuality,* 28.

tangible masculinity substance the tribal males believed was found in a man's semen.

Notably, while fellatio performed on adult males remained mandatory for adolescent boys, strong taboos existed concurrently against same-sex behaviors outside the culturally institutionalized form. Of course, the very existence of the taboos tacitly acknowledges that instances of "illicit" same sex behavior occurred.

Additionally, whereas nearly all boys successfully transitioned into arranged marriages as adults, a rare few demonstrated some kind of indisposition toward heterosexual relationships. Those who failed in marriages were ridiculed and excluded from serving as semen donors because of their questionable effectiveness in nourishing manhood. Within this culture and its heterosexual gender connectivity, these uncommon instances of illicit, same-sex behavior and failed heterosexual relationships reveal biological components causing a variation in typical gender connectivity.

Notice that I do *not* cite the institutionalized form of same-sex behavior in this culture as evidence of biological causation of homosexuality. If anything, the institutionalized behavior establishes the biological causation of heterosexuality. Early exposure to same-sex behavior did not steer young New Guinea boys into a homosexual lifestyle, as many in our culture fear would happen to our young boys. Almost all adolescents of the New Guinea and Melanesian cultures remained heterosexual, despite the compulsory fellatio they performed through adolescence. They grew up with the same heterosexual, erotic, fantasies as virile boys in our culture.[28] Therefore, the New Guinea culture appears to demonstrate that a man's socially stigmatized venture into illicit same-sex behavior, or his difficulty in adapting to heterosexual relationships is likely attributable to some sort of predication (what one

---

[28] For a detailed description of sexual identity issues in cultures other than Western culture, and specifically a thorough discussion of the effects of institutional same-sex behavior on male sexual development within Melanesian cultures, see anthropologist Patrick Chapman's book *Thou Shalt Not Love*.

does as a result of who one is) rather than predilection (what one does because one likes to).

Although the last several paragraphs refer almost exclusively to male same-sex gender connectivity, the absence of references to female same-sex gender connectivity should not be inferred as an attempt to belittle the significance of female same-sex gender connectivity or disparage the biological significance of female same-sex gender connectivity in particular.

Among most cultures and for most of human history, women have been defined by male prerogative and controlled by male domination. The sexual implications are that males arrogate the importance of their sexuality over women's sexuality, and, in some cases, create the cultural norms and mores that establish absolute control over female sexuality. Even in our enlightened, post-Renaissance, Western culture, scholarly opinion (by men) maintained for a time that women experienced no sexual eroticism at all: their functional design remained limited to impregnation and birthing children. Thus, female same-sex gender connectivity has remained unexplored chiefly due to males' lack of interest in female sexuality, largely denied because males exercise such thorough sexual control as to submerge issues of female same-sex gender connectivity under heterosexual strictures.

A Muslim Pakistani woman from a religiously conservative region, for example, would most likely be invisible if she experienced a lesbian predication. In the first place, she would likely not be able to formulate in her mind the concept of 'lesbian' because her culture offers no scripts to help her identify such same-sex feelings and attractions. All she could recognize is the divergence, seemingly not shared by other women, between her experiences and what her culture expects. Secondly, she would completely disappear in a culture that forces women to marry at a young age, a culture that imposes total female economic dependence upon a husband due to the scarcity of jobs even for educated women, and a culture where fear makes even chance gossip within a gender-segregated group of women dangerous to any girl who dares confide any same-sex predication. Lesbian women who have escaped from this repression to a more tolerant society confide that many women like them are forced to surrender to heterosexual norms and cannot admit their homosexuality. These minority women, forced to live a lie, tragically represent instances of sexual repression that provide eloquent testimony that homosexuality is not a choice, but the constituent nature of their being. They represent a variety of same-sex gender connectivity that is forcibly scripted to appear heterosexual.

In short, institutionalized same-sex *behavior* does not in itself indicate a biological component of same-sex gender connectivity, nor does the apparent "absence" of same-sex behavior, as some morally conservative societies claim, prove that instances of innate, same-sex gender connectivity does not exist within them.

Other circumstances illustrate the same principle that common instances of same-sex behavior do not indicate innate same-sex gender connectivity. Same-sex behavior frequently occurs in prisons, naval ships, or any grouping of males experiencing long-term inaccessibility to females. In cultures that tolerate open prostitution, males lacking options for economic survival frequently turn to prostitution for the same reasons as women in similar economic plight. Such instances of homosexual behavior simply indicate *non*-innate gender connectivity as opposed to the far more rare instances of *innate* same-sex gender connectivity.

A sex act does not in itself establish the nature of gender connectivity. Same-sex arousal alone (leading to orgasm), attraction alone (manifest in fantasies, emotional obsessions or romantic interests), and attachment alone (in the form of same-sex bonding or intense friendships) do not each separately indicate a biological component either to same-sex or other-sex gender connectivity. Only the *integration* of arousal, attraction, and attachment together—toward the same sex or another sex—constitutes a kind of gender connectivity experienced as something innate, thereby indicating a sexual identity one may call an 'orientation,' such as heterosexual or homosexual.

Integration of the three aspects of gender connectivity does not require the actualization of one or all aspects. An unmarried, virgin, heterosexual female is not something other than heterosexual because she has not yet satisfied her natural attraction to and intrinsic capacity for arousal with a man through sexual intercourse, nor fulfilled her innate aspiration for attachment in a heterosexual marriage. Neither is a celibate priest, who happens to be gay, something other than homosexual because he defers his natural attraction to men and creates no occasion for arousal leading to sex with another man. In order to detect the *intrinsic* nature of an individual's gender connectivity, we must determine the main or exclusive gender of the primary relationships an individual is innately motivated to establish, in which all three aspects of gender connectivity—arousal, attraction and attachment—integrate in fact or in prospect.

At a recent PFLAG[29] gathering, a twenty something Japanese-American woman, exquisitely beautiful, related her experience when she first indicated to her mother the nature of her gender connectivity. She was eight when she took a magazine to her mother, pointed to the picture of an attractive Olympic figure skating champion and said, "I want her." Her mother responded, "You don't mean you want her, dear. You mean you want to be like her." "No mother, I want her," she insisted. Imbedded in her use of the word 'want' was the profound desire to be integrally enclosed in relationship with another person, somewhat like the lost child who sobs, "I want my mother." In that childhood moment of actual attraction to the skater in the picture, the young girl understood the attachment she desired in prospect with someone toward whom she might also eventually experience incipient forms of arousal.

Integrated gender connectivity, whether integrated toward an individual of the same sex or of the other sex, must be given

---

[29] PFLAG is a national organization of Parents and Friends of Lesbians and Gays, together with bisexual and transgendered persons.

prominent consideration in the dramatic development of sexual identity that occurs in adolescence. During this period of development, the varieties of gender connectivity are frequently divulged. Therefore, it is mandatory that mentors and counselors responsible for guiding youth in their journey of self-discovery recognize the possible variations of gender connectivity. It is as important for adolescents to discover who they are *not* as sexual beings, as it is for them to discover who they *are*. It should not be assumed that an adolescent who experiences homosexual eroticism is gay, nor that an adolescent who perfectly enacts the expected roles of heterosexual relationships is straight. Sexual identity is perfectly clear to some youth as they develop. But for others, it proves confusing. Those who experience confusion require adult counselors with patience, a listening ear, and wise understanding to enable them to find their authentic identity.

Again, reflection upon one's *own* sexual identity, particularly for those who identify as heterosexual, proves invaluable. If an individual were asked to pinpoint when she decided she was most aroused by someone of the other sex, or when he adjusted his sexual attractions toward individuals of the other sex only, or when she limited her dating and marriage aspirations to a person of the other sex only, most likely individuals would respond, "I didn't ever make those choices. Its just part of the package of who I am." Most heterosexual persons take for granted the innate nature of their integrated other-sex gender connectivity. Nevertheless, gender connectivity, whether same-sex or other-sex, remains a part of the innate nature of *every* human being.

I argue that gender connectivity, when all three aspects—arousal, attachment, and attachment—are integrated, constitutes an innate part of sexual identity; and thus far, I have framed the argument in terms of a homosexual and heterosexual dichotomy. This structure requires a disclaimer. Because our culture war over homosexuality casts the divide between homosexual and heterosexual, one cannot engage the issue without acknowledging where the battle lines are drawn. In reality, however, we cannot reduce the issue of gender connectivity into binary categories of homosexuality and heterosexuality. Neither biological realities nor environmental realities allow us to catalog things so neatly on one side or the other. Therefore, I do not argue on behalf of a clean division of people into heterosexual or homosexual categories. Sexual identity, comprised of sex definition, gender definition, gender identity, and gender connectivity, remains too varied and complex to settle for such binary or bipolar conceptualizations or any other strict categorization. This reality proves truthful even though dominant tendencies exist in gender connectivity toward a heterosexual and a homosexual classification, dominant tendencies in sex definition include a male or a female classification, and dominant tendencies in gender identification support a masculine or a feminine classification. Nevertheless, the attempt to fit all individuals somewhere along a bipolar scale or to catalog each person within a delimiting definition of sexual identity is bound to fail.

Alfred Kinsey's seven-step scale of male sexuality remains one of the most oft-quoted studies in identifying the nature of homosexuality as a behavior whose incidents can be measured on a bipolar scale from exclusively homosexual to heterosexual behavior. To some extent, homosexual and heterosexual fantasies can also be measured scientifically, but as internal psychological experiences they cannot be verified in the same way as external behavior. Believing no biological evidence proved innate homosexuality, Kinsey approached the question of homosexuality from a position of pure science. On the basis of pure science, only instances of sexual behavior may be qualified and empirically measured. Love cannot be scientifically measured or examined; neither can the typically subjective aspect of gender connectivity we identify as *attraction*. The part of sexuality related to desire and attraction still remains something of a mystery from the standpoint of pure science (though studies in neurobiology and brain imaging may prove helpful in the future).

Problematically, Kinsey's numerical scale fails to take into consideration the person who has strong feelings of erotic arousal toward same-sex individuals and strong attraction toward those of the same sex, but who has never had a homosexual experience and will not acknowledge same-sex erotic feelings. On the basis of scientifically verifiable behavior, that individual must be placed on the exclusively heterosexual side of the Kinsey scale, which would be false in terms of the individual's *subjective* experience. Still another problem with Kinsey's one dimensional bipolar scale relates to its failure to acknowledge the important involvement of gender identification characteristics. At what point does the scale weigh gender characteristics like "butch" or "femme" lesbian, or "nellie" or "guy" gays relative to sexual orientation? These terms employ the language of stereotypes; yet one cannot assume that a masculine female or a feminine male is homosexual, or that a masculine male or a feminine female is heterosexual. Many people may assume wrongly that a stereotypically masculine man like Rock Hudson—a handsome, muscular, athletic "ladies man"— belongs on the heterosexual side of Kinsey's scale. A one-dimensional scale based on the single factor of sexual behavior, "scientific" as it may be, simply cannot support an adequate understanding of the varieties of gender connectivity.

Edward Stein, in *The Mismeasure of Desire* (1999), attempts to improve on Kinsey's one-dimensional heterosexual-to-homosexual scale. On Kinsey's scale, bisexuality would be based on the comparable degree of sexual activity with same-sex or other-sex partners. This determination, however, does not consider that a person may harbor intense sexual desires for a person of the same sex but rarely engages in same-sex activities, meanwhile possessing limited sexual interest in but frequently engaging in sexual activity with persons of the opposite sex.

Stein adds an additional set of axes to Kinsey's scale to form a two-dimensional bipolar scale: one axis measures the degree of desire for and actual sexual activity with same sex partners, and another measures the degree of desire and actual sexual activity with other sex partners.[30] One must question, however, why only two dimensions should appear on the bipolar scale of sexual orientation. Why not three or four dimensions, or even more?

Designing bipolar scales of any dimension is inadequate for characterizing the complexities of human gender connectivity. Gender connectivity cannot be simplified to a heterosexual/homosexual scale based upon purely measurable data. For this reason, and for others associated with sexual identity characteristics of gender definition and gender identity, we should try not to locate people on scales between sets of polarities based on single attributes of gender connectivity. Any single human being possesses too many overlapping facets to his or her being that frustrate our efforts to place unequivocally that individual onto some arbitrary point between two poles. Thus, gender connectivity, like most other uniquely human experiences, proves too complex to be explained except in human terms. As Mondimore asserts, "If our most human quality is our enormous diversity of capacities and capabilities, especially in our relationships with each other, it should not be at all surprising that in some of us, the capacity for love becomes oriented toward members of the same sex."[31]

Therefore, I strongly advocate *against* considering and using 'gender connectivity' as a synonym for 'sexual orientation.' According to Roger L. Worthington, *sexual orientation* technically refers to one's sexuality-related predispositions, whether constructed genetically, biologically, environmentally, and/or socially. When a person recognizes and accepts his or her sexual

---

[30] Stein, *The Mismeasure of Desire*, 54–61. For purposes of developing a consistent and powerful account of sexual orientation that fits to a considerable extent with our intuitions, the two-dimensional account of sexual orientation, however the axes are drawn, seems like a good choice, better at least than the more popular binary or bipolar views of sexual orientation.

[31] Mondimore, *A Natural History*, 157.

orientation, it is called *sexual orientation identity.*[32] To be sure, we often talk in terms of *orientation*, whether that means a homosexual orientation, a bisexual orientation, or a heterosexual orientation. But what remains implied in such loaded verbiage is the assumption that sexual orientation is about *sex*. 'Sexual orientation' seems to lean in the direction of identifying the gender of those whom one is predisposed to "take to bed." 'Gender connectivity,' on the other hand, reaches into the full range of attitudes and relationships established with other people.

In its more specific connotation, gender connectivity points to the identity of the primary personal relationship within which we seek the closest sense of belonging (attachment), the strongest desire to be together (attraction), and the most intense mutuality of physical closeness (arousal). In its broadest connotation, gender connectivity recognizes the complexity of human gender relationships with other gendered human beings in society. For example, in human society we are not so gender simplistic as are animal herds and flocks; hence, we recognize positive and negative ways people interact with each other in the workplace or marketplace, etc., and how our relationships have distinct dynamics between and among gendered people. The hiring standard of "attractive women" for certain occupations (television news anchors comes to mind), sexual harassment in the workplace, as well as sorties of teenage guys and girls scoping each other out in shopping malls, illustrate that a broader social scope of gender connectivity exists than represented in only dyadic, interpersonal connections.

Also, for the purpose of avoiding arbitrary labeling, I prefer to use the term 'gender connectivity' and its associated attributes of *arousal*, *attraction*, and *attachment*, rather than using the term 'sexual orientation.' These components of our identity better lead us into the rich and complex nature of our sexual identity, unique to each individual and expressing the varied ways persons connect with other gendered persons. The concept of gender connectivity helps us better appreciate the diverse human qualities in

---

[32] Worthington, "Heterosexual Identity Development," 497.

our relationships with one another than does the concept of sexual orientation. Advantageously, the concept does not require categorical determinations of the exact nature of an individual's sexual identity. We may recognize that most people are transparently integrated in their gender connectivity so that they are conspicuously same-sex or other-sex in their innate nature. But the concept of gender connectivity also allows us to appreciate the person who may indeed be homosexual, but chooses to remain in and sustain a heterosexual marriage. It also allows us to appreciate the heterosexual individual who chooses never to have other-sex conjugal relationships, as well as the homosexual individual who chooses celibacy. And it allows us to appreciate the individual who fits none of the typical combinations by which we attempt to slice and dice human relationships into some segment of the heterosexual/homosexual scale.

Gender connectivity also recognizes that dysfunctional personality development can lead to some individuals' inability to integrate its three attributes. A rapist or child molester experiences sexual arousal in connection with internal rage and frustration rather than as part of interpersonal attraction or mutual progression toward attachment. A physically and sexually abused woman, who cannot trust men or be attracted to them because of a past history of psychological and emotional trauma caused by men, is likely to be non-integrated in her gender connectivity.

Therefore, to appreciate and understand sexual identity, we ought to recognize that terms such as 'homosexual' or 'heterosexual' cannot support an all-encompassing description of any one individual. To label anyone tends to impose upon individuals an arbitrary notion of who they are. Persons who do not fit under the label of our predefined definitions may individually experience life in a kind of scripted social limbo in which even self-understanding becomes difficult. Misunderstanding increases whenever society's need to hang definitive labels on people prevails. In an area as complicated as sexuality, labels become onerous, and comparisons to heterosexuals and homosexuals prove unconvincing.[33]

Unique life experiences interact with unique biological potentials to produce each individual's unique sexual identity. Because of this complex interaction, we must recognize that sexuality may involve certain choices in the way we respond and interact with our environment; but sexuality also involves discovery leading to a progressive recognition of our constituent nature—*not* a choice—in our expeditionary journey through life. Our sexuality is not just the physical magnetism of sexual attraction, but also a matter of affection, integrity, fidelity, and yearning to love and to be loved in enduring partnership with another human being. Sexuality "involves not only the urges of the body but longings of heart, mind, and spirit for life-giving companionship and lifelong friendship."[34]

Dissent Regarding Gender Connectivity

Homonegative groups intensely resist arguments favoring innate same-sex gender connectivity with a bias that sometimes leads to outright rejection of a biological component that shapes it, or prompts them to claim a higher, religious authority to dismiss the relevance of scientific evidence supporting it. We all have biases, but 'bias' is not synonymous with prejudice until one refuses to consider seriously evidence on both sides of an issue.

Repeatedly, I have encountered resistance from some family members, friends, colleagues, and agitators to look honestly at both sides of the issue, as they continue to voice homonegative sentiments. Some of them start with the premise that homosexuality is evil and subsequently search only for seemingly credible information to support their premise. Some persons refuse to engage in dialogue with articulate gay men and women,

---

[33] Chandler, *Passages of Pride*, 146.

[34] Chilstrom and Erdahl, *Sexual Fulfillment*, 105.

yet quickly form or support groups and alliances designed to indoctrinate others with anti-gay views and propaganda.

Some individuals, who have strongly dogmatic and moralistic religious views, typically reduce ethical issues in society to clear black-and-white distinctions. Believing that God's Word provides the start and end point for understanding one's self, history, and the cosmos, they declare that because the Bible reveals that God created human beings male and female, clearly homosexual sexual identity is contrary to God's purpose in creation.

Some persons have strong biases against homosexuality because they were once hurt by a homosexual person who abused, raped, or abandoned them. Or a spouse or child was shocked and hurt by their spouse's or parent's disclosure of a gay, lesbian, or transgender identity.

Some who are the most relentless in their opposition to homo-sexuality are those who, in denial about their *own* homosexuality, project self-loathing upon everyone and everything that brings the issue close to home. And further, some relentless opponents of homosexuality are admittedly homosexual themselves, yet they renounce their homosexuality out of profound guilt and internal conflict from trying to resolve their inner turmoil.

Public as well as personal biases persist, supported by denial of evidence, restricting evidence, distorting evidence, and in some cases, outright lying about evidence.

One example of denying evidence is the rejection, misrepre-sentation, and cover up of the astounding amount and variety of scientific information on animal homosexuality that began to emerge more than 200 years ago. According to Bruce Bagemihl, much of this information was buried out of sight intentionally, thereby obstructing the public from realizing the "full extent to which homosexuality permeates the natural world."[35]

---

[35] In *Biological Exuberance*, Bagemihl states:

Most of it is inaccessible even to biologists, much less to the general public. What has managed to appear in print is often

An example of restricting evidence occurred in a bizarre episode at the end of the nineteenth century—one that profoundly affected later scientific inquiry and opinion, to some degree even to the present day. German neurologist, professor of psychiatry, and director of the psychiatric clinic of the University of Vienna, Richard von Krafft-Ebing, wrote *Psychopathia Sexualis*, published in 1886. This compendium presents more than 200 case studies of individuals whose lives were "bizarre" and "pathological." Using about forty case studies of homosexuals derived from police records, mental asylums, and other psychiatrists' case studies, Krafft-Ebing fashioned a 'scientific' foundation about the psychopathological, dysfunctional nature of homosexuals, concluding that they were over-sexed, shallow people prone to mental illness and incapable of having mature relationships.[36]

At the same time, a prominent literary figure of late nineteenth-century England, John Addington Symonds, wrote autobiographical diaries chronicling his own homosexuality and referencing the homosexuality of many of his acquaintances. A significant amount of Symonds' autobiographical work, as well as his philosophical and ethical reflection about homosexuality, became incorporated in the book *Sexual Inversion* by Henry Havelock Ellis, an English physician and one of the foremost authorities on sexuality in the English-speaking world. The book

---

hidden away in obscure journals and unpublished dissertations, or buried even further under outdated value judgments and cryptic terminology. Most of this information, however, simply remains unpublished, the result of a general climate of ignorance, disinterest, and even fear and hostility surrounding discussion of homosexuality that exists to this day—not only in primatology, but throughout the field of zoology. Equally disconcerting, popular works on animals routinely omit any mention of homosexuality, even when the authors are clearly aware that such information is available in the original scientific material. As a result, most people don't realize the full extent to which homosexuality permeates the natural world. (87)

[36] Mondimore, *A Natural History*, 38–39.

contained more than thirty case studies of homosexuals—essentially clinically boring descriptions of men and women not only emotionally stable but also socially integrated members of their communities. These examples provided a stark contrast to the lurid details of Krafft-Ebing's case studies of criminals and psychopaths. Describing the contrast between the two books, Francis Mondimore writes,

> In contrast to reading through *Psychopathia Sexualis*, at times not unlike picking up a rock and finding all sorts of slimy and grotesque creatures slithering and skittering for cover, the 'inverts' revealed by reading *Sexual Inversion* are notable for their normality.[37]

What is remarkable about the publication of the two books is the dismal betrayal of truth and fairness manifest in the official response to them. Krafft-Ebing's lurid book went through multiple publications to meet reader demand, became a standard authority among physicians and psychiatrists on the nature of homosexuality, and perpetuated decades of research whose purpose was to bear out the pathological nature of homosexuality. In contrast, Ellis' book, revolutionary for describing homosexuality as an innate, biological predisposition and for describing homosexuals as normal people, was banned as lewd and wicked.

Distortion of information—reshaping information to frighten people—also characterizes one-sided bias. Referring to the legalization of same-sex marriage in Holland, and the liberalization of attitudes toward homosexual persons in Scandinavian countries, alarmists purported that the demographic information in those countries demonstrated that relaxing moral censures against homosexuals also led to a steady decline in heterosexual marriages and the deterioration of the family institution.

As a point of fact, the decline of heterosexual marriages began in these countries *before* any liberalization of social attitude and legalization of same-sex marriage . . . and for reasons having

---

[37] Mondimore, *A Natural History*, 48–49.

nothing to do with these factors. The decline of heterosexual marriage reflected post-World War II economic issues as well as changes in emerging social dynamics: women's shifting role in the professions and workplace resulted in greater economic independence from men, and women's new reproductive control allowed them to postpone childbearing and to separate sexual activity from procreation. These dynamics, *not* liberal attitudes toward homosexuality, produced a greater number of households consisting of non-married couples choosing to postpone marriage and parenthood, and, in some cases, to defer marriage permanently.

Granted, much confusing information exists about homosexuality that makes a balanced view difficult to acquire for someone who believes it an inherently evil behavior. One problem lies with the seemingly higher profile of promiscuity among some gay men than among straight men. Citing statistics about gay men's short-term relationships, one-night-stands, and frequenting of gay bars and baths, some individuals conclude that gays therefore are more debauched than promiscuous straight men.

But quantifying sexual promiscuity among homosexuals does not prove anything lewd about homosexuality, but rather only suggests that promiscuity is prominent in male sexual behavior in general. Driven by hormones and instructed by society to be aggressors, males, regardless of whether they are gay or straight, are more apt than women to pursue their sexual desires.[38] But perhaps the assumption that women remain more reticent about casual sex no longer holds true, given the extent of sexual activity among college-age women who, with contraceptives to control their reproductive choices, are less worried about unplanned pregnancy than were women a generation ago.

Some who maintain a homonegative bias argue that statistics confirm the notion that homosexuality is a spiritual disease leading to personal misery, mental illness, and a life hounded by guilt. The natural question, however, is whether homosexuality

---

[38] Chandler, *Passages of Pride*, 152.

per se causes these personality disorders, or are they attributable instead to the demonizing of the homosexual individual, as well as to lurid cultural depictions of homosexual behavior that intensify social rejection, censure, and too frequently, lead to abuse and violence against homosexuals?

Several scenarios well illustrate the problem. Consider what a gay or lesbian teenager, compensating and coping with same-sex desire during the critical period of sexual development in adolescence, might do under the pressure of verbal abuse and bullying by schoolmates. For some homosexual youth, the harassment and impossible expectation to conform to heterosexual standards causes them to break. Suicide rates among gay teens are double that of their straight peers,[39] perhaps even higher.

Parents and siblings should try to comprehend the damage to self-image upon an adolescent child when they deprecate a child, or turn that child out of the family upon discovery that the child or brother/sister is homosexual.[40]

Religious leaders likewise should consider the effect their public and frequent denunciation of homosexuality as an abomination to God might have upon devoutly religious, but closeted, gay or lesbian parishioners. What should a deeply religious homosexual person feel when told that truly godly believers must abstain from this abomination and must earnestly commit to the divine power that helps overcome wicked lusts. Might not we expect a profound spiritual crisis in the parishioner who, for all his or her earnest faith and prayer, still experiences these attractions and urges, and more and more despairs over a secret and "sinful" condition?

An acquaintance once shared the deep pain he felt when a close friend of many decades, for whom he was even a groomsman in his wedding, hung up the phone on him as soon as he

---

[39] *2005 Massachusetts Youth Risk Behavior Survey*, 50.

[40] Greenberg, *The Construction of Homosexuality*, 341.

heard his voice because, having learned he was gay, the friend wanted nothing more to do with a homosexual.

No wonder individuals who have undergone psychotherapy or religious exit counseling based on homonegative premises *sometimes* come to hate themselves. Not surprisingly, self-identified homosexual individuals who engage in such reparative therapy often announce that they are miserable and declare of their homosexuality, 'I detest it!'[41]

Most emphatically, one should *not* generalize that all or even most homosexuals are innately unhappy and mentally diseased. In fact, I witnessed quite the opposite in my personal interactions with hundreds of homosexual individuals in a Dallas church whose membership included more than 3,000 gay, lesbian, bisexual, and transgender people. Most of those I knew demonstrated, at least outwardly, innate happiness and mental stability.

Many individuals with a homonegative bias demonstrate a strong preference to define homosexuality as a behavior. Such a definition seems a fairly simple concept to grasp, and has the advantage of characterizing a person in a way that is objective and scientifically accessible.[42] To determine who is homosexual, one must only identify the sex acts a person performs and whether these sex acts involve someone of the same sex. This definition has an even greater "advantage" of reinforcing the opinion that homosexuality is mutable—changing one's sexual orientation is as simple as selecting a sex partner of a different gender! This way of identifying homosexuality, according to Mondimore, loses sight of the fact that sexual identity and sexual behavior are not the same.

> [D]evelopment of a homosexual identity and the decision to engage in same-sex intimacy are quite independent processes. Individuals may engage in homosexual behaviors for a variety of purposes and may or may not be

---

[41] Greenberg, *The Construction of Homosexuality*, 428–29.

[42] Stein, *The Mismeasure of Desire*, 42–44.

homosexual in orientation. Homosexual contact during adolescence, as an expression of sexual exploring and defining, is common. Teenage male prostitutes, found throughout the United States and the world, exhibit what might be called 'economic' homosexuality—many, perhaps most, of these young men consider themselves heterosexual. Homosexuality in closed institutions like prisons and boarding schools has been called 'situational homosexuality.' When same-sex intimacy is the only available outlet for sexual release, many individuals engage in homosexual activity.[43]

In other words, under some circumstances anyone could perform same-sex acts without necessarily having a 'homosexual orientation.' This reduction again supports the idea that homosexuality is mutable, a choice. The fallacy of such reasoning, however, is that homosexuality is not solely behavioral; same-sex sexual behavior, while it may be part of what characterizes homosexuality, is not its only defining factor.

One deeply problematic circumstance for some people with homonegative biases is the person who "becomes" homosexual at some point in life, because this later identification as gay or lesbian seems to conflict with that individual's claim that homosexuality is immutable. Those who hold such biases must acknowledge that they lack privileged access not only to an individual's general thoughts and feelings, but also particular sexual desires, fantasies, and so forth; yet they nevertheless refuse to accept an individual's personal assessment of his or her sexuality and to conclude that the person who claims to be gay or lesbian is indeed immutably homosexual. Holding such a bias may prevent a person from acknowledging that the reason a person may come to recognize their homosexuality later in life is because same-sex desires have been deeply repressed in a

---

[43] Mondimore, *A Natural History*, 169.

person's subconscious. Theoretically, because social stigma upon some individuals causes them to bury same-sex desires in the subconscious, those desires may not surface until much later in life.[44] For example, a 45-year-old woman with three children who suddenly leaves her husband of twenty-five years and claims, "I'm a lesbian," obviously poses a great difficulty to the person who refutes the notion that homosexuality is an intrinsic element of someone's nature.

But what about the homosexual innateness of an individual in opposite circumstances? How does a person who believes homosexuality is *not* innate understand the "happily" married-with-two-children youth director of a conservative church, who gives testimonies about his "liberation" from a former life as a practicing homosexual, yet admits under questioning that he continues to have homosexual thoughts and desires? Do they assume that as long as this youth director does not practice homosexuality, he is now heterosexual?

This young youth director fits a dispositional view of homosexuality that says a person may be internally disposed to homosexuality but will not or cannot enter into a homosexual experience with someone. That is, strong moral restraint may cause one person to reject homosexual acts with another person; and for others, life circumstance may make experiencing homosexual acts with another person impossible. With respect to persons with dispositional homosexuality, we have no more privileged access to their general thoughts or feelings nor their particular sexual desires, fantasies, and the like than for persons with self-identified homosexuality, whose repressed and unconscious homosexual feelings finally come to awareness later in life. How then, should we understand a person living with specific geographical (rural, small-town America), social (demanding work schedule that limits social contact), or emotional (self-hatred or high religious

---

[44] Stein, *The Mismeasure of Desire*, 44f.

commitments) circumstances in which they may find no appropriate sexual partners with whom to engage their desires?[45]

Self-identification at an earlier stage becomes difficult to assess when questioning what a person might do or feel erotically whose unconscious repressed desires surface later in life. Likewise, assessing a person's feelings and same-sex consciousness from a dispositional view becomes complicated when that individual will not or cannot have homosexual experiences. In the former example, was the person *not* homosexual until he or she acted upon same-sex desires; or in the latter example, is the person *no longer* a homosexual simply because he or she cannot or does not act on same-sex desires? It is easier for a person who is homo-negative to answer these questions by merely clinging to the belief that homosexuality is simply behavior.

Undeniably, a limited number of persons who believe their gender connectivity is same-sex appear to change to a heterosexual mode of gender connectivity. Persons who undergo such a change represent unique individuals, whose experience reflects the end result of the developmental dynamics that have shaped them. But if we assume that *all* can change because *some* can change, we do violence to the vast majority who cannot change. The assumption that *all* can change is absolutely false and dangerous. To postulate that every homosexual is a product of environmentally developed behavior that can be altered by psychological reparation and/or spiritual disciplines risks imposing profoundly destructive consequences on those who cannot change even when they earnestly try. In cases of biologically innate gender connectivity, it is not uncommon under compelling circumstances to make people adopt *behaviors* opposite to their biological constitution, be it same-sex or other-sex; but the constitution itself remains unchanged.

On the other hand, some individuals experience tragically destructive interpersonal relationships with people they should be able to trust most and from whom they should receive the most

---

[45] Stein, *The Mismeasure of Desire*, 45–46.

love and support. Due to these negative experiences, they may indeed experience confusion regarding their sexual identity. This grave confusion may lead some to adopt same-sex behavior and relationships that result in the person self-identifying as homosexual. If we assume homosexuality is innate for everyone who self-identifies as such—a false and dangerous assumption—we will do violence to some persons by insisting that they not question their homosexuality. The postulation that no one can change homosexual identity risks glossing over the potentially destructive effect of unresolved sexual conflicts potentially exacerbated by the perpetuation of same-sex relationships contrary to one's essential other-sex nature. Such individuals need encouragement to identify and manage their sexual conflicts and, in the context of healthy individuation, to help them realize the nature of gender connectivity that authentically belongs to them.

Unfortunately, one of the strongest defenders of homonegative bias, and also one of the greatest violators of human dignity is the institution that ought to, above any other, understand and appreciate persons who are different: the religious institution. Religious institutions perpetrate violation by making absolutes of moral codes regarding homosexuality in spite of scientific evidence that, at minimum, calls for re-examination of these codes, and that selectively borrows outdated or unsubstantiated findings of social sciences to contemporize and substantiate religious convictions.

An American Lutheran Publicity Bureau publication revealed this unfortunate bias about homosexuality by answering the title question "Can Homosexual Love Be Blessed?" with an unequivocal "No." Despite scientific and anecdotal evidence that homosexuality cannot be reduced to a behavior, the pamphlet declared in three statements that homosexuality is indeed a behavior.

The first statement identifies homosexuality with sexual "acts" in citing Biblical texts and stating, "The Bible clearly condemns homosexual *acts* as a violation of God's will" (emphasis mine). The second statement implies homosexuality is an unacceptable act by stating that only one valid sexual act exists: "The Bible also teaches that there is only one place where *sexual union* serves God's purposes—in the union of a man and a woman in marriage" (emphasis mine). The third statement assumes that homosexuality is an act of sin resulting from disordered desires expressed in violation of God's will: "The Christian doctrine of sin teaches us that our human desires are disordered, that we don't naturally seek God's will." In other words, homosexuality is an *expression* of unbridled desire. It is a *behavior* enacted when bent homoerotic desire is unchecked.[46]

Based on the premise that homosexuality is a sinful behavior, the pamphlet expands its argument that homosexual love cannot be tolerated by referencing marriage, self-satisfaction, and justice. Concerning marriage, the pamphlet blames society for losing the link between sex and family. Specifically, because homosexual behavior lies outside of marriage, it thereby violates the link between sex and family. Concerning self-satisfaction, the pamphlet blames society for equating happiness with self-satisfaction. By implication, a sexual act is pleasurable, therefore homosexuality, understood as pleasurable behavior, is wrongly justified in claiming that it results in happiness. Concerning justice, the pamphlet distinguishes between justly safeguarding individual's rights against discrimination and violence because of who they are, and extending those protections to individual participants in wrongful behavior as though such behaviors should receive full acceptance and approval. The author implies that self-identified homosexuals should have no special rights because rights ought not be extended on the basis of sinful behavior. The clear principle of the pamphlet is that homosexuality is behavior—evil behavior.

This conclusion raises an important ethical issue. The premise and declarations throughout the pamphlet seem to demonstrate that the writer defines homosexuality without respect for the persons defined, and without evidence of mitigating information. If indeed, the writer did *not* take into account current scholarly

---

[46] American Lutheran Publicity Bureau. "Can Homosexual Love Be Blessed?", CM06.

research, or factual and anecdotal evidence from interviews with homosexual persons themselves, then to reach such arbitrary conclusions proves not merely suspect but morally irresponsible. In essence, the pamphlet disparages the character of men and women of same-sex gender connectivity by reducing the nature of their gender connection to the physical dimension of *arousal* only, thereby disregarding the interpersonal dimension of *attachment*. The author vilifies loving, faithful, caring same-sex relationships by denigrating love's natural desire for physical expression—a desire shared by every heterosexual couple. In sum, such verbiage and proclamations prove negligent and abusive.

Other ethical issues will be considered later. But the subsequent chapter, *Breaking from Traditional Bias*, focuses on the uneasy relationship between science and religion, and addresses the question why so many religious institutions zealously reject available evidence concerning the nature of homosexuality, and in so doing, reject better understanding persons whose gender connectivity is of the same sex. Chapter 5: *Same-Sex Relationships and the Bible* then examines the Biblical texts traditionally used against homosexuality.

CHAPTER FOUR

Breaking from Traditional Bias

Personal Profile: Uncertain Certainties

The young man in his mid-twenties did not tell me he was gay. Nor did he offer an explanation for asking me, "What do you believe about homosexuality?" As pastor of a Lutheran church in Portland, Oregon, and barely older than the young man sitting across from me in my office, I was totally unprepared for his question. In hindsight I should have learned more about him and the motivation behind his question before I so readily propounded an answer. Had I listened more intently than I spoke, I might have gained some insight into his concern over this issue. But before that occasion in the early 1970s, no one ever requested a personal audience to ask my view about homosexuality. Maybe the question came up once, possibly twice before in an adult study group. But this young man was someone with a personal concern, his eyes searching mine, asking me what *I* believed about homosexuality. At the time, I possessed only sketchy beliefs and information about homosexuality. I had no depth of experience and study from which to formulate a response.

If he was homosexual, he was the first one I had met (to my knowledge). I assumed a few effeminate men I had known in the past might be homosexual. I heard the stories my mother and father shared about a troubled man they counseled many times, a man who, they later confided to me, was homosexual. I heard from some of my fellow clergy to watch out for brother so-and-so who allegedly propositioned his roommate at a church convention. My personal experience provided only minimal grounds on which to respond to the young man's question.

I had only three sources of information on which to base an answer. The first, stereotypical impressions of homosexuals formed by cultural images in the media, such as movie portrayals of "perverted" and sinister men, and news stories about homosexual predators arrested in public parks and restrooms. The second source was Biblical judgments against same-sex rape in the Sodom and Gomorrah stories and the Apostle Paul's comments about unnatural same-sex behavior in the first chapter of Romans. The last source was the bit of scientific information I picked up about the hypothalamus being the "Central Station" of sexual desire. Based, upon my limited sources of information, therefore, I gave him an answer in proper ecclesiastical style.

"I believe the Bible is most concerned about what action comes out of a person's heart," I told him, explaining that the desires, prompted in the lower brain center and processed by reason, must be contained first, then the homosexual act proceeding from it. The concern ought to be one of controlling the desires that might move individuals toward homosexual behavior and redirect them toward the good purpose for which God created our sexuality.

After asking me a couple of questions for clarification, he thanked me politely and left. I never saw him again.

I suppose he saw me as a religious authority ready to deliver "dogmatically correct" answers—*not* a compassionate person with empathy for his concerns. Or, perhaps, he recognized an insensitive fool pontificating opinions with greater vocal than mental profundity. He met someone who stood by religious dogma, but not someone who appreciated his personal dilemma. In the years following our son's admission that he was gay, I finally experienced standing on that young man's side of the question.

The first time occurred when I first disclosed to my clergy colleagues that my son was gay. The national Church body was engaged in a study of human sexuality, one part of which dealt with homosexuality. At one of our monthly clergy conference meetings, the subject of the study was brought up amid significant disapproval about the inclusion of homosexuality. They believed the Church spoke clearly enough in the past about homosexuality's incompatibility with Scripture and the Church's traditions. Several of my colleagues were quite vocal against what they perceived to be a liberalizing tendency in the Church's stand toward homosexuals.

I told them my son was gay, and that out of the process of coming to understand him and his homosexuality, I now had concerns about some of the assumptions underlying their arguments. After my brief comments, a silence lasted for several moments . . . and then someone changed the subject. At no other time thereafter did my colleagues, with one exception, mention another word about the subject in my presence.

Similar occasions followed. The one pastor in the conference who had been openly empathetic toward me, and knew some of my personal and theological history, invited my wife and me to share our family story at a spring conference meeting for clergy and lay people. During the business meeting preceding the program, a delegation of lay people and their pastor from one of the conference congregations submitted a resolution to terminate all discussion about homosexuality in that conference and to appeal to the national Church body to affirm its traditional position on homosexuality. The immediate intent of the resolution was to cancel the very program we were to present, and secondarily, to subscribe the conference to the "truth and authority" inherent in the Church's past declarations about homosexuality.

In all, my colleagues reacted to the disconcerting circumstance of homosexuality as I did with the young man I encountered—with little knowledge and skimpy comprehension, but with grand certainty that our response was righteous. Unfortunately, most of us did not personally know gays and lesbians of great character and faith (at least, that we were aware of), and had not explored the abundant amount of scientific information about the nature of homosexuality. Based upon what we knew from cultural aversions toward homosexuality and from what we believed the Bible taught about it, we comprehended very little of the devastating impact of rejection and condemnation on gays, lesbians, and their families. No wonder gays and lesbians, as well as gender-variant individuals, feel stifled when relating to people who resort to standard, righteous opinions instead of engaging in personal dialogue that might risk controversy or, worst of all, might risk a seismic shift in mindset.

We all tend to feel uneasy when we have few cut-and-dried answers to the perplexing questions that assault our comfortable biases. Certainly, for all the questions about sexual identity, we feel more comfortable having definitive answers corroborated by empirical, scientific investigation. Many arguments about the nature and cause of homosexuality could be settled if only unequivocal answers existed. Then again, maybe unequivocal answers are not so persuasive after all. The human intellect can remain highly adamant against facts that unsettle cherished beliefs, especially when facts are evidential, but not conclusive; that are rationally and empirically substantive, but not quantitatively and unequivocally provable. In Western religion, particularly Christianity, we have inherited St. Augustine's (354 CE) guideline for deciding what to accept (or not accept) when science conflicts with Scripture: science should be preferred when its evidence is conclusive; Scripture should be preferred when scientific evidence is inconclusive.

This dictum is all well and good for natural science, which often offers measurable or quantifiable evidence about nature and its laws. But problems arise when applying the maxim to sciences that extract evidence from data that is difficult to measure and quantify: data related to the psyche, society, and culture.

The dilemma we face regarding the question of homosexuality is that, at this point in time, while we have considerable and weighty evidence from natural science pointing to biological causation, we cannot categorically close the case. The dilemma is exacerbated by the tendency, particularly among those of a conservative bent, to prefer the clear assurance of traditional mores and dogmas to the muddle of divergent, perplexing evidence. Tenaciously clutching cultural biases against homosexuality, they summon the Bible's sexual biases to buttress the conviction that age-old tradition demands condemnation of homosexuality. Seriously considering scientific evidence that conflicts with our bias therefore introduces ambiguity into the dilemma—ambiguity that proves sorely disquieting to traditional convictions.

Nevertheless, the noted general complexity about the cause of human sexual identity compels us to pose more sophisticated questions about the cause of this or that aspect of sexual identity. It also compels us to cope with realities that provoke questions for which no easy answers exist. We must accept considerable ambiguity in what we do and do not know about sexual identity, and we must realize that causes of specific aspects of sexual identity will not always be simple to identify and define. That no such proven answers exist to all our questions exacerbates a cultural dilemma rooted in two main issues—ambiguity and analogy.

Ambiguity and Analogy

Ambiguity

Ambiguity occurs when the only appropriate response to a quandary involving a "this" or a "that" is, "I don't know for certain." We noted ambiguity while discussing causes of variety within the four classes of sexual identity. At times we must confess that, at present, science does not conclusively know the cause of this variation or that.

For example, respecting *sex definition*, the general cause of a one- or two-chromosome variation in sex definition may seem to result clearly from biological influences, yet we face ambiguity regarding the precise combination of biological and environmental causation. The same ambiguity exists within *gender definition* when, during prenatal development, the ducts that form internal sex organs and the gonads that form external sex organs develop in ways incongruent with the sex of the fetus.

Whereas we more easily live with ambiguity regarding sex definition and gender definition, many become progressively more uncomfortable with ambiguities regarding *gender identification* and *gender connectivity*. Considerable ambiguity occurs regarding gender-variant or homosexual persons because the discrimination between biological influence and environmental influence within the characteristics of gender identification and gender connectivity proves more elusive to identify and define. More critically, the ambiguity concerning these characteristics often becomes especially troublesome when accepted standards of social and religious morality enter into the discussion.

Every so often op-ed pundits, writers of letters to editors, and speakers in conversational debate about homosexuality, dismiss the ambiguity about same-sex gender connectivity with the claim that a two-thousand-year tradition condemning homosexuality "proves" that we should not change now. This argument from tradition, however, does not mitigate ambiguity: it intensifies it. In the first place, it stems from the tradition of *Western* culture only, without acknowledging that not all cultures condemned same-sex relationships. In the second place, the contemporary notion of 'homosexuality' cannot be equated with what tradition supposedly condemned because modern conceptions of homosexuality represent a *recent* (within the last 200 years) understanding that does not necessarily correlate with the varied historical attitudes and responses of "traditional" Western culture toward same-sex behavior. And finally, the claim does not address the crucial question of *why* Western culture has, for more than 2000 years, and unlike some other major civilizations, maintained negative views about human sexuality in general.[47]

---

[47] Herdt, *Same Sex Different Cultures*, 10. "Over the decades anthropologists and other scholars, most notably beginning with Bronislaw, Malinowski, Ruth Benedict, and Margaret Mead have articulated several

The tension that ambiguity generates when moral issues are at stake is intensified by the confrontation of two fundamentally different and incompatible responses to ambiguity. One response to ambiguity demonstrates openness and acceptance; the other reflects suspicion and rejection.

To be sure, the degree to which ambiguity proves problematic depends upon the inherent significance of the specific issues. The ambiguity of playing outdoors when rain threatens probably does not bother children who are eager to play outside regardless of the weather. But the ambiguity of stepping into an unknown, darkened room would likely weigh heavily on children, fearful about whether that room is safe or scary. Likewise, ambiguity relating to sexual identity becomes more or less problematic depending upon the issue. Not knowing what happened at conception to cause a child to be inter-sex represents an ambiguity that, though severely disconcerting to the parents, does not create the divisive moral quandary for our society as does the ambiguity of not knowing what causes same-sex gender connectivity.

In the current conflict about homosexuality, great difficulty arises from the fact that formal science itself is filled with numerous ambiguities about the cause and nature of same-sex gender connectivity. However, the advantage of such ambiguity in

---

principles about the relationship between culture and sexuality. Four of these concern us here. First, nonwestern societies, past and present, have sexual cultures and codes of sexual practice as complex as our own system of sexuality. Second, sexuality is a part of the social fabric of custom, kinship, and family relations and must be understood in this broader sense of the total social system. Third, sexual variations in behavior are common across human groups, and a high degree of tolerance is accorded to same-gender relations in the majority of societies. This challenges us not to assume but rather to explain the powerful influence of heteronormativity as a social fact in western cultures. Fourth, the accumulation of anthropological knowledge in all societies has enabled us to reflect on the history of sexuality in western culture and to humanize the laws, which historically rendered gays and lesbians outlaws in their own civilization."

science is that debate is not only a legitimate but necessary function, and research continues to further more knowledge. Science relies on the basic assumption that its conclusions are fallible and subject to correction.

The response to ambiguity from the side of religion, however, is typically very different. Particularly with "revealed" religions like Judaism, Christianity, and Islam that hold sacred the divine authorship of scripture, religion tends to suppress or to demote the importance of information that conflicts with theological or moral conclusions drawn from "infallibly inspired" Scripture.

Although theological seminary faculties are sometimes theologically and socially progressive in their response to cultural change, the denominational, administrative leadership, the clergy, and the rank and file believers within religious institutions commonly find themselves in a severe dilemma when pressures of culture and science push in directions that the religious establishment perceives as not only dangerous but without warrant. The religious hierarchy, responsible for preserving the integrity of the religious community's body of truth, tends to take an adversarial posture toward any contrary challenge. As a result, ordinary believers often follow suit because the issues at hand prove too complex to investigate for themselves, and the issues become too unsettling not only to their belief system but, perhaps more importantly, to their concerns for preserving cultural integrity as they know it. Not surprisingly, therefore, religious leaders will use alarmism as a means to incite the faithful to resist information and/or trends that conflict with existing religious convictions. "We've got trouble right here in River City!" cries the alarmist, like the salesman in *The Music Man*, who goes on to delineate the awful consequences of letting an idea or a trend insert its way into the status quo.

Generally speaking, uncertainty is the native atmosphere in which science thrives. Certainty, in contrast, is the native atmosphere in which many Western religions thrive. Science relentlessly searches for truth; and where truth is seemingly found, science does not rest but proceeds to challenge the findings, testing them again and again. Religion defines doctrine and tends to relent-lessly defend the "truth" of its dogma. Where that truth is questioned, subscription to dogma and tradition is often mandated. Science impudently believes that no truth is sacred. Religion reveres the sacred truth of its doctrines and believes that challenging the inviolability of its divine source is blasphemous impudence. All truth, for the scientist, should be subject to empiri-cal testing and the scrutiny of reason. Truth, for the caretaker of sacred oracles, must be buttressed by certainty in its doctrines, even when dogma conflicts with reason and ordinary experience. Science *questions* the truth of every conclusion while religion *confirms* truth's absolute conclusions. For religion, doubt of dogma must be dispelled with certainty, not more ambiguity. Where ambiguity reigns, science feels comfortable, but religion feels acutely uncomfortable. Thus, ambiguity proves the flash point at which the conflict between science and religion greatly intensifies.

This assertion does not mean to generalize that all scientists are fair and unbiased, while religious believers are never inquir-ing and open-minded. Individuals, whether scientists or theolo-gians, are subject to preconceptions and prejudices like any other person. Anyone can be predisposed to biases that narrow our vision, that slyly thicken our inventive capacity to think beyond the philosophical status quo, and that harden our mindset, rendering us impervious to the influence of factual documenta-tion. Information, instead of producing more clarity, produces only more obfuscating interpretations that individuals use to support or refute various positions according to their particular viewpoint. As previously mentioned, Bagemihl provides an example of such clouding in noting that scientists have disputed the naturalness of animal homosexuality, *despite* concrete facts and comprehensive information about it.[48]

At the heart of the conflict lies the deadlock that results when science systematically examines experience through reflection, induction, and reason, and religion theologically interprets

---

[48] Bagemihl, *Biological Exuberance*, 78.

experience through tradition, scripture, and dogma—and proponents of *both* sides fall prey to dogmatism. Dogmatism of either
science or religion causes heated, factional debate among ordinary
men and women whose positions are conditioned by their level of
comfort with progressive science or level of discomfort with
religious (and moral) uncertainty.

Confronting Ambiguity with Bias

Ambiguity becomes even more problematic when a religious
community grounds its warnings about deviating from religious
traditions and authority in the defense of cultural biases
supported by Biblical biases. Several times throughout history,
supposedly infallible Biblical truth (God's truth) has been exposed
as the purported truth of a Biblical interpretation incorporating
the Bible's cultural biases. When, from the hindsight of historical
perspective, we look at past conflicts between science and religion,
we frequently observe that the issues at stake in a conflict are
fundamentally as much cultural as religious. At the time of the
conflict, a culture's status quo may be threatened by views that
potentially destabilize, if not destroy, certain centuries-old social
institutions and/or values. Because the existing social orders reflect institutionalized Biblical biases, the threat to the existing
social order appears as an attack on divine truth, the consequence
of which might pitch civilization into ruinous chaos.

The response of religious authorities, therefore, is to turn to
the Bible's cultural biases perpetuated in contemporary culture,
and to use those biases for authorization to oppose the threat of
new ideas. The appeal to Biblical biases to defend cultural biases,
as though they are infallible truths, lies at the heart of the science/
religion conflict and remains a significant part of the problem in
the current debate about homosexuality.

Does the Bible have biases? Of course. But what constitutes a
"Biblical bias"? A bias, as used in this context, reflects a preference
or inclination inhibiting impartial judgment. In this sense, a 'bias'

is not the same as a 'prejudice,' which carries negative connotations of adverse judgments made without sound evidence, irrational or unreasonable preconceived convictions. Bias, on the other hand, suggests judgments or convictions based upon sound knowledge, but knowledge that may not yet have been tested by other or additional information, or that may seem so complete and self-contained that it becomes difficult to consider other points of view impartially.

The Bible, for example, possesses a geocentric cosmological bias. From the Biblical record, a description of the universe emerges in which sun and stars rise and fall against a dome, above which God resides in heaven. The heavenly bodies move from one side to the other over a platter-like surface resting on two pillars whose foundations are anchored in Sheol. Having no available empirical evidence to the contrary, and in the face of simple observation (in which the sun "obviously" moved across the sky), Biblical writers could not conceive of the earth's revolving around the sun.

The Bible also possesses a patriarchal, hierarchical bias. In the society it describes, males dominate a realm in which the elders maintain chief authority. The Bible passage often quoted these days to defend a particular pattern of marriage expresses this patriarchal bias: "For this cause shall a man leave his father and mother and cleave to his wife" (Gen 2:25). Only males had the privilege to leave father and mother and become independent. Females were the property of males: the property of their father until he transferred his right of ownership to the husband, who then claimed her as his property.

Analogy

When the certainties of the past encounter the ambiguities of a new age, deciding between when to hold fast to the old and when to embrace the new becomes difficult. Admittedly, and unfortunately, situations arise when challenging accepted truth reflects simply fashionable, avant-garde rebelliousness. Although the challenge may be popular and widely supported by many respected people, its success would ultimately compromise the health of the human community. The reverse of avant-garde rebelliousness proves equally unhealthy, however. This occurs when the caretakers of religious truth vigorously obstruct the acceptance of a valid challenge to accepted truth with arguments rooted in tradition. They define what is culturally sacrosanct according to ancient religious biases and thereby eliminate the possibility for an evolution in our understanding of sacred truth.

Analogies help us more effectively discriminate between *substantive* challenges and those that are merely fashionable. We look back at past moments of crisis when, after a period of severe conflict, old "truths" at last surrendered to new realities. We note times when the caretakers of sacred truth ultimately had to admit that the truth they defended was not absolute divine truth, but an assumed truth based on ancient biases. We examine those times to see if any similarity exists between a contemporary conflict and a past conflict that finally resolved when antagonists realized they did not possess all available information, and recognized that their interpretation of the sacred writing proved flawed.

For example, ancient conflicts over adherence to Old Testament ritual and purity laws, like those that prohibited eating pork, led to the decision that many no longer applied to a later society. In addition, we no longer believe the earth is flat, or that the sun and other heavenly bodies revolve around the earth. We no longer believe that kings rule by divine right. We no longer believe slavery is a valid station in the social hierarchy. Although some religious groups persist in believing so, most people in Western cultures no longer believe a women's place should be limited exclusively to bearing and nurturing children, and to domestic management. Thus, previous conflicts allow us to extrapolate similarities between past and present issues. These analogies then illustrate how we might proceed in safely accepting issues previously opposed.

Analogies within the homosexuality debate, however, have *themselves* become part of the debate. They become problematic because the principal focus of the analogy, that is, the basic premise for making an analogy, has not been defined clearly in the context of the discussion. Consequently, those who defend the validity of the analogy and those who reject it cannot establish a fundamental basis for discussion.

For example, one analogy draws a parallel between the unjust denial of civil rights to blacks and the unjust denial of civil rights to homosexual persons. Some African-American individuals take offence at this comparison and maintain that injustice against persons of color, whose skin color is immutable and cannot be hidden, cannot be equated with denial of rights to people whose only identification is by how they behave in private. Others object to the analogy's validity by arguing that the Bible does not condemn slavery, but does condemn homosexuality. The Bible favors liberating slaves but expresses no favor toward homosexuality.[49]

The fallacy, however, lies in making the validity of the analogy stand or fall upon the similarities, or lack thereof, between the two subjects: persons of color whose race is immutable and homosexuals whose behavior is considered immoral. Clearly, the African-American experience and the homosexual experience in society are not strictly analogous. Yet the similarity of methodology used to condemn abolition and to condemn homosexuality does prove truly analogous. At the heart of the analogous methodology between the abolition and homosexual controversies lies the use of Biblical bias to support and defend cultural biases.

---

[49] Gagnon, Robert A. J. *The Bible and Homosexual Practice: Theology, Analogies, and Genes*. Theology Matters: A Publication of Presbyterians for Faith, Family and Ministry, 6.

Abolition Controversy Biases: Hierarchism and Elitism

Hierarchism

The dominant social structure throughout the historical periods covered by the Biblical writings is patriarchal–hierarchal. Tribal elders, kings, or high priests occupied the top stratum of the social structure. Indentured servants and slaves were at the bottom. This social structure perpetuated the institution of slavery in the New Land that, ironically, proclaimed boldly that all men were created equal. The hierarchical bias favored a social structure that blinded most people from recognizing the inconsistency of upholding slavery in a society that declared itself egalitarian.

The Bible never condemns slavery—not in the Old Testament and not in the teaching of Jesus. Its character transformed in the New Testament, but was not abrogated by the Apostles, specifically not by Paul. According to the Apostle Paul, although master and slave roles were socially prescribed by the hierarchical structure, in Christ they became peers who fulfilled their personal roles toward one another with mutual love and respect. In the workplace they were unequal, but in the Christian community they were equals in Christ.

The Bible's benign tolerance of slavery flowed into the culture of the societies that subsequently embraced Christianity. The slave systems that existed in cultures where Christianity spread remained even in those areas where Christianity became a major cultural and political force.[50] From the time of medieval Europe to the opening of new lands in North America, the theology of slavery provided by Augustine guided Christian understanding. Augustine asserted: (1) people before the Fall were equal; (2) the universal sinfulness entailed by the Fall required the establishment of institutions of coercion, including slavery; (3) slaves should be obedient and masters kindly; and (4) sin itself is the

---

[50] Sherer, *Slavery and the Churches*, 13.

worst slavery, no matter what one's civil status.[51] In other words, slavery was evidence of sin in the world, but was not itself sinful.

In nineteenth-century America, in an address printed in the Southern Presbyterian Review (XIV, 1862, 541), the Rev. Dr. Thornwell echoed Augustine's assertion in the following way:

> Slavery is a part of the curse which sin has introduced into the world and stands in the same general relations to Christianity as poverty, sickness, disease, or death. In other words, it is a relation that can only be conceived as taking place among fallen beings—tainted with a curse. It springs not from the nature of man as man, nor from the nature of society as such, but from the nature of man as sinful, and the nature of society as disordered.

In the fallen state of misery and sin in which man lived, slavery was necessary.[52] Some men were destined to rule so that order might be maintained among those destined to serve. Providence appointed some to be masters and some servants; and rather than destroying these distinctions, Christianity assumed responsibility for establishing and regulating them—and enjoining every individual to conform.[53]

Nothing suggested to a great many Christians in Colonial America, therefore, that regarding some humans as property might be unlawful or ungodly.[54] The Bible substantiated the notion that slavery existed as a part of society that must be administered with equity for the good of the governed. In the patriarchal form of slavery that the Church taught, slaves were considered a part of the household wherein the head of the house

---

[51] Sherer, *Slavery and the Churches*, 15.

[52] Jenkins, *Pro-Slavery Thought in the Old South*, 215.

[53] Sherer, *Slavery and the Churches*, 95.

[54] Sherer, *Slavery and the Churches*, 18.

owed as definite duties to the slaves as to his children; both came under the same benevolent discipline of the family.[55]

In the eighteenth-century American colonies, slavery increased dramatically in order to meet the economic imperatives of a struggling new nation. Not only did slavery increase, it took on an even more dehumanizing character in the importation of men and women from "dark" Africa, whose "primitive" character, in the view of "civilized" Europeans and Americans, gave license to the most monstrous violations of human rights in history. In response to these violations, opposition to slavery in America began to increase concurrently with slavery's growth.

In colonial America, a more aggressive position against slavery, in contrast to previous eras, advanced regarding the relationship of master and slave. According to this aggressive abolitionist position, slavery was not a sinless social structure necessitated by conditions in a Fallen world and to be regulated benignly by kind and godly masters. Slavery was *in and of itself* sin, and slaveholding was immoral.

Against this attack, pro-slavery advocates turned to the Bible, where the basic, traditional support of slavery was drawn out in order to prepare a moral defense against the accusation that slavery was immoral.[56] As one would expect, the "orthodox" Christians asserted, in a similar manner to the present-day clash of fundamentalism versus modernism,[57] that the "liberal" anti-slavery advocates who labeled slavery "sin" and slaveholders "sinful," were not merely incorrect—they fundamentally defied the Holy Word of God. Obviously, calling something a "sin" that God condoned was to suggest that God condoned sin. Such a conclusion was considered blasphemous and those who argued that position were guilty of persistently placing human reason above the authority of Divine truth. Pro-slavery theologians

---

[55] Jenkins, *Pro-Slavery Thought in the Old South*, 209.

[56] Jenkins, *Pro Slavery Thought in the Old South*, 200.

[57] Jenkins, *Pro-Slavery Thought in the Old South*, 238.

charged that abolitionists reached conclusions drawn from "the abstrusest speculations," based on "strained application of passages from the Bible" and "forced inferences from doctrine."[58]

To the anti-abolitionist theologian, Scripture made absolutely clear that God approved slavery, as long as it existed in the manner in which the relation was of mutual benefit to master and slave, that is, the servant was directed to "obey in all things your masters," and the master was commanded "to give unto your slaves that which is just and equal."

Elitism

The socially and economically elite entered the fray against the abolitionist views for the sake of the socio-economic stability that slavery sustained for them. In order to support their proposition, however, they had to embrace another Biblical bias, the bias of ethnic elitism, as a way of supporting the notion that slaves, consigned to their social status, could actually benefit from their unfortunate station.

Biblical elitism is a common thread of both Old Testament and New Testament Scripture. The Israelite descendants of Abraham are identified in the Bible as a "special people," a "chosen people" favored by God for the purpose of being a blessing to all humanity. In contrast, the pagan nations surrounding Israel are identified as a cursed people against whom God's wrath lashes out, especially when those nations rise up against the People of God. Even the "chosen" people could incur divine wrath usually reserved for the ungodly nations if they turned away from their God.

These views fit well with rationalizations supporting slavery. African slaves—whose primitive customs and moral behavior contrasted so drastically from the concept of godliness in the new, enlightened democratic society—accommodated the idea that God favored godly, cultured Europeans, but God disfavored rebellious people and willed that they should be subservient to the favored.

---

[58] Jenkins, *Pro-Slavery Thought in the Old South*, 219.

Slavery was an appropriate hierarchical position suited for those whom God placed in low estate as a means of putting their disobedience and rebellion in check. The privileged elite was entrusted with supervision and management to rule the slave and to hold the slave's wildness in bounds.

It is important to note that elitism and hierarchism create a hegemony—a predominant influence over others. Within hegemony, the privileged arrogate the right to define the non-privileged who, with no power or voice for self-identification or definition, commonly give consent to such definitions out of accommodation to their own powerlessness. Consequently, those in power defined slaves in terms that validated the supposed benefits of enslaving them. The pro-slavery Anglican evangelist, George Whitefield, made the following assertion:

> In permitting slavery God had some wise end in view which, though unfathomable, would undoubtedly end up to the advantage of the Africans. Considering the miserable condition of the blacks in Africa which might cause a father to sell his family into slavery, how much better must their condition be, when disposed of in a Christian country, where they are treated with mildness and humanity, and required to perform no more than that portion of labor which in some way or other is the common lot of the human race.[59]

Although abundant evidence proved that Christian slaveholders in the South ignored the Pauline admonition about the Christian master's responsibility toward slaves, African slaves were defined as barely superior to animals and therefore deserving of harsh treatment, similar to a mulish beast. Although more than adequate evidence identified among the dehumanized slaves, men and women of superb intellect, skill, character, and nobility, Southern church leaders chose to sustain a debased definition of blacks, support slavery, and protect the socio-economic structures

---

[59] Sherer, *Slavery and the Churches*, 76.

that depended on slavery. It remained only for pro-slavery extremists to extend the principle, showing that Africans were so inferior that they properly belonged in slavery for everyone's benefit. The crassness with which extremists distinguished blacks from human beings, and associated them with animals is illustrated by the following citation:

> [T]hey are already slaves *to the tyrannizing power of lust and passion*, they are clothed in *brutal stupidity* and *savage barbarity*. The African is *a creature in human shape, (for in such a state of degradation one can hardly call him a man)*, a compound of *child, idiot, and madman, who is altogether incapable of choosing for himself.* A condition of slavery is therefore consistent in this case with the law of nature since it tends to everyone's greater happiness, including the slave's. (emphasis mine)[60]

The abolition controversy clearly shows how Biblical bias served current cultural biases. This methodology in the cause of anti-abolitionists took advantage of the legitimacy of the hegemony that the hierarchical and elitist biases supported. It justified the authority of those in power *to define* those they ruled in ways that secured their right to oppress them. In the same way, a long tradition of heterosexual and religious hegemony continues to exercise its right *to define* gays and lesbians in ways that validate the prejudices held against them, and to oppress homosexuals as a perverted blight upon decent society. Concurrently, until recently, most homosexuals gave implied consent to those definitions by closeting themselves and by mimicking heterosexual behavior.

---

[60] Sherer, *Slavery and the Churches*, 110.

Cosmology Controversy Bias: Geocentricity

Perhaps the clearest analogy to the conflict over homosexuality is the conflict over cosmology in the seventeenth century, particularly the highly public conflict between Galileo and the Roman Catholic Church. Comparing this scientific issue with what many consider a purely moral issue may seem odd. However, the homosexuality controversy is indeed a scientific issue as well as moral. And conversely, the sixteenth- and seventeenth-century cosmology controversy was as much a moral issue as scientific.

The notion that the center of the universe was not the earth, abetted by the emerging enlightenment emphasis upon humanistic ideals, caused tremendous moral repercussions. The geocentric view of the cosmos (the earth as the center of the universe) supported the belief that human beings represented the climax of God's creative design. But if the center of the universe shifted from earth to sun, the moral center also shifted from the idea of human beings ruled by God toward a view of human beings ruled by scientific laws inherent in the impersonal forces of nature.

Ancient Greek philosophers first considered the idea that the earth might not be the center of the universe. But the sixteenth-century scholar Copernicus, considered the father of the modern view of the universe, first proposed the mathematical theory that the sun was the center of the universe, although he was not convinced himself of the accuracy of his mathematical theory of the universe.

Scholars who followed Copernicus did not fully embrace conclusions regarding a heliocentric universe, conclusions that at that time proved extremely fragile and fallible. Sixteenth-century mathematician Peter Ramus, a believer in Copernicus' sound mathematical basis and reliable observations, met 24-year-old Danish scholar Tycho Brahe in 1569 and tried to convince him of the truth of his views about mathematics and astronomy. Persuaded by Ramus to start from scratch and construct a correct mathematical theory of the orbits of the planets (earth included) around the sun, Brahe devoted his entire life to making precise

observations of the universe and to drawing significant conclusions about its nature.[61]

Ironically, Brahe did not fulfill Ramus' desire to carry forward
Copernicus' heliocentric theory. In fact, the Copernican model of
the solar system disturbed Brahe because, on the one hand, he was
greatly attracted to the model's simplicity and elegance, but on the
other, he felt repelled by the concept of a moving earth. In part,
Brahe rejected the motion of the earth because as a basically
devout man, he could not reconcile the motion of the earth with
certain passages in the Scriptures.

During the last eighteen months of Tycho Brahe's life, the
young mathematician, Johannes Kepler, became his collaborator.
Kepler, unlike Brahe, believed in the correctness of Copernicus'
heliocentric theory. He was convinced that Brahe's highly accurate
observations of the planets were essential to his attempts to prove
the correctness of the Copernican heliocentric model of the solar
system.[62] From Brahe's astronomical observations, Kepler eventually deduced his laws of planetary motion and changed the course
of human perception regarding the heavens.[63]

Amazingly, even Kepler, known as the father of modern astronomy and a predecessor of Galileo, did not embrace Copernicus'
theory of a heliocentric universe on scientific grounds alone. Not
enough empirical, scientific evidence existed. Many mathematical
calculations and logical hypotheses supported the theory of a
heliocentric universe, but not enough practical evidence existed to
prove its reality. Ultimately Kepler found a close relationship
between the Copernican world structure and the doctrine of the
Holy Trinity: "That I dared so much was due to the splendid harmony of those things which are at rest, the sun, the fixed stars,
and the intermediate space, with God the Father, and the Son, and

---

[61] Booker, "Cultural Crisis Then and Now," 72–74.

[62] Booker, "Cultural Crisis Then and Now," 77–78.

[63] Elkind, "The Moral Code and the Trials That Test Our Adherence to
It," 32.

the Holy Spirit."[64] Kepler believed that because God is supremely true, a system that reflected the Godhead must also be true. Thus his religious ideas could show that the Copernican system was true and uniquely true.[65]

Born in 1564 in Pisa, Italy, Galileo Galilei, a professor of mathematics at the University of Padua, was required to teach geocentric astronomy to medical students. But contrary to his mandated teaching, Galileo was a Copernican. He made no public sign of his belief until many years later. Having read a report about a spyglass that a Dutchman had shown in Venice, Galileo used the information from the report together with his own skills in craftsmanship and mathematics to make a series of telescopes. When he turned his telescope to the night sky, Galileo began to make remarkable discoveries that finally provided the practical, empirical evidence proving the correctness of Copernicus' heliocentric view of the universe.[66]

Until then, the Catholic Church did not display much anxiety toward Copernicus' heliocentric view, which seemed little more than an abstract, mathematical theory. At this time, the Catholic Church's authority for dealing with interpretations of the Holy Scripture, Cardinal Robert Bellarmine, saw little reason for the Church to be concerned as long as Copernicus' view, supported by Galileo, remained hypothetical—a mathematical theory enabling a more simple calculation of the positions of the heavenly bodies. However, if taken as a literal account of the structure and movement of the heavens, the theory would prove dangerous because it undermined the faith and authority of the Scriptures.

Bellarmine stated that it was error to say that the motion of the sun and the immobility of the earth were not "matters of faith and morals," as mentioned in the decree of the Fourth Session of the Council of Trent. They were in the Bible, all of whose statements

---

[64] Elkind. "The Moral Code," 139.

[65] Elkind. "The Moral Code," 141.

[66] O'Connor and Robertson, "Galileo Galilei," paragraph 12.

must be true because of its divine authorship. And finally, using Augustine's maxim, Bellarmine conceded that if and when the Copernican theory were ever proven, the Church would need either to reinterpret the contrary Biblical passages, or at least to say it did not understand them. But Bellarmine believed no such proof had been produced to date, and he maintained great doubt that it could be produced.[67]

At this time in the Church's history, Western culture could not afford another challenge to its stability. The Holy Roman Empire and the Roman Catholic Church were reeling from the tempestuous decades of the Reformation and the incursion of the Turks into southern Europe. Church authority was also disrupted by the implications of Renaissance humanism that put the locus of human value on man's assumptions about himself rather than his place in a divine scheme.

As part of the effort to bring stability to these troubled times, the Church, through the Council of Trent, endeavored to seal up the divine truth, which the Holy See was obligated to defend and define. Allied with the conventional scientific understanding of the universe and with the Biblical witness, the Church was obliged to preserve the accepted truth. Threatened by the perceived peril to Church authority, religious authorities used a Biblical cosmic bias to support the current scientific geocentric bias, and declared the heliocentric theory to be heretical. It banned all writing, investigation, and conversation about the subject and put Galileo on trial as a heretic.

Not only within the Roman Catholic Church, but also within Protestant churches, powerful leaders fought vigorously against the spread of the Copernican doctrine of a heliocentric universe. In Germany, Martin Luther denounced Copernicans as "scoundrels" and labeled Copernicus as "the fool [who] will upset the whole science of astronomy," and the one who defies the "Holy Scripture [which] shows that it was the sun and not the earth

---

[67] Blackwell, *Science, Religion and Authority*, 31.

which Joshua ordered to stand still."[68] Philosopher Philipp Melanchthon, a Lutheran scholar and religious reformer, strongly supported Luther's condemnation of the Copernicans and recommended to a correspondent that "wise rulers should suppress such unbridled license of mind."

Remarkably, in framing the current debate about homosexuality within this cosmology analogy from the early 1600s, far less empirical, scientific evidence supported a heliocentric cosmology than exists today to support the view of homosexuality as an immutable form of gender connectivity. Yet those who oppose homosexuality use the biases of the Bible to support their condemnation of homosexuality in the same manner that the clerics and scientists of the sixteenth and seventeenth centuries used the Biblical, geocentric bias to oppose a heliocentric cosmology.

Homosexuality Controversy Bias: Procreation

The controversy over homosexuality proves analogous to the cosmology and abolition controversies with respect to the way the Biblical biases are used to sustain cultural biases. The Biblical bias used to defend cultural homonegative biases is procreation. The procreative bias consists of two premises based upon the belief that sex and procreation represent a divinely architected order of nature. The first premise is that sex is binary, comprised of male and female. Scripture states that God created human beings in his own image: *male and female* he created them (Gen 1:27). The second premise is that male and female are complementary for the purpose of conjugal and procreative union. The divine imperative in Scripture is "be fruitful and multiply" (Gen 1:28), and the divine intent is that *man* leave father and mother, cleave to his wife (*woman*), and become one flesh (Gen 2:24).

---

[68] Motts and Weaver, *The Story of Astronomy*, 74–75.

This divine order, according to those who subscribe to it, is conclusively and unequivocally ratified by Jesus, the divine Son of God when, concerning the question about divorce, he quotes the Genesis passages referred to above.

> But from the beginning of creation, 'God made them male and female.' 'For this reason a man shall leave his father and mother and be joined to his wife, and the two shall become one. So they are no longer two but one.' What therefore God has joined together, let no man put asunder." (Mark 10:6–9)

The question that arises about this "order of nature," supposedly designed by God and ratified by Jesus, is: "Can this be a bias?" Clearly no species, not least the human species, will last longer than a generation without procreating. Logically, for procreation, there must be a male and female. Hence, the divine order, both for humans and all other creatures, seems explicit in the creation stories of Genesis. The Bible sustains the common conclusion that the natural order consists of a binary division of humans, and all other creatures, into male and female for the purpose of conjugal and procreative union. Thus, the earlier mentioned quip, "God made Adam and Eve, *not* Adam and Steve."

The procreation bias remained an untested and unchallenged conviction about human sexuality for most of Western history. Not until the second half of the nineteenth century, with Gregor Mendel's groundbreaking work in plant genetics, did we learn about such entities as chromosomes that passed traits from generation to generation. The subsequent discovery of sex chromosomes paved the way for the modern, scientific means of understanding that an individual's sex is defined by the diverse combination of two sex chromosomes rather than by simple observation of binary male and female anatomy. Yet those who argue that the "gay agenda" contradicts millennia of tradition continue to cite the centuries-old premise concerning binary male/female, as well as the premise that male and female are "obliged" to be fruitful and multiply. Therefore, reviewing the evolving character of that tradition proves useful here.

A procreative underscore in Gen 1, "Be fruitful and multiply," turns out to be missing in the *second* creation story in Gen 2. In place of emphasizing procreation, Gen 2 focuses upon affirming the goodness of human sexuality. The man and woman were naked and were not ashamed. The procreative dimension of their sexuality is euphemistically disguised in the phrase that the two should become "one flesh." In this euphemism, the reference to sexual intercourse implicitly emphasizes human capacity for interpersonal union over the limited capacity of procreation. The understanding of sex in Gen 2 is rooted in the view that the man and the woman are to be interpersonally united for a purpose larger than to be fruitful and multiply. Procreation was one function of relationship but not the primary function. The larger, more complex issue centers upon interpersonal union: it was not good for the man to be *alone*. The remedy for that aloneness was to unite two human beings, one male and one female. In that sense, the euphemism for sexual intercourse, "to know," commonly used in the Bible to refer to conjugal relations, points to the larger issue of human relationships than solely procreation. Adam "knew" Eve and she conceived. Before Joseph had "known" Mary, he discovered she was already pregnant. Incipient in this Bible euphemism lies an understanding that physical sexual engagement is not exclusively a matter of procreation, but an expression of a deeper intimacy between two human beings.

Nevertheless, emphasis upon procreation's importance grows in the Jewish tradition based, first of all, upon a concern shared by many other cultures of that age: the concern regarding infertility. Infertility, to the ancients, was a female issue, not male. The male, so they believed, provided the seed that, like any other kind of seed, was a self-contained form of incipient life needing only a fertile environment in which to grow. Women, therefore, provided the fertile environment of the womb in which to incubate men's seed. If the seed did not grow, the infertility was the fault of a barren womb, comparable to barren soil. Understandably, barrenness was a problem for people in a time of short life expectancy, high infant mortality, and a high fatality rate of women from childbirth.

Progeny was a Hebrew man's eternity. If no progeny perpetuated his line, nothing was left of a man beyond his own death. Levitical laws encapsulated the importance of this concern by mandating that the brother of a deceased man must copulate with his deceased brother's wife as often as necessary until she conceived and bore a child. Therefore, by means of the brother's surrogacy, the deceased man's lineage lived after him.

A highly significant factor contributing to an increased importance placed upon procreation at the time was the practical implication of the promise to the patriarch Abraham that he was to be the father of a great nation whose numbers exceed the stars in the sky. Infertility, obviously, would prove a terrible threat to the fulfillment of that promise. In fact, part of the Abraham story reveals Abraham's anxiety about the barrenness of his wife, Sarah: her barrenness stood in the way of fulfilling God's promise.

The later history of the Hebrews brought about conditions that both heightened prudishness about sex and concomitantly elevated the importance of procreation. Their national humiliation taught them the hard way that concession to the base impulses of human nature led to ruin, not happiness. The conquest of the Hebrew nations of Judah and Israel, and the subsequent dispersion of the population into the Mesopotamian region, necessitated for the Israelites a profound reflection upon their understanding of themselves as God's chosen people. In their dispersion, the institution of the synagogue developed to provide centers where the people were taught their ancestral faith and where their cultural identity was maintained against the adaptation to or the intrusion of alien philosophical and cultural views. Into the Israelite identity crisis created by dispersion into the Fertile Crescent, entered one of the great intellectual movements of the age that, to one degree or another, affected the entire world of the Mediterranean rim: Stoicism.

Stoicism grew as a major philosophical view beginning in the last quarter of the third century before the Christian era. It placed great ethical emphasis upon virtue characterized not simply by ethical conduct, but by a will controlled by reason and not passion. Its ascetic approach was not merely to control passion, but to eliminate all passion whose feelings are opposite from reason.

Although the Jews were disinclined to embrace Stoicism, nevertheless a spiritual link existed between Stoicism's emphasis upon controlling sensuality and Jewish priestly admonitions against pagan sensuality. Banished from their holy place in Jerusalem, the temple in ruin, the intellectual leaders of Israel turned not to the philosophy of the Stoics to inform their rallying cry for personal and national reform, but to priestly admonitions to keep God's Law. The disciplined life, guided by reason for the Stoics and the Torah for Hebrews, encouraged the development of asceticism in both cultures as a prominent feature of morality. This asceticism not only encouraged a more conscientious emphasis upon procreation as the legitimate purpose of sexual intercourse, it also instilled a more negative view of sex in general. Although the Hebrews believed the world with its sensual passions must not be rejected as the Stoic ascetic insisted, Hebrew and Stoic alike agreed that such passions must be controlled. For the Hebrew, human sexual desire represented a part of this world that needed disciplined control, but that should be embraced as good and necessary for human reproduction. [69]

Although Judaism in general had little interest in the philosophies of the time, a few Jewish scholars did study them. One of them was Philo, a Jewish scholar in Alexandria (and a contemporary of the Apostle Paul), whose work profoundly influenced later Christian scholars. Pertaining to procreation, Philo embraced the view that the male provided the seed and the female the fertile field to incubate the seed. From the Stoic

---

[69] Brown, *The Body and Society*, 63–64.

influence, Philo embraced the view that the sexual urge represented an irrational passion that must be annihilated. The rational synthesis of these two views determined that the pleasure of sexual intercourse was of no importance in itself, but only part of the ejaculatory event for transferring seed to the womb in order to produce another life. Therefore, God made the male to produce seed and created sexual stimulation only for the purpose of releasing seed. God made women fertile in order to provide the environment in which the seed could flourish and grow. Philo's conclusion was, therefore, that all unions without reproduction as their purpose should be prohibited.

Though early Christian Church fathers embraced Philo's view, they tended to have a much more negative view of sex itself—even more severe than St. Paul, who counseled, "It is well for a man not to touch a woman. But because of the temptation to immorality, each man should have his own wife and each woman her own husband" (1 Cor 7:1–2). Increasingly, marital sexual intercourse became defined as a *concession* to sexual desire, subsumed under the negative label 'Lust,' which should be controlled in the ongoing struggle between the flesh and the spirit.

St. Augustine, the fourth-century theologian, did not maintain as negative a view of sex as some earlier Church fathers. For Augustine, the critical opposition was not between flesh and spirit, but the Stoic distinction between passion and reason. Consequently, virginity did not necessarily represent the supreme good. Sex could be good, too, if governed by reason, not concupiscence. Such would be the case when married couples engaged in sex, without lust, to produce children.[70]

Moving through Western history, the potential for procreation increasingly becomes the standard by which human sexual acts are judged. Thirteenth-century medieval philosopher and theologian, Thomas Aquinas recognized that the broad category of human sexual activity was comprised of various, distinctive acts.

---

[70] Greenberg, *The Construction of Homosexuality*, 225.

The distinctions between them, however, were less important to him than that they be judged by their potential for procreation.[71]

Puritan ideology in the early New England colonies frowned on sensuality of any kind that might jeopardize commitment to work and family. The family was perceived to be the core social institution, responsible for production, reproduction, and the transmission of property from one generation to the next.[72]

In the nineteenth century, Krafft-Ebing, a European physician, proponent of the Degeneracy Theory and staunch Roman Catholic, wrote numerous articles about sexual perversions based on hundreds of his own case studies. According to Krafft-Ebing, sex is a perversion if reproduction is not its goal.[73]

Even this simple sketch of historical views on what constitutes ethically acceptable human sexual intercourse shows a development that increasingly preferences procreation as the prime justification for sexual behavior.

In Western culture, a negative view of human sexuality in general developed alongside the procreation bias of justifying sexual intercourse. Of course, the notion that procreation remains the only justification for sex seems itself an inherently negative view. However, an added impetus to this negativism arose in the new religion that became known as Christian.

Within a few decades after the death of Jesus, an entirely new dimension of religious belief emerged that tremendously impacted the sexual ethics of the Western world. Its view of the world was not that of the Stoics, who conceived of the world dualistically as soul and matter. Neither was its view an apocalyptic one of an indeterminately future, cataclysmic end to this evil world that would be replaced by a new kingdom of God. Like the apocalyptic view, it anticipated the world's end; but in contrast, it saw the

---

[71] Greenberg, *The Construction of Homosexuality*, 491.

[72] Greenberg, *The Construction of Homosexuality*, 344–45.

[73] Greenberg, *The Construction of Homosexuality*, 414.

new Kingdom of God as having already begun in the present age through Jesus Christ. In Christ, all things were now new, and supreme fulfillment would occur when he came again: soon. Thus, a "new creation" was so imminent that its approach could already be anticipated and foretasted in the present.

A small number of prominent Christian men and women made a dramatic gesture to embody this immanent, "here and now" new age by devoting themselves permanently to life-long sexual chastity and the renunciation of marriage. Time was running short, after all; a Christian society possessed the capacity to break the flow of human sexual nature that caused life to continue from generation to generation: "For them the continent body stood for a principle of reversibility; the flow of life itself could be halted. The renunciation of marriage laid bare the fragility of a seemingly changeless order. The means by which society was continued could be abandoned. Chastity announced the imminent approach of a *new creation*."[74]

Filled with personal disgust for the sexual license rampant in Greco-Roman cities, the Apostle Paul, like these radical Christians, preferred that Christians live in celibate chastity (as he did himself). But unlike these radical Christians, and cognizant of the sexual nature of the present human condition, he made concessions regarding marriage.

> [25] Now concerning the unmarried, I have no command of the Lord, but I give my opinion as one who by the Lord's mercy is trust worthy. [26]I think that in view of the impending distress it is well for a person to remain as he is. [27]Are you bound to a wife? Do not seek to be free. Are you free from a wife? Do not seek marriage. [28]But if you marry, you do not sin, and if a girl marries she does not sin. Yet those who marry will have worldly troubles, and I would spare you that. [29]I mean, brethren, the appointed time has grown very short; from now on, let those who have wives live as

---

[74] Brown, *The Body and Society*, 63–64.

though they had none . . . [31] For the form of this world is passing away. (1 Cor 7:25–29, 31)

The Apostle Paul was born in Tarsus, a city located in present day south-central Turkey that the Roman Empire eventually absorbed in 67 BCE. It prided itself in its university that became a prominent center for the study of Greek philosophy, rivaled only by the universities in Athens and Alexandria. Evidence that the Stoic influence flowing from that seat of learning had some effect upon the young Saul of Tarsus appears in his personally ascetic view of marriage, and in the warnings he gives about the dangers of *porneia* (fornication, sexual immorality, un-chastity), resulting from sexual frustration when sexual intercourse is not allowed within marriage.

Nothing in Paul's writing suggests that sexual urges could be wholesome and good in and of themselves when ordered within a warm, conjugal expression of intimacy. Instead, Paul provides an essentially negative impression. Life would be better without sex, but husbands and wives must not refuse sex with one another lest Satan tempt them through lack of self-control. Peter Brown charges that the legacy of Paul's essentially negative strategy, stating his preference for celibacy but allowing for conjugal rights and encouraging the young to marry and have children, "slid imperceptibly into an attitude that viewed marriage itself as no more than a defense against desire. In the future, a sense of the presence of 'Satan' in the form of a constant and ill-defined risk of lust, lay like a heavy shadow in the corner of every Christian church."[75]

This historical development results in the perception that human sex is a morally volatile condition of human life possessing only two legitimate elements: procreation and family nurturing. First, as a fundamental behavior requisite for reproduction, sex is moral only between a man and woman—because obviously only a male and female can procreate. Second, sex defines the nature of the

---

[75] Brown, *The Body and Society*, 55.

family: the morality of sexual behavior is conditioned upon the formation of a family inaugurated by marriage and providing the male and female role of nurture for the children born of their union. Thus, the moral *sine qua non* of human sexuality: in marriage, a male to sire and a female to bear children; a father to provide the male component of nurture and a mother to provide the female component of nurture in a complementary union of male and female. This, it is argued, is the divine order of creation against which other definitions—including same-sex marriage—are prideful rejections of God and the order God sanctioned. Any other order is "a violation of the anatomical and procreative sexual complementariness of male and female in creation—by definition an instance of pride, a supplanting of God's design in creation for sexuality in favor of one's own design." [76]

Even among those with a more tolerant view toward gays and lesbians, the procreative bias occurs when the issue of same-sex marriage is raised. A Fort Worth, Texas, editorialist suggests that gays have every right to consider themselves "married" by the criteria that count: love, commitment, and devotion. He also suggests that gays should receive a number of privileges afforded married couples, such as beneficiary designation and hospital visitation. But he does not believe society and law should so easily allow them the status of marriage: "Marriage is a union between one man and one woman. It is the foundation upon which our society advances. We grow up, we marry, we have kids, they grow up, they marry, they have kids, and on and on." [77] In other words, having kids, reproducing the species, is the fundamental purpose of marriage; procreation is the basic argument against gay marriage. He continues, "Children are the lasting, glorious byproduct of marriage, and a prime reason against equating gay and straight marriage." Supposedly, this rationale for opposing gay marriage is not anti-gay, but rather reflects a basic statement

---

[76] Gagnon, *The Bible and Homosexual Practice,* 86.

[77] Davis, "Is 'Gay Marriage' an oxymoron?", B15.

of what marriage is and why marriage should be "protected." Protecting marriage is purportedly not a slap against gays, but "an acknowledgement of the societal value of marriage, specifically as defined by God and man throughout human history."

Problems with the Procreative Bias

One problem with the procreative bias is that the first premise—that sex definition is binary, male and female—is false. Unquestionably, male and female sex definition dominates. But as a matter of empirical science, sex definition is not limited to male and female, but also includes what is called inter-sex (see Chapter 1, *Sex Definition*).

Another problem with the procreative bias is that its binary view of sex fails to account for the tremendous sexual variety within creation. With respect to non-human sex, one can probably assume ancient people did not have sophisticated zoological classifications of thousands of species of marine, aviary, insect, and mammalian creatures. Considering that the Bible says that God created all creatures as well as humans, God apparently did not consider it important to inform the Bible writers of His delight in creating a boisterous variety of sexual expression among the creatures of the earth that far exceeds the conventional male/ female, heterosexual pairing. Bagemihl writes:

> The animal world—right now, here on earth—is brimming with countless gender variations and shimmering sexual possibilities: entire lizard species that consist only of females who reproduce by virgin birth and also have sex with each other; or the multi-gendered society of the Ruff, with four distinct categories of male birds, some of whom court and mate with one another; or female Spotted Hyenas and Bears who copulate and give birth through their "penile" clitorides, and male Greater Rheas who possess "vaginal" phalluses (like the females of their species) and raise young in two-father families; or the vibrant

transsexualities of coral reef fish and the dazzling intersexualities of gynandromorphs and chimeras.[78]

The Biblical writers simply did not know that their God created such varied species with an accompanying variety of sexual activity. On the contrary, the Noah's Ark story (Gen 7) explicitly states that a male and its mate, two of every sort of living thing, including birds and creeping things, should be brought aboard: "two and two, male and female, went into the ark with Noah" (Gen 7:9). Not only does such binary sexuality hardly reflect the reality of nature, Noah supposedly abandons thousands of species to mass extinction whose sexual identity did not qualify them to board the ark. If we hold to the notion that sex is divinely good only as the behavior of a binary male and female couple for purposes of procreation, then nature displays a contrary reality. In fact, if we assert that God created this amazing variety, then the Bible, based on its own standards, portrays a rather prudish God. Why, even the table-delicacy oyster is a sexual misfit in the Biblical "divine order." The oyster is a male for the first year and half of his life and releases sperm to fertilize oyster eggs. Then he becomes a female for the rest of her life and releases eggs to be fertilized by her younger oyster neighbors. A good reason may exist why the Bible's kosher laws forbid eating all mollusks, including oysters, but more than likely, it has nothing to do with oysters' sexual identity!

Sex is manifest in great variety in creation, all of it good from the hand of a sexually imaginative God—*if* we take literally the Genesis refrain that God looks at what God has made and calls it good. Nature exhibits a variety far exceeding the sexuality cited in the creation stories in the book of Genesis or the Noah's ark story, in which all heterosexual pairs of animals enter the ark.

Some may rightly argue that animal characteristics and behavior do not automatically legitimate comparable characteristics and

---

[78] Bagemihl, *Biological Exuberance*, 260.

behavior among humans. But the point in referencing animal sexual variety is not to claim that animal characteristics validate the same characteristics among humans. The point rather, is to challenge the narrow viewpoint that negates so much human sexuality when nature is filled with such abundant variety.

A kind of innate hypocrisy arises in using the Biblical procreative bias against homosexuality. In our current era, those who employ the procreative bias know that human sexuality encompasses far more than genital intercourse, but they still apply the bias indiscriminately against gays and lesbians. The bias appears when they approve non-procreative heterosexual sex among couples who cannot or choose not to have children, but condemn homosexual couples because their sexual union is non-procreative.

The hypocrisy of the bias also emerges when we look at religious liberal views about sex in recent decades. The sexual revolution inaugurated in the late nineteenth century, and brought into full bloom by the counter culture of the 1950s and 1960s, brought about a substantial change in public mores as well as in religious views toward sexuality. A more positive and open view toward sex and its pleasurable expression emerged when representatives of some church institutions began to talk candidly and positively about sex, and to affirm the pleasure of conjugal sex rather than merely allowing for the pleasure as an unavoidable side affect of procreation. Now we encounter far less frequently the heavy moralizing in Western countries that all sex should be for reproduction, and that sexual pleasure per se is wrong.[79] Such reproductive logic is antiquated—until it relates to the issue of homosexuality. Then the traditional Judeo-Christian morality is summoned to deny the integrity of same-sex relationships by insisting that homosexual persons must remain chastely celibate.

Couples must no longer procreate of necessity; but they continue to enjoy the pleasure of sex. Technology enables women

---

[79] Herdt, *Same Sex Different Cultures*, 29.

to control reproduction and extends longevity for men and women far beyond the childbearing years. Yet even though the era of modern birth-control methods renders procreation optional, the human, physiological *capability* of procreation is cited as the reason why the divine order of sexual intercourse should be an exclusive and fundamental moral principle that excludes same-sex sexual relationships. Arguing from the anatomical nature of procreation, Robert Gagnon writes, "The fact that the semen ejaculated by the penis 'takes root' (we should say, 'effects the fertilization of an egg') and nurtures life only when penetration of a woman's vagina occurs is clear and convincing proof of God's exclusive design in nature of heterosexual intercourse. God/nature obviously intended the female vagina to be the complementary sex organ for the male penis."[80]

One can argue justifiably that what *is* truly "against nature" is the reduction of sexual pleasure to the function of procreation alone. Evidence proves that the stigmatization of sexual pleasure as something evil, apart from the intent to procreate, is a major causative factor in sexual dysfunction and contributes to marital disintegration, sexual abuse, pornography, and prostitution. Moral purity between a husband and wife does not mean suppressing the desire for sexual pleasure in deference to procreation, but rather a wholesome sharing of sexual pleasure in mutual respect, sensitivity, love, and fidelity. Men and women who love a person of the same sex are equally capable of this moral purity, regardless of the inability to engage in procreative sex with one other.

Idealization of Male/Female Complementariness

One argument upholds that the capacity for procreation establishes the basis for a unique complementariness of male and female. From a limited physiological, anatomical view the argument is correct: male and female are complementary, in the

---

[80] Gagnon, *The Bible and Homosexual Practice*, 169.

way that a plug-and-socket relation exists between penis and vagina, and that procreation requires the male sperm and the female egg. Beyond that, a great many questions about sexual relationships raise doubts about whether complementariness remains anything more than a romanticized ideal, not to mention whether it proves God's exclusive design in nature of hetero-sexual intercourse.

As the argument goes, the first man ("Adam" or "Earth Creature") can be complete only when the longing for sexual in-tercourse and marriage is fulfilled in someone not merely like the man (male, of course) but in a sexual opposite, a female who be-comes a complementary fit for the man, a complementary sexual "other."[81] The procreative role, as well as the companionship and support of this heterosexual couple, thus means that maleness and femaleness are essential to their completeness. Human com-pleteness ultimately rests upon binary gender opposites.

A closer look at the supposed complementariness of binary sexuality, however, reveals that it is not as complementary as one might assume. Genitalia, the seemingly most complementary as-pect, have significant disparities. Because of varying anatomical genitalia structure for any given individual, commonly the penis and clitoris of many couples do not make contact sufficiently during vaginal intercourse to stimulate female orgasm. Therefore, vaginal intercourse will rarely be completed in orgasm for both parties unless couples include methods of sexual foreplay to bring the female to full sexual arousal.

In fact, the purpose of the female clitoris is a curious physiological contradiction to the idea of sexual complementari-ness. Its function in female orgasm has no purpose for procreation as it has for male orgasm, which ejaculates semen from the penis. Its sole purpose is for sexual arousal leading to orgasm. One might argue that female orgasm plays a small role in procreation because female orgasm causes clonic spasms of the uterus that help draw spermatozoa up the cervical canal to where egg and

---

[81] Gagnon, *The Bible and Homosexual Practice*, 59–61.

spermatozoa can meet and effect fertilization. But before jumping to the conclusion that these spasms illustrate the complementariness of male and female functions, one should recognize that the spasm is a nearly useless redundancy for procreation, in as much as spermatozoa "know" where to go to fertilize an egg without the aid of the spasm. For the most part, the vagina and uterus are actually hostile environments for sperm that cause the massacre of hundreds of thousands of spermatozoa by the female immune system before they reach the place of impregnation.

Only 150 years ago, women were not even considered to have sexual feelings, not to mention orgasm. This chauvinistic assumption, especially before modern obstetrics, must have engendered in many women the sense that they were abused or exploited by men to whom they were expected to submit their body as an obedient "companion" (wife) and who realized, if impregnated, they faced the dreaded possibility of dying in childbirth, a not uncommon occurrence.

Differences between the male and the female brain also tend more to accentuate how men and women compete more than complete. The gender distinctions between male and female cerebral hemisphere lateralization support broad generalizations such as that the male is an "aggressive warrior" and the female a "nurturing caregiver." The differences in brain function between male and female may be as much a source of conflict as complement, as suggested by the phrase "battle of the sexes."

Common problems of sexual dysfunction among married couples underscore the difference between male and female sexual response that frequently emphasizes how sexual differences are a vexing mystery, not a fulfilling complement to the partner of the other sex. And the oft-touted virtue of raising children in households headed by both a man and a woman because of the differing emotional and social modeling necessary for child development assumes, without warrant, that those "complementary" emotional and social attributes are gender exclusive.

Overall, the idealistically purported complementariness of male and female is highly questionable for many aspects of male and female relationships. Instead, an enormous amount of incompleteness exists in the supposed complementariness of male and female pairs. In fact, this incompleteness is true not only of male and female relationships, it is also a simple fact of human relationship at many levels that requires from each person in a relationship the kind of patience, care, understanding, sensitivity, awareness, openness, and honesty that enables the development of the uniqueness of each human person. Particularly in extended, committed relationships, patiently working through the demands of dis-complementariness with grace, forgiveness, and acceptance proves mandatory for both other-sex and same-sex relationships, if they are to mature into life-long fidelity and intimacy.

This generally universal need to form closeness in a human relationship represents the profound implication of the phrase, "Bone of my bone and flesh of my flesh" in the Genesis creation story. This bone-of-my-bone closeness is first and foremost an issue of ordinary humanity. Adam is made complete *not* primarily because Eve is a complementary woman, but because she is *human* like Adam, thereby making possible completeness for *both* Adam and Eve. The closeness we cannot share with animals—"but for the man there was not found a helper fit for him" (Gen 2:20)—we can share with other human beings. Our common humanity makes possible a shared relationship that cannot be shared with any other kind of creature.

Our individual uniqueness calls forth from each of us the mandate for candor and trust that enables us to experience unity in our common humanity. Individual human uniqueness and the requirements for achieving intimacy are as applicable for same-sex couples as for other-sex couples. The challenge to achieve interpersonal intimacy and completeness—*this* is what is basic to the "divine order" cited in the Gen 2 creation story when God observed that it is not good for the man to be alone. This fundamental challenge exists for all human beings, independent of any ideological claims of the supposed importance of male/female sexual complementariness.[82]

Scrapping Sexual Reductionism

We owe a debt of gratitude to the sexual revolution and modern reproductive technology for their influence upon our understanding of human sexuality. In spite of the more salacious or libertine aspects of their influence, they have helped our culture view human sexuality more positively, and to better appreciate that being a human being, a sexual human being, involves far more than the physicality of sex. Human beings, of course, are not merely physical beings, but mental beings, emotional beings, spiritual beings, and social beings. Our sexuality permeates our whole being, touching all of what we are: physical, emotional, intellectual, social, and spiritual.

Homonegative heterosexuals, contrary to the view that sexuality permeates the entirety of being human, presumptively reduce homosexual couples' relationships to physical behavior alone. Homosexual couples, accordingly, are persons delimited by same-sex behavior whose association with each other is dismissed as a "chosen lifestyle." Even the label under which homosexual persons are lumped is sometimes reduced from 'homosexuality' to 'homosex'; and whole books, devoted to proving homosexuality's inherent wickedness, focus on the sinfulness of same-sex intercourse or "homosexual practice."[83]

---

[82] Gagnon, *The Bible and Homosexual Practice*, 176. "[O]ne fact remains indisputable: in the very act of male–male intercourse one partner (or both, if active–passive roles alternate) is taking the place of a woman. As far as the fittedness of the sex organs is concerned, only a woman is anatomically complementary to a man. For a man to take on that role is an obvious distortion of the gender distinctions endowed in nature by God."

[83] Gagnon, *The Bible and Homosexual Practice*, 37.

The presumption heterosexuals assume in defining homosexuals is analogous to that of elite, white European descendents in eighteenth- and nineteenth-century America, who presumed to define African slaves as non-human brutes and Native Americans as savages. Having defined Negroes and "Indians," anti-abolitionists defended the legitimacy of slavery and of forcing relocation to reservations upon entire tribes of people. The heterosexual hegemony defines homosexuals similarly, basing their definition upon the sexual behavior of same-sex couples. Consequently, who homosexuals are as *persons* becomes a matter of indifference in the same manner in which African slaves and Native Americans were dehumanized. Homosexuality is ever and always a perverse act of 'homosex.' With such reductionism as a basis for viewing same-sex relationships, the Bible indeed cites same-sex intercourse for censure and condemns each instance of it. With such reductionism, distinguishing between same-sex behavior in Bible times and same-sex behavior today becomes irrelevant. Eliminating distinctions means that male rape by the men of ancient Sodom, or pederasty among the aristocrats of Greece, or the temple prostitution practiced in the temples of Rome, is no different from the committed, loving, human relationships among many homosexual persons today. All that matters is that homosexuality is a sinful, genital behavior. Under the premises of reductionism, this judgment remains unmitigated even when a same-sex couple, like an other-sex couple, may have lived together for ten, twenty, thirty, forty, or more years in faithful commitment equivalent to any enduring heterosexual couple. Unlike the other-sex couple, whose sexual activity is seen as only one piece of a whole loving relationship, a same-sex couple's relationship is *qualified* only by one piece—physical sex, which is deemed incompatible with the Divine Order.

The incessant determination by reductionists to define homosexuality as a behavior of same-sex sexual intercourse makes difficult engaging in mutually respectful dialogue about homosexuality. Defined as a behavior, the logical corollary is that homosexuality cannot be immutable. It only identifies a numeric marker that indicates how often same-sex activity occurs in a given individual's experience. The behavioral definition also justifies the odd, moral distinction adjudging that homosexual *feelings* are not sinful, only *acting* on those feelings is sinful.

Some who oppose homosexuality wish to distance themselves somewhat from this extreme view. Increasingly, one encounters a willingness to concede that some people have persistent interests in persons of the same sex that begin in early childhood. They hesitate, however, to call homosexuality an 'orientation' versus a prevailing inclination. Rather than conceding that homosexuality is essential to a person's being, they assert that it is merely a behavior in response to erotic attractions established in early childhood that must be controlled in order to prevent falling into sin.

Thomas Schmidt states explicitly that he cannot use the term 'homosexuality' while allowing that "there appears to be sufficient evidence that some people do not *desire* physical intimacy with members of the opposite sex, and they do *desire* intimacy with members of their own sex. Furthermore, some people have known this *desire* for as long as they can remember" (emphasis mine).[84] The preceding statement demonstrates the resolve to dismiss the evidence for integrated same-sex gender connectivity in favor of the traditional opinion—that misdirected erotic desire leads some individuals to make the sinful choice of engaging in homosexual behavior. This erotic desire sounds very much like the demon "Lust."

Opponents of homosexuality, therefore, have difficulty with persons who claim their homosexuality is immutable because their entire rationale for opposing homosexuality is heavily invested in calling homosexuality a *behavior* borne out of lust. The motivation for behavior is an attitude, a desire that may be common to every person (as in the case of lust), but that can be controlled by the will, especially a spiritually sanctified will, so as not to allow it to choose immoral behaviors.

---

[84] Schmidt, *Straight & Narrow*, 150.

The moral mandate to control same-sex desire often means more than managing the desire or lust: it usually means eliminating it. In fact, some evangelical churches teach that when Jesus said a man who lusts after a woman commits adultery with her in his heart, he essentially meant, "Thinking it is the same as doing it." Consequently, merely abstaining from same-sex desire is not sufficient—one must never think about it at all. For a homosexual person, attempting abstinence from thought becomes, literally, a nightmare. They dream. And whereas thoughts can be controlled to some degree during the day, they cannot be controlled at night. Any erotic, emotionally fulfilling dreams supposedly indicate a hidden desire. And because God condemns homosexuals (defined to include those who even *think* about same-sex behavior), and because homosexuals *do* think about it (consciously or otherwise), they are categorically condemned at the outset.

In contrast to the behavioral definition of homosexuality, same-sex gender connectivity identifies what and who persons are *by nature*. Who I am by nature implies inevitability: I can be nothing else but who I am. Behavior is but one manifestation of who I am. If I am left-handed, I use my left hand because I am a left-handed person. The person who professes "I AM homosexual" poses a problem to those opposed to homosexuality because the claim to an innate homosexual nature means that such a person not only insists his or her same-sex behavior is inevitable, but it is *justifiable*. This assertion remains unacceptable to those who reject homosexuality as innate in some persons. To reject the notion of inevitability, therefore, the term 'orientation,' if those who oppose homosexuality use it at all, becomes redefined in order to avoid the implication of homosexuality's inevitability and its concomitant moral justification. As Thomas Schmidt says, "when I use the term orientation I mean only what a person desires, not what a person has a right to do, much less what a person is compelled to do as an expression of his or her being."[85]

---

[85] Schmidt, *Straight & Narrow*, 150.

People often become highly defensive when the theological convictions that sustain their rejection of innate homosexual identity are challenged by the claim of gay or lesbian persons: "I was born this way," or worse, "God made me this way." Many ridicule this presumption as either willful self-justification before God, or outright blasphemy. The implication, of course, which incites such protest, is that if one truly is born a certain way, then something or someone *other* than oneself is responsible. If not me, the pious soul then says, "God is responsible."

Rather than raising the question, "Did God make me this way?" the homosexual person might be encouraged to ask, "Does God *care* about me?" Even the person who opposes homosexuality agrees that God cares about homosexual persons. They would agree that God cares, but because they believe homosexuality is not innate, their admonition continues, "God cares enough about you to enable you to change. Therefore, you can and must change." Unfortunately, persons who have already suffered through long, anguishing, unsuccessful efforts to change "with God's help" often end up abandoning the belief that God cares.

Some homosexual persons, convinced they must change to heterosexual, have ultimately discovered that God cares about them even when they cannot change. Frustrated by others' insistence that they *can* choose to change "with God's help," no wonder they finally retort with the simple rejoinder, "God made me this way." As an expression of faith, they acknowledge that they did not make themselves: they earnestly *tried* to make themselves something else and could not. In some way, therefore, God must have been graciously involved in the process of their becoming who they are.

But not just theological issues regarding marriage and procreation remain at stake in the current controversy about homosexuality. As when debate raged over cosmology and abolition, the fabric of culture itself is being rent by enormous forces.

Our American culture is awash in explicit sexuality, eroticism in advertising, and pornography accessible with a click of a button on the Internet. Statistical reports of divorce, physical and emotional abuse within the family, infidelity, and abandonment quantify society's belief that The Family is in jeopardy, not only because of pressure from sexual liberalism, but also because of economic pressures caused by the importance modern society places on success and self-gratification. Economic pressure forces both spouses to work—sometimes two or more jobs—in order to maintain a standard of living only two incomes can provide. All too often, fractured families result, increasing the numbers of single-parent or blended families. Fortunately, many of these families survive amazingly well. Unfortunately, many, many do not. Our society is gripped by the fear that when the family fails, society will fail. At a time like this, politicians, social service workers, educators, and clergy feel a tremendous obligation to defend the family, to strengthen the family, to affirm family values in order to help the family survive.

Mixed with this urgency to strengthen families, much alarmist talk echoes about the purportedly last days of the United States. The collapse of Life As We Know It appears on the horizon unless we resist an attack by any threatening force. Among these "attacks"?—the recent trend of some Western nations, including the United States, to normalize homosexuality. Many religious alarmists accuse advocates of civil rights for gay and lesbian families of launching an explicit effort to destroy Christian culture. Against this perceived threat, the Biblical bias for conjugal procreation is used to support cultural biases in fighting against the erosion of society's stability by the blight of homosexuality.

Despite those who trumpet the threat of homosexuality to Christian culture, tolerance toward gays and lesbians progresses. It progresses in measure with positive encounters of heterosexual individuals with openly gay and lesbian individuals of human dignity. Open and candid homosexual people, who have embraced their sexual identity and are self-assured of their worth as human beings, make visible to society that they are men and women of great integrity, character, talent, compassion, fidelity, and faith *equal to* heterosexual men and women. They also are our great artists, statesmen and stateswomen, teachers, doctors, attorneys, civil servants, farmers, athletes, corporate executives, clergy, etc. They also are the brave laborers and homemakers forced by low wages and diminishing public support to live in impoverished ghettos and substandard housing next door to drug dens, villains, and prostitutes. These people of great dignity do not warrant the vilification of moral dogmatists. Religious bigotry and tabloid-style media exposés often imply that lewd, scandalous stories of pathetic sexual deviants, such as those about pedophiles, reflect typical homosexual behavior, and thereby they throw a guilt-by-association stereotype over all homosexual persons. Of course they neglect to tell us that such sexual deviants are as likely to be heterosexual persons as homosexual.

Long shaped by limited anecdotal evidence recorded in the patient files of psychotherapy clinics, negative definitions and descriptions of homosexuality by scientists of a generation ago were based mostly upon reports of that segment of the homosexual community having personality and psychological disorders for which they sought treatment. In recent years, researchers have revealed that emotionally and psychologically stable homosexual men and women, who of course never visited such clinics, probably comprised a far larger segment of the homosexual community than previously acknowledged or realized. Such individuals existed in society, but because they were hidden in their closets, no one saw them.

Many scientists willingly question their assumptions about the nature of homosexuality. Homonegative members of the religious community must also be willing to question their assumptions of truth, and to struggle honestly with the ambiguity surrounding the origin and cause of homosexuality. To facilitate the process of sincere reassessment, the following chapter, *Same-Sex Relationships and the Bible,* explores in more detail the Bible texts referring to same-sex behavior.

CHAPTER FIVE

Same-Sex Relationships and the Bible

Personal Profile: I've Been Bible Thumped

Anger rose in me as Beth described her luncheon experience with a friend. On several previous occasions over a cup of coffee, the acquaintance listened attentively to Beth's conversational references to our gay son and to the primarily gay and lesbian membership of the church where we worshipped. Knowing that the woman's pastor strongly opposed homosexuality, and that she attended his adult Sunday School class that maintained the Bible's condemnation of homosexual behavior, we realized she did not agree with our point of view. But she never argued nor proselytized in her response to Beth's sharing . . . and neither did Beth toward her. Although her response always reflected compassion toward our family, she honestly admitted she was puzzled by our approval of our homosexual son.

One day she finally reached an emotionally compelling decision to confront Beth about the ungodliness of homosexuality. After all, those who harbor concerns for friends often cannot help but say something they hope will effect change. And so with sweet and firm conviction, this woman said, "Beth, I just don't understand how you and Gib can approve your son's lifestyle. The Bible is so clear. In the book of Jude, verse seven, it says that Sodom and Gomorrah indulged in homosexuality and were punished with eternal fire." Her admonition was clear: our gay son was on the path toward eternal fire. Not as clear, yet implicit, was the implication that Beth and I, by approving of our son and other homosexual persons, would also feel the heat.

Her concern echoed the saying among Christians that "Jesus was sent to deliver his people *from* their sins, not *in* their sins." Christians who use this adage tend to assume that homosexuality is sinful behavior from which gays and lesbians must be delivered. The underlying premise, frequently echoed, is: "Love the sinner, and hate the sin." Like their view of any other sin, they believe homosexuality is behavior that can be forgiven, but that must also be forsaken. Because sin is persistent and difficult to forsake, they urge the homosexual person to rely on Jesus' help to renounce such sinful behavior. Basic to Christian doctrine is the belief that Jesus loves and forgives every sinner, and—by means of the Holy Spirit—leads the sinner to repentance, and transforms the penitent's heart to forsake sin. Consequently, many Christians will say they love homosexuals like any other person; but when the homosexual person asks approval for his/her "sinful lifestyle," the Christian adamantly says, "No!" Although they may love the sinner, they *cannot*, in their obligation to represent the love and mercy of Jesus, minimize or disregard the seriousness of the sin, thereby risking the spiritual welfare of the sinner. To grant approval to the sin of homosexuality is tantamount to disobeying Jesus. Granting permission to remain *in* sin essentially contradicts Jesus' stated purpose of delivering people *from* sin.

After my initial anger subsided, I decided to take Beth's friend seriously, turn to the Scripture she referenced, and honestly search for its meaning. I took out my Bible and opened it to Jude, a little book of twenty-five verses tucked tightly into the end of the New Testament between the Third Letter of John and the Revelation to John. Quickly looking up verse seven, I read pretty much what Beth's acquaintance told her: "Sodom and Gomorrah and the surrounding cities, which likewise acted immorally and indulged in unnatural lust, serve as an example by undergoing a punishment of eternal fire" (Jude 7-8).

Pretty straightforward stuff, not much wiggle room here, it would seem. This Bible passage is definitely one upon which people base the statement, "It is absolutely clear that the Bible condemns homosexuality." Clearly, Sodom and Gomorrah were judged for wickedness. Clearly, indulging in unnatural lust evokes the passage in the Apostle Paul's letter to the Romans where he cites those who "exchanged natural relations for unnatural" (Rom 1:26). And it seems vividly and terrifyingly clear what "undergoing a punishment of eternal fire" (Jude 8) is all about. I'm not surprised Beth's friend wanted to convey her profound concern for us with a clear statement she hoped might transform our thinking from "hell bound" to "straight and narrow."

But before I take any single verse at face value, I always want to look at the *context* of a particular reference—the ideas a writer records before and after a verse, and what those ideas mean *within* the writer's cultural environment. Not a hard task concerning Jude, with only twenty-five verses in the entire book.

First I looked at the beginning of the letter, where a writer often explicitly or implicitly explains the purpose for writing. After a brief salutation, Jude gets right to the point. He is "eager to write" (Jude 3), and even more emphatically he states that it is "necessary to write" (Jude 3) because of something called 'apostasy'—the abandonment of one's faith or principles, the renunciation of religious belief and allegiance. In no uncertain terms Jude appeals to his readers "to contend for the faith" (Jude 3). He raises the alarm that Christians face a deadly, serious conflict inside the Church because of subversives who surreptitiously entered the Church to pervert the faith, deny Jesus Christ as Lord, cause members of the Church to forsake the teaching of the apostles, and embrace the scoffers' ungodly ways.

At the end of this short missive, Jude restates his concern about apostasy. He expresses his confidence that God is able "to keep you from falling and to present you without blemish" (Jude 24) before Him in the end. In other words, he encourages his readers to trust God to preserve them from abandoning their faith, and to strengthen them to maintain allegiance to Jesus Christ until they stand before God's glorious presence.

The author moves into the main body of his letter by citing three instances in the Biblical narrative when God took action against apostates. The first citation details the Hebrews' exodus from Egypt under the leadership of Moses, when many of them, impatient for Moses to return from his private pilgrimage on the Mount of Sinai, reverted to the idolatrous worship they practiced in Egypt. Through God's mercy, the people experienced freedom from their miserable bondage in Egypt, yet they incurred divine wrath when some abandoned the teaching of Moses to worship the golden calf—"he who saved a people out of the land of Egypt, afterward destroyed those who did not believe" (Jude 5).

The second citation refers to a story told among Christians (see 2 Pet 2:4) about angels who enjoyed the heavenly privilege of standing in the presence of God, but who, because they renounced righteousness for unrighteousness, were expelled from heaven into Hell. When they turn to unrighteousness, God puts even angels under subjection and keeps them "in eternal chains in the nether gloom until the judgment of the great day" (Jude 6).

Finally Jude reaches the citation of Sodom, Gomorrah, and the surrounding cities. He states that they acted just like the people of the Exodus and just like the fallen angels. Specifically, the people of these cities are condemned for acting immorally and indulging in unnatural lust—literally, to go after strange (or other) flesh—like the apostate Israelites and angels cited before.

The sin of "going after other flesh" implies that Sodom and Gomorrah's sin was a parallel but not necessarily identical act to that of the angels and Israelites. The parallelism consists of immoral behavior, but the contexts prove dissimilar. The "other flesh" of the Israelites consisted of intermarriage with persons of the pagan neighbor tribes (see Deut 7:1–4). Of the angels, "other flesh" consisted of immortals cohabiting with mortal women, if we are to read the passage in 2 Pet 2:4 as an interpretation of the "sons of God marrying the sons of men" (Gen 6:1–4). The men of Sodom and Gomorrah are condemned because they have sex with "other flesh" outside the "male and female" order. For any and all of the sins of "going after other flesh" or immorality, God's punishment is expected. Therefore Jude correlates the sin of the Israelites and angels with the sin of Sodom and Gomorrah; they were examples of divinely punished sinners "just as Sodom and Gomorrah" (Jude 7). Sodom and Gomorrah were guilty of sin like the Israelites and angels because they "likewise acted immorally and indulged in unnatural lust" (Jude 7). Although the behavior is different, the sin of Sodom and Gomorrah is of the same character as the sin of the apostate Israelites and angels, and the punishment of apostate Israelites and angels is of the same character as the punishment of Sodom and Gomorrah.

But, if the parallelism of the sin of immorality and unnatural lust among the three groups makes them comparable, what shall we make of Jude's close linkage of the men of Sodom and Gomorrah with *apostasy*, specifically with the apostasy of angels and the people of the Exodus? The men of Sodom and Gomorrah hardly fit the definition of 'apostate.' What Biblical evidence existed to suggest that these people had a faith in the Hebrew God to abandon, or allegiance to a righteous God to repudiate? "What was the *apostasy* of the men of Sodom and Gomorrah?" I wondered.

I recognized the Sodom and Gomorrah narrative primarily from Gen 18 and 19, a narrative that became particularly familiar through emphatic and frequent references used to condemn homosexuality. Yet nothing in those chapters suggests *apostasy*, only evil—such that, according to the Biblical narrative, Sodom and Gomorrah were burned to cinders in an almighty downpour of fire and brimstone because fewer than five persons in the entire population could be counted righteous. For what reason does Jude make this direct association between Sodom and Gomorrah and Hebrew apostasy? The question continued to intrigue me.

Old Testament Apostasy and Same-Sex Behavior

Faith and Unfaith

Personally, I consider highly remarkable the distinctiveness of the Hebrew faith that emerges from the dominant cultures in which it took shape. Taking into account the powerful and overwhelming cultural pressure from surrounding cultures, the historically inconsequential Hebrews should have disappeared into archival oblivion along with many other minority groups of antiquity. Mesopotamia in the Euphrates valley, the neighboring Canaanite tribes with their sensually appealing culture, Egypt with its ancient splendor, the philosophically and culturally influential Greeks—these cultures dominated the ancient world and should have swallowed up the comparatively tiny group of Hebrews. But the Hebrew faith's distinctiveness persevered in spite of the intense cultural potency of surrounding empires, a testimony to the mystery of inspiration animating the human spirit to rise above the innumerable challenges and threats to sustaining human communities. In the Old Testament, a narrative thread recurs about a patient and persistent upward call of God to a human community, a call with a vision of justice and an empowerment of individuals to live lives of righteous character.

The narrative of the Old Testament most constitutive of Israel's identity as a unique people with a distinctive faith is the story of Moses and the Hebrew exodus from Egyptian slavery. Although no evidence proves that Moses existed or that the exodus indisputably occurred, as with the Hebrew tales of ancient patriarchs such as Abraham, these stories prove authentic in the sense that a nation did exist and *continues* to exist as a culturally distinct ethnic group . . . whose *contemporary* story is still powerfully shaped by the ancient story of Moses and the exodus.

The distinctiveness is reflected for example, in the story of a conversation between Moses and God (Exod 33:19–23), in which the portrayal of God, on the one hand, is personal enough to "speak" with Moses, yet so transcendent that Moses must be tucked into a cleft of a rock with his back to the cleft's mouth so as not to be consumed by the glory of divine holiness. God is anthropomorphized as having a hand placed over the opening of the cleft to shield Moses from this glory of divine holiness.

This imagery points to an understanding of God quite unlike the common deification of natural and human forces in the pantheon of gods found in nature religions. This imagery diverges from the embodiment of deity in immortal cultic heroes or in the divinization of a kingly lineage. The story implies the utter transcendence of God beyond any possible natural association, yet also suggests that God is capable of personal engagement in human experience. In the story, God tells Moses, "I will be gracious to whom I will be gracious, and will show mercy on whom I will show mercy" (Exod 33:19). This characterization of God's grace and mercy repeats in the next chapter: "The Lord, the Lord, a God merciful and gracious, slow to anger, and abounding in steadfast love and faithfulness" (Exod 34: 6).

Stories about God's graciousness to the Hebrews that reflect this merciful attribute include the narrative about God freeing them from Egyptian bondage, caring for them in the wilderness, and ultimately establishing them in the region of Canaan. The narrative made clear that God's graciousness represented more than a Divine attribute. Henceforth, the Hebrews themselves were expected to express the same attribute in their interactions with those around them, particularly with strangers and sojourners in their midst. God's people were to express *cultural* superiority through acts of hospitality respecting and welcoming strangers who came into their midst, rather than practice the *brutal* superiority some of the neighboring Canaanite tribes demonstrated against their neighbors with barbarous acts of cruelty.

In actual practice, Israel often found itself embroiled in conflict with its neighbors over the pragmatic necessity of land acquisition and occupation that led to open warfare with Canaanite tribes. In this conflict over which people should legitimately occupy the land, Israel's belief in Divine favor appears unmistakably, but also they adopted syncretistic religious practices in common with their enemy neighbors. In spite of the genocides and battles they executed in the name of God and purportedly at God's behest, the principal vision of a God of universal mercy, whose mercy was to be reflected in the national and personal lives of Israel, remained embedded, however dimly at times, in the self-understanding of the Hebrew people.[86]

The great requirement of Deuteronomy epitomized this vision:

> "And now Israel, what does the Lord your God require of you, but to fear the Lord your God, to walk in all his ways, to love him, to serve the Lord your God with all your heart and with all your soul . . . For the Lord your God is God of gods and Lord of lords, the great, the mighty, and the terrible God, who is not partial and takes no bribe. He executes justice for the fatherless and the widow, and loves the sojourner, giving him food and clothing. *Love the sojourner therefore; for you were sojourners in the land of Egypt.*" (emphasis mine)[87] (Deut 10:12–19)

The distinctiveness of the Hebrew vision of God may be traced throughout the narrative of the nation's historical development among other regional Canaanite nations. This vision also appears in the narratives of the post-exilic period, especially in the prophetic literature, as the Hebrews in Babylonian exile struggled with self-identity. The struggle to maintain an authentic identity continued during successive periods of domination under Persians, Medes, Greeks, and Romans.

A tension occurs in Israel's historical narrative between those who articulated a more prophetic voice, calling Israel to be faithful to a universal call for justice and mercy, and the more priestly voice, calling Israel to be faithful to an exclusionary call to keep

---

[86] Miller, *The Religion of Ancient Israel*. 12–13. These repeated characterizations of Yahweh as merciful and gracious and acting in steadfast love define this deity in a way that lifts up mercy alongside justice as indicating the particular "bent" of the God of Israel.

[87] In all subsequent Bible quotations, italicized text represents emphasis that I have added.

pure its cultic practices and individual piety. A quote from the prophet Amos clearly articulates this struggle, and was invoked in the appeal for justice during the 1960s American Civil Rights Movement: "I hate, I despise your feasts, and I take no delight in your solemn assemblies. But let justice roll down like waters, and righteousness like an everflowing stream" (Amos 5:21, 24).

In every articulation of Israel's vision of God, the plea to remain faithful resounds. Yet alongside the transforming upward call to the Hebrews, a deteriorating downward drag ensues. Throughout Israel's history, inspiration to higher standards drew sparks of friction against the resistance of debasing attractions. Where seeds of faithfulness were planted also grew the weeds of faithlessness. Fidelity to God was all too often abandoned for the sirens of pagan sensuality. In short, apostasy was an ever-present danger. With that, we return full circle to the Bible passage from Jude quoted to Beth by her compassionate friend.

Segue to Sodom

As for the ancient Hebrews living in Canaan and so also for Jude's contemporaries, the appeal of cult religions, particularly the rampant sensuality practiced commonly in Greek and Roman culture, proved strong. People in the Church began to make compromises between their Christian faith and their desire to fit into the prevailing culture. Therefore, Jude makes an association between the instances of the apostasy he observes in his age with those of Israel's ancient narratives, when apostasy and wicked, immoral, perverse behavior went hand in hand. Curiously, he includes Sodom and Gomorrah among the list of apostates. Because Jude raises the issue of Sodom and Gomorrah among that list, we must look more closely at the Sodom and Gomorrah narrative in the book of Genesis, one of the most commonly cited Biblical passage relating to homosexuality.

The only portion of the Sodom story commonly cited in the contemporary homosexuality debate is the intended rape of the guests in the home of Lot (Gen 19). Highlighting just this particular incident, however, misses the point of the Sodom narrative *in toto*. Sodom proves an exemplar of apostasy, one that Hebrew Scriptures repeatedly hold up as a warning against the apostate tendencies of the Hebrew population. Interestingly, when Biblical writers chastise the Hebrews' apostasy, they sometimes chide them with the claim that the apostasy of God's own people is more severe than that of Sodom (see Ezek 16:47–60). Clearly the issue more critical to Biblical writers than the men of Sodom's same-sex behavior is the cultural corruption permeating an apostate culture (see Isa 1:10–17). What, therefore, is Sodom's extreme apostasy?

Before addressing that question, we must remember that the dominant religions of Canaan deified nature itself. The Sun, moon and stars, as well as the basic forces of the earth, were believed to be the visible manifestation of divine presence and power that controlled all other dimensions of nature. Gods and goddesses existed as anthropomorphic extrapolations of these natural powers; and the stories of their lives and antics both reflected and influenced human experience. A dominant characteristic of nature religion included fertility cults, found among agrarian tribes dependent on prolific crops, as well as among nomadic tribes dependent upon prolific herds. Economic prosperity in the ancient world related directly to prolific flocks of sheep or herds of cattle, abundant harvests of crops, as well as the procreation of human descendants. Fertility cults among some tribes evolved into highly sexual rites intended not only to mimic the sexual activity of the gods and goddesses upon whose favor prosperity depended, but also to manipulate the gods' and goddesses' favor to improve the chance of prosperity, to re-enact the sexual behavior of the gods and goddesses whose fecundity, they believed, blessed the earth with good harvests and prolific livestock.

The Old Testament refers often to Asherah, idolatrous images of the shape of a nude woman, often heavy with child, and with full, sometimes multiple breasts. Biblical references to pagan festivals suggest wild and orgiastic rituals involving cult prostitutes, both male and female, with whom sexual activity was intended to honor the fertility gods and to curry their favor. In actuality, these references probably reflected intense hostility toward Canaanite culture, expressed through exaggerated propaganda that projected fantasized sexual perversion onto the Canaanites[88] (much like in white American culture, we can identify numerous instances of fantasized exaggerated sexual appetites projected onto black males).

Therefore, when reading the Bible writers' castigation of sexual immorality, we must perform a cultural translation away from our cultural mores to those of the ancient world. We must shift from the contemporary idea of immorality as personal behavior that transgresses moral codes of public decency. Instead,

---

[88] Biale, *Eros and the Jews*, 24. "It has been generally assumed that the Canaanites, following a pagan, polytheistic religion, practiced fertility rites in which male and female ritual prostitutes (*kedashim* and *kedashot*) engaged in sexual intercourse as a way of promoting intercourse between the gods. Thus, the prophet Hosea thundered against Israelites who followed Canaanite religion:

> They sacrifice on the mountaintops And offer on the hills, Under oaks, poplars and terebinths. Whose shade is so pleasant. That is why their daughters fornicate. And their daughters-in-law commit adultery . . . For they themselves turn aside with whores. And sacrifice with kedashot. (Hos 4:13-14)

Yet lack of corroboration of such practices in the Canaanite texts themselves suggests that these graphic images prove little more than propaganda. Just as the covenant with the Israelite God was understood as a metaphorical marriage, so worship of a foreign God came to be seen as metaphorical adultery. The prophets regarded Canaanite religion with such hostility that they may have projected a whole range of sexual fantasies onto their enemies, much as later anti-Semites were to accuse the Jews of a variety of deviant sexual practices."

we must see that the immorality observed by Biblical writers in their pagan neighbors represented legitimately established behavior *within* pagan social conduct. In sum, these behaviors occurred not as personal transgressions of moral codes, but as communal behaviors reflecting a specific time and culture, and considered integral to religious and social integrity.

One must recall that some Biblical writers believed that the experience of divine grace inherently demands expression in the life of the *recipient* of grace. Into the Christian era we are reminded to love one another, *as God first loved us*: love for one another is the evidence that we are the disciples of Jesus. Israel's historical legacy, its hallmark of godliness, required the nation's community life to make evident in its own behavior that God established that very community by divine grace; and they believed the practice of hospitality best expressed this demonstrated faith. To use a modern analogy, hospitality for the Israelites served like a shortcut icon on a computer screen. Clicking on the icon initiates the program that lies behind the shortcut. Thus, for the Israelites,[89] a click on "Hospitality" brings up the God who delivered Israel from adversity, provided sanctuary, food and drink in the harsh wilderness, and, above all, gave worth, identity, and a prosperous land of their own to a people who would have had no national identity without God's gracious redemption from slavery.

Fully mindful of God's mercy, they tried to exemplify the divine blessing they received by sheltering and protecting the stranger who came into their midst, providing food and clothing if needed, and bestowing upon the stranger/sojourner/foreigner all the dignity of worthy guests in their homes. Divine compassion from God converted into human compassion for the poor, the widow, and the orphan.

---

[89] Classical Greece also commended hospitality toward the sojourner; but there, the motivation for the practice derived from a humanistic ideal of just relationships among mortals, whereas Hebrew hospitality arose from an internalized recognition of God's gracious justice executed for the well-being of humans.

Gen 14–19 — Sodom and Gomorrah

The question remains, *why* are pagan sensuality and the Hebrew concept of hospitality so crucial to understanding the Sodom and Gomorrah incident recorded in Gen 19? First, however, we must look at the earliest Biblical reference to Sodom found in Gen 14—earliest, that is, except for references to Sodom's geographic location in Gen 10 and 13, and the general indictment "Now the people of Sodom were wicked, great sinners against the LORD" (Gen 13:13).

During the time of the patriarch Abram (later renamed Abraham), the Genesis narrative identifies the aggressive military campaigns of King Chedorlaomer of Elam and his allies as the greatest international threat over the region of Canaan. After twelve years under Chedorlaomer's repressive military occupation, the conquered tribes of Canaan rebelled. War broke out in the valley of Sidim near Sodom and Gomorrah, where the Kings of Sodom and Gomorrah joined forces against the alliance. But things went badly. During the ensuing battle, many of the rebel forces became mired in the bitumen pits in the valley and were massacred. The rest fled to the hills. King Chedorlaomer and his allies went on to plunder Sodom and Gomorrah and the other nearby cities, and took captive their women and children.

The Biblical account of this regional conflict tells that when Abram learned of the disaster, he gathered 312 of his men and set out in pursuit of the alliance army. Though vastly outnumbered, Abram "routed them and pursued them to Hobah, north of Damascus. Then he brought back all the goods, and also brought back his kinsman Lot with his goods, and the women and the people" (Gen 14:15–16). Then begins the narration of this remarkable event:

> After his return from the defeat of Chedorlaomer and the kings who were with him, the king of Sodom went out to meet him at the Valley of Shaveh (that is, the King's Valley). And King Melchizedek king of Salem brought out

bread and wine; he was priest of God Most High. He blessed him and said,

> "Blessed be Abram by God Most High,
> maker of heaven and earth;
> *and blessed be God Most High,*
> *Who has delivered your enemies into your hand!"*

And Abram gave him one-tenth of everything. And the king of Sodom said to Abram, "Give me the persons, but take the goods for yourself." *But Abram said to the king of Sodom, "I have sworn to the LORD, God Most High, maker of heaven and earth, that I would not take a thread or a sandal-thong or anything that is yours, lest you should say, 'I have made Abram rich.'* I will take nothing but what the young men have eaten, and the share of the men who went with me—let Aner, Eshcol, and Mamre take their share." (Gen 14:17–24)

Obviously, the King of Sodom experienced a remarkable phenomenon of national redemption that King Melchizedek, the mysterious Messianic figure of the Old Testament, describes as an act of God executed through the instrumentality of Abram.

But also note the righteous actions of Abram. He humbly defers the success of military victory to God and refuses to capitalize on the situation for his own gain. God is believed the unseen source of deliverance, and Abram visibly implements his mercy. In practical reality, it was Abram who won the victory over the alliance. But in this event, interpreted as God's act through Abram, the King of Sodom experiences Abram's unique act of grace: a concrete expression of the theological abstraction of divine victory. The mundane experience of Abram's mercy confirms in practical reality God's mercy.

One might expect the King of Sodom, impressed by the circumstances of his nation's deliverance, to ponder the experience of divine mercy and, at minimum, recommend personal emulation of Abram's noble character. But apparently he did not. Far from becoming a grateful people, Sodom and Gomorrah perpetuate such cruel barbarity that they earn a despicable reputation among their neighbors.

The ominous threat of judgment against Sodom and Gomorrah first emerges in the second half of Gen 18. Not only did Sodom's king and citizens *not* take heart from their deliverance, they lived as people so malicious in their evil that others cried out to God for deliverance from their savagery (see Gen 18:20).

The narrative dramatically depicts Sodom as so far removed from the God who won their national deliverance that God appears completely in the dark about the extreme adversity created by Sodom. Thus, God must investigate, must see for himself if the harsh complaints against Sodom are legitimate (see Gen 18:21).

Canaanite cities in the ancient world typically organized into tribes, with small cities or clustered encampments of nomadic groups ruled by patriarchal warlords or kings. Often dissension and conflict arose between tribes with little to hold them together. Although they shared a common religion, each tribe saw its gods as especially favoring their particular tribe and more powerful than the gods of a neighboring tribe. Among many tribes, suspicion toward outsiders and hostility to tribal enemies proved so intense that they perpetrated vicious acts of cruelty upon strangers unfortunate enough to be caught in their tribal territory. Travel through their regions became extremely dangerous.

Among the more aggressive, hostile tribes, a common practice was to sexually abuse and harass strangers or members of alien tribes who fell into their hands. Believing their own gods to be stronger than those of their neighbors, they demonstrated superiority by subjecting captives to sadistic brutality. Male captives were emasculated by rape, in order to denigrate them and subject them to the height of indignity—putting them into the sexual role of a woman.

This extreme apostasy of Sodom and Gomorrah must provide the context for examining the judgment upon them in Gen 19. Having experienced deliverance from a gracious God, they ignored God in favor of a sensual idolatry that encouraged a variety of sexual immoralities and perversions. In utter contrast, as a demonstration of a living remembrance of God's grace, Israelites extended God's favor by graciously including strangers within their gates. Thus, on the one hand, a people were consecrated to do justice, and on the other hand, a people were consumed to do injustice. Such injustice and violent sexual abuse lies at the heart of Sodom's wickedness in this text:

> The two angels came to Sodom in the evening; and Lot was sitting in the gateway of Sodom. When Lot saw them, he rose to meet them, and bowed himself with his face to the earth, and said, "My lords, turn aside, I pray you, to your servant's house and spend the night, and wash your feet; then you can rise early and go on your way." They said, "No; we will spend the night in the street." But he urged them strongly; so they turned aside to him and entered his house; and he made them a feast, and baked unleavened bread, and they ate. *But before they lay down, the men of the city, the men of Sodom, both young and old, all the people to the last man, surrounded the house; and they called to Lot, "Where are the men who came to you tonight? Bring them out to us, that we may know them."* Lot went out of the door to the men, shut the door after him, and said, "I beg you, my brothers, do not act so wickedly." But they said, "Stand back!" And they said, "This fellow came here to sojourn, and he would play the judge! Now we will deal worse with you than with them." Then they pressed hard against the man Lot, and came near to break the door. (Gen 19:1–7, 9)

Clearly, taking this entire historical and cultural context into consideration, one simply cannot equate the sadistic, brutal sexual abusiveness of the men of Sodom with gay and lesbian people today, nor suggest that they risk the eternal fire as Jude declares of Sodom, without risking what essentially amounts to slander and spiritual abuse.

Judg 19—The Gibeah Story

To further underscore the context of apostasy and institutionalized sexual aggression as the basic grounds for which the Bible
condemns specific same-sex behavior, we turn to a seeming
adaptation of the Sodom and Gomorrah story: the narrative of
Gibeah's immorality in Judg 19. Like its counterpart in Gen 19, the
Gibeah story appears to underscore the evil of apostasy, especially
involving a return to the practices of Canaanite religion. Although
the text does not explicitly state the nature of Gibeah's apostasy,
the parallelism with Sodom and the absence of hospitality in
Gibeah imply a gross failure of Hebrew citizens to live up to their
divine calling.

The story begins by introducing a Levite (that is, a member of
Israel's priesthood) whose newly acquired concubine ran away
and returned to her father's house in Bethlehem (see Judg 19:1–2).
Several months later, the Levite traveled to Bethlehem to retrieve
her; however, for several days, the woman's father delayed hand-
ing over his daughter. Finally, rather late one day, the Levite
persuaded the father to relinquish his daughter so they could
begin their journey home before nightfall. The Levite, concubine,
and the Levite's servant managed to reach Jebus, a tribal village of
the Jebusites (Judg 19:10), where the servant urged the Levite to
stop for the night because travel so late in the day was dangerous.
But the Levite refused:

> "We will not turn aside into the city of *foreigners, who do not
> belong to the people of Israel;* but we will continue on to
> Gibeah." And he said to his servant, "Come and let us
> draw near to one of these places, and spend the night at
> Gibeah or at Ramah." (Judg 19:12–13)

The story appears to reflect the separatist element of Hebrew
belief, concerned with preserving a Holy people against contamination by alien influences. It also seems to suggest the danger of
spending the night in a place where aggression and abuse from
hostile tribes may occur. And so the Levite insists instead that

they should extend their travel into dusk in order to reach a city of Israelites, where he might expect hospitality. Unfortunately, he was wrong. Turning into Gibeah, "he went in and sat down in the open square of the city, *for no man took them into his house to spend the night*" (Judg 19:15). At this point, the Levite could well suspect something amiss.

The narrative continues with remarkable parallels to the story of Sodom. The Gibeah story includes a character much like Lot, Abraham's nephew in Sodom. He is an outsider, from the country of Ephraim, who somehow resides safely in this inhospitable city of Benjaminites, and who offers to the Levite the hospitality the Benjaminite citizens should have provided —but did not.

> And behold, an old man was coming from his work in the field at evening; the man was from the hill country of Ephraim, and he was sojourning in Gibeah; the men of the place were Benjaminites. And he lifted up his eyes, and saw the wayfarer in the open square of the city, . . . And the old man said, "Peace be to you. I will care for all your wants; only do not spend the night in the square." [21]So he brought him into his house, and gave the asses provender; and they washed their feet, and ate and drank. (Judg 19:16–17, 20–21)

As evidence from Judges and 1 and 2 Kings suggests, Gibeah's apostasy, most likely syncretistic of Hebrew and Canaanite religions, proved commonplace in the development of Israel's cultural and religious history. In other words, these examples likely do not reflect the outright abandonment of Israelite religion, but rather the tendency to worship the Hebrew God while simultaneously courting the fertility gods' favor for good crops and livestock. King Solomon tried to be faithful to God; but at the same time he kept his foreign wives happy by building temples to their favorite deities, including Astarte, mostly likely the fertility goddess Asherah with a different name. Regardless of historical setting, openness to alien influence demonstrated an adulterous defilement and compromise of Israel's fidelity to a Holy God.

The writer of Judges, by relating the Gibeah incident, seems to emphasize the vileness of Israel's apostasy by drawing a parallel to Sodom. In both instances, men come pounding on the door at night with the intent of raping the foreigner in their midst.

> As they were making their hearts merry, behold, the men of the city, base fellows, beset the house round about, beating on the door; and they said to the old man, the master of the house, "Bring out the man who came into your house, so that we may know[90] him." (Judg 19:22)

Like Lot in Sodom, the old man tries to protect his guest and even offers innocent women, his virgin daughter and the Levite's concubine—chattel nonetheless—to assuage male rapaciousness.[91]

> And the man, the master of the house, went out to them and said to them, "No, my brethren, do not act so wickedly; seeing that this man has come into my house, do not do this vile thing. Behold, here are my virgin daughter and his concubine; let me bring them out now. Ravish them and do with them what seems good to you; but against this man do not do such a vile thing." (Judg 19:23–24)

But the sadistic intentions of the men of Gibeah could not be deterred any more than Lot could dissuade the men of Sodom.

---

[90] "Know" used here is a euphemism for sexual intercourse.

[91] Note again the patriarchal presumption of antiquity about the status and worth of women. This recurring premise offers further reason to reject the notion of Divine inspiration of Scripture as a *literal* recording of God's word and for acknowledging the actuality of Biblical bias. We cannot forget that the patriarchal bias denigrating women, exemplified so blatantly here (and without any kind of 'divine' censure), found avid proponents in modern times in several contemporary cultures. Not too long ago, spousal abuse by male Christian leaders toward their wives was justified as a means to ensure the godly reputation of the leader by enforcing the wife's submissive compliance to her husband.

The Levite seized his concubine, and put her out where the men raped and abused her through the night, until morning when she collapsed at the door of the house. No indication suggests that these men were consumed with homoerotic lust, and searched for same-sex relations as part of a sensual night on the town. No, they were abusive men bent on the feminization of strangers to demonstrate their god's superiority over them. They sought any victims, male or female, to defile them with erotic, sadistic passion.

Both Gen 19 and Judg 19 describe incidents of rape used as tools of culturally acceptable, sadistic brutality against other human beings. Those who committed these acts do *not* demonstrate a homosexual identity in the sense that we understand today—as persons innately oriented toward gender connectivity with members of the same sex. Nor does the behavior of those Biblical men reflect homosexual behavior in general. Homosexual relationships cannot be summarized as a single behavior, male-on-male intercourse, and be equated with the men of Sodom and Gibeah, whose cruel practices of rape represented a socially approved expression of contempt toward foreigners and strangers.

Leviticus — The Holiness Code

This discussion of culturally sanctioned sexual abuse, employed to dominate others, leads us to another Scripture passage frequently used to condemn homosexuals: "You shall not lie with a male as with a woman; it is an abomination" (Lev 18:22). The command is repeated in Lev 20:13 with the additional penalty that for such an act, the persons involved shall be put to death. The appended capital punishment of Lev 20 applies to both partners of same-sex intercourse, whereas Lev 18 does not assign any blame to the penetrated partner.

A question emerges from the command that a man should not lie with a male *as with a woman*. The expression "to lie with" is a Biblical euphemism for sexual intercourse, an expression just as clear as our contemporary euphemism to "sleep with." Saying a male should not lie with a male clearly connotes a same-sex experience; so why take the trouble to amplify the obvious by adding that this behavior should not be in the same manner "as with a woman"?

The phrase emphasizes that the role of the one involved in this illegitimate sexual intercourse is the 'inserter' or the 'penetrator,' as opposed to the passive, penetrated partner.[92] The distinctiveness of this emphasis is important in the context of the cultural mores regarding male-to-male sex acts among the Hebrew's neighboring societies. The bans against same-sex intercourse in neighboring societies, particularly Egypt and most notably Greece, are closely tied to the notion that legitimate sex is related to status rather than to gender. The penetrator or active partner in sex must always be superior/dominant in status, and the penetrated or passive partner must always be subordinate. *Legitimate sexual behavior* for a freeman, therefore, included not merely penetration of a woman, but also a male slave, a boy, or a male non-citizen, none of whom could claim the rights and privileges of a freeborn male. A freeborn male who assumed a passive, penetrated role in sexual relation was considered degraded and immoral.

Consequently, *class status* is the critical background issue regarding sexual relationships for the writers of Leviticus. Status becomes the basis for sexual mores that belong to idolatrous neighbors and therefore must be kept alien among the Hebrews. But in the foreground, *gender* represents the critical issue as to acceptable or unacceptable sexual behavior for the Hebrews. The principle of status among pagan nations, and gender among Hebrews, prove contrasting principles. That which a Hebrew man

---

[92] Olyan, "And with a Male You Shall Not Lie the Lying Down of a Woman," 186. "In fact, in the wider context of biblical law, the idiom 'to lie with' is used exclusively of insertive partners. I suspect that the same is true of Lev. 18:22 and 20:13: the laws address the insertive partner in a male-male coupling."

experiences in vaginal intercourse with a woman should not be experienced with a man, as it is among the pagans.

Seen against this background, several reasons—all connected to the issue of apostasy—emerge why the distinction "as with a woman" might be made. But first, we must examine more closely the phrase "*it is an abomination.*" The Hebrew word translated into English as "abomination" is variously transliterated *toeba* or *toevah*. With few exceptions, the word *toevah* is used in the Bible to describe God's disposition toward *idolatrous* practices, not to things that are evil in-and-of themselves. Biblical writers who referred to things that are depraved, wicked, evil in-and-of themselves, commonly used the word *zimah*.

The choice of word proves interesting. A man may not lie with a man *as with a woman* because it is *toevah*, an idolatrous act, not *zimah*, an act that is evil in-and-of itself. The resulting implication suggests that lying with a male *as with a woman* is vile because it represents an idolatrous act associated with the religion or culture of neighboring societies who sanctioned same-sex behavior that was abusive, or that serviced the rituals of idolatrous cults.

Therefore, in this Leviticus passage, same-sex behavior is censured primarily because of its association with idolatry.[93] In this

---

[93] Gagnon, *The Bible and Homosexual Practice*, 117–18. "The word 'toeba' is restricted in Leviticus to forms of sexual immorality that can be characterized in three ways: (1) a sexual act regarded by Yahweh as utterly detestable and abhorrent, (2) a sexual act which rendered the individual participants liable to the death penalty or being 'cut off' from God's people; (3) a sexual act which, if left unpunished by the nation, put the entire nation at risk of God's consuming wrath, God's departure from the midst of the people, and expulsion of the people from the land of Canaan (19:22, 26–30; 20:13). Homosexual intercourse is singled out among other abominable sexual acts in Leviticus 19 and 20 as a form of sexual misconduct particularly worthy of the designation 'toeba'. It is difficult to see how one can speak of this or other acts in Leviticus 18 and 20 as 'ceremonially unclean rather than inherently evil' for the author or even for ourselves." Here Gagnon reveals both his premise that the

regard the censure of male-to-male sex very much relates to the Sodom and Gomorrah and Gibeah stories described earlier, in which the degrading rape of strangers proves utterly incompatible with hospitality to strangers expected from the people of God.

The first critical reason that the writers of Leviticus would oppose same-sex intercourse relates to the bias of procreation, as mentioned before. Procreation *must* occur to promote the blood-line of Abraham into future generations. It involves a sense of ultimate destiny, a destiny shaped by Israel's understanding of God's purpose for choosing them for a unique purpose. God promised Abraham that the entire world of human beings would be blessed by his descendents. At stake lies no less than the survival of Israel in order to bless the nations: and same-sex intercourse cannot further that mission.

A second, closely related reason: not only did Israel have a responsibility to procreate to perpetuate the divine purpose for which it had been called into existence, but also the 'seed' (semen) that made the perpetuation possible was *intrinsically* valuable and should not be wasted. Male seed, like a seed of grain, contained within it the entirety of life that would germinate and grow *only* when placed in fertile soil, i.e., the woman's womb.

Third, we cannot dismiss the significance of the canonical development of the book of Leviticus, created over many genera-tions of oral transmission and tenuous written preservation. Specific references to the neighbors comprised of Canaan and Egypt reflect the period of the Kings when Israel controlled most of the land between the Mediterranean Sea and the Jordan River. Substantial evidence in Leviticus suggests at least two textual sources. Lev 1–16 appear to be written from a Priestly source that emphasizes the importance of the *cultic* purity of Hebrew life. Beginning with Lev 17, the language and style change signifi-cantly, and the content appears to be written from a Holiness source that emphasizes instead the importance of the *personal*

---

nature of homosexuality is behavior, "a sexual act," and his unfortunate designation of same-sex intercourse as something "inherently evil."

purity of life. Holiness is understood as a kind of separation. God is Holy, and therefore separate, distinct from unholy humans. Thus, the people of God are also to be holy, that is, separate, distinct from the idolatrous cultures surrounding them. Israel is, in effect, meant to be a segregated people, a people carved out of the morass of impure and profane cultures among which they exist, a nation that must be safeguarded against the impure incursions of virulent and seductive idolatry.[94]

The final form of Leviticus was not published and edited until later in Israel's exilic period, well into the Hellenistic era of an emerging Western civilization. By that time, Stoicism was already one of the most dominant philosophical schools of its time, profoundly impacting the Greco-Roman world and the provinces under its control for centuries to come. Heavily negative toward any kind of excess—ethical, intellectual, emotional, etc.—Stoicism provided the moral principles that gave rise to an asceticism that was especially rigid about sexual purity and self-control. The ascetics' repudiation of pederasty and cultic sexual practices in the Greco-Roman culture resonated positively with the priestly faction in post-exilic Israel as well as the spirit of the Holiness code. The priestly faction was prone to assign the cause of Israel's misfortunes (conquests and oppression) on the laxity of cultic and personal moral integrity and disobedience to the commandments of God. In this religious environment, for example, same-sex intercourse and intercourse with one's menstruating wife (and exposure to her unclean menstrual blood) were perceived as equal defilements that imperiled the Jews' distinct (segregated) identity as the People of God.

For these reasons, specifically centered around apostasy, we can surmise that same-sex intercourse would be abhorrent to the Levitical writers. The abhorrence would be amplified by using the phrase *as with a woman* because it not only brings to mind anal rape commonly practiced by men of pagan tribes against their enemies, but also, given the historical period in which Leviticus

---

[94] Milgrom, Jacob. "Leviticus 17–22," 1398.

later developed, it refers to the readily available information about fertility goddess rituals. Sexual excesses were highly visible to Jews living in the Hellenistic culture of the Mediterranean region. The temples erected to the goddesses Astarte, Venus, and Cyble dotted the urban landscape of the Greco-Roman world. What transpired inside these temples was known not only through the tales of inside practitioners, but also through temple-sponsored rituals, dances, and processions that passed through city streets. The votaries who served in these temples consisted of not only female cult prostitutes, but male cult prostitutes as well. Sensuous and bizarre acts of debauchery occurred in which the distinction between men and women was blurred. As a result, the connotation of *as with a woman* evoked highly graphic images of pagan sexual debauchery.

Also crucial to understanding this section of scripture is the positioning within the text itself of this passage about same-sex intercourse. It appears following sixteen verses of prohibition against sexual indiscretions, which, in turn, follow immediately after the preface of Lev 18. The preface to the entire section on sexual immorality is as follows:

> And the LORD said to Moses,
> Say to the people of Israel and say to them: I am the LORD your God. You shall not do as they do in the land of Egypt, where you dwelt, *and you shall not do as they do in the land of Canaan, to which I am bringing you. You shall not walk in their statutes.* (Lev 18:1–3)

The gist of the preface is, "Don't behave like your pagan Canaanite and Egyptian neighbors, who engage in the kinds of acts identified in the following examples." The practices of Israel's neighbors illustrate *unholy* idolatry. Israel, in contrast, must remain holy, as the Lord their God is holy. They must not engage in practices that defile a holy people faithful to a holy God, nor to defile the holy ground that God provided for their place of residence. This passage expresses the concerns of a writer unmistakably worried about the problem of Israelite contamination from paganism. The cultural context of Lev 18:22 is unambiguous: fertility cults and pagan rituals.

To interpret the passage in Leviticus properly, we must retain its context and not impose our modern assumptions about homosexuality that have been shaped within the historical development of Western cultural attitudes about human sexuality. Regardless of our speculations about the Leviticus writers' attitudes toward what we call homosexuality today, the plain and clear basis for their condemnation of same-sex behaviors *in their time* are specifically the behaviors well known among pagan cults. The explicit cause of condemnation remains immorality rooted in idolatry. The basis upon which the writers of Leviticus declared a strict censure on same-sex behavior was fundamentally shaped by their concern about apostasy, not by issues we know of regarding later developments in Jewish and Christian theological attitudes.

Ezekiel — References to Sodom

God's anger against the apostasy of his people is perhaps expressed most vividly in the book of the prophet Ezekiel. Here, Israel is cast in the sexual imagery of a wife who becomes a whore, thus illustrating the seriousness of Israel's apostasy in the same-sexual language as the fertility cults God's people were embracing. In these verses, God cries out as a wronged husband:

> Have you not committed lewdness beyond all your abominations? Behold, everyone who uses proverbs will use this proverb about you, "Like mother, like daughter." You are the daughter of your mother, who loathed her husband and her children; and you are the sister of your sisters, who loathed their husbands and their children. Your mother was a Hittite and your father an Amorite. And your elder sister is Samaria, who lived with her daughters to the north of you; *and your younger sister, who lived to the south of you, is Sodom* with her daughters. Yet you were not content to walk in their ways, or do

according to their abominations; within a very little time you were more corrupt than they in all your ways. *As I live, says the Lord GOD, your sister Sodom and her daughters have not done as you and your daughters have done.* [49]*Behold, this was the guilt of your sister Sodom: she and her daughters had pride, excess of food, and prosperous ease, but did not aid the poor and needy.* [50]*They were haughty, and did abominable things before me; therefore I removed them when I saw it.* [51]Samaria has not committed half your sins; you have committed more abominations than they, and have made your sisters appear righteous by all the abominations that you have committed. (Ezek 16: 43–51)

If we took to heart the spirit of Ezekiel's condemnations today, we would undoubtedly worry about more than what people may or may not do in the privacy of their bedrooms. Fundamentalist and conservative religious groups attack homosexuality in our culture as though it is the "Sin of sins," despite far greater threats from other sources of societal degradation. The fervor they rouse against homosexual issues becomes a distraction that takes an inordinate amount of government time, expense, and energy away from justice issues of public education, health care, economic opportunity, and foreign policy.

New Testament Apostasy and Same-Sex Behavior

Rom 1:26–27

Like the Old Testament examples discussed previously, the context of Paul's reference to homosexual behavior in Rom 1:26–27 focuses on idolatry and apostasy: "for *although they knew God they did not honor him as God* or give thanks to him, but they became futile in their thinking, and their senseless minds were darkened" (Rom 1:21). Notably, when Paul wrote the letter, he resided in Corinth, notorious throughout the ancient world for its sensuous immorality. Before Paul's time, it had been the most active Greek center for the worship of the goddess Aphrodite. In the temple devoted to her, the active practice of temple prostitution flourished and, at one time, was said to have employed a thousand prostitutes serving the goddess. The temple's ritualized prostitution, and the city's prevalent brothels, provided sex and entertainment to a crowded city enriched by these services.

Additionally, the recipients of Paul's letter lived in Rome, the center of a relatively new, but extremely popular and growing cult of Cybele, the great mother of the gods, and her lover-grandson Attis. Among its religious activities, men practiced wild, sometimes brutally masochistic, sexually orgiastic trance-inducing rituals that sometimes culminated in self-castration. Such excesses come quickly to mind regarding Paul's reference to "shameless acts with men and receiving in their own persons the due penalty for their error" (Rom 1:27).

Paul need not have visited Rome personally to be familiar with the pagan cult of Cybele and Attis. The cult worship was widely practiced throughout major cities of the Greco-Roman world. He would have heard second-hand reports about the practices in Rome, and would have encountered similar practices elsewhere in the Greco-Roman world during his missionary journeys. Thus, one may confidently assume that Paul was generally familiar with the sexual excesses of pagan idolatry, given the extent to which he traveled about the Greco-Roman world; and he was obviously dismayed that people chose to practice sensuous idolatry when the *true* God was plainly knowable. In this context of idolatry, and the danger of apostasy among members of the Church, Paul writes:

> For this reason God gave them up to dishonorable passions. Their women exchanged natural relations for unnatural, [27]and the men likewise gave up natural relations with women and were consumed with passion for one another, men committing shameless acts with men and received in their own persons the due penalty for their error. (Rom 1:26–27)

Some theologians might discount the significance of Paul's familiarity with pagan sexual cult practices. They might argue that Paul's primary concern is not to moralize about particular sin, but rather to emphasize that, regardless of whether one is a pagan Gentile, a devout Jew, or a Gentile Christian, "all have sinned and fall short of the glory of God" (Rom 3:23). The antidote to this universal human condition, therefore, becomes justification by God's "grace as a gift, through the redemption which is in Christ Jesus" (Rom 3:24). Indeed, this interpretation may possess validity. However, his references to men and women being consumed with passion for their own sex does not arise in isolation from a definite familiarity with the pagan practices with which those behaviors are associated. Paul's concerns about immorality has a clear, cultural context.

We may not be able to discern what Paul knew about same-sex relationships in general, but when speaking of degrading passions among men and women, certainly the same-sex practices within the cults of Aphrodite and Cybelle proved the most referential behaviors. Also, most certainly Paul knew of the socially institutionalized practice of pederasty common among the male elite of Greco-Roman upper-class society. Paul would understandably be highly concerned about the danger that Roman Christians might be pulled back into the sensually attractive practices of the goddess cults or of the pederasty of the socially elite.

The Influence of Stoicism upon Paul

Even if the scope of Paul's condemnation of same-sex activity in Rom 1 remains limited to practices commonly found in pagan idolatry or Greek pederasty, Paul would likely adopt a negative view of same-sex practice in general because of his exposure to Greek Stoicism. The full extent of Stoicism's influence upon Paul cannot be determined with as much certainty as his familiarity with pagan idolatry. But one may assume that the influence was probably significant.

To understand the relevance of Paul's exposure to Stoicism, one must briefly review the significant change in Jewish thought that emerged in the centuries just prior to the Christian era, and particularly Stoicism's role in effecting that change.

In the eighth century before the Christian era, the twelve Hebrew tribes that constituted Israel in Canaan split in two: the northern kingdom of Israel and the southern kingdom of Judah. The Assyrians conquered Israel in 722 BCE, and the Babylonians conquered Judah in 586 BCE. With the destruction of Jerusalem and the Temple, the population was enslaved and scattered throughout the empires of the Middle East. In time, contingents of Jews returned from exile in Babylonia, settled, and rebuilt Jerusalem and the Temple. Over several generations, they experienced a mixture of peace, conquest, civil war, autonomy, revolts, and persecutions. Overall, reality for the Jews proved dismally short of their expectations for their lives when God restored their nation. Naturally the searching question of Jews in the Diaspora, as well as the disappointed restorers of the Hebrew state would be, "Why do God's chosen people experience so much suffering and humiliation?" One critical answer reasoned, "We suffer because we were careless in our observance of God's law and because we compromised our religion by too much tolerance toward alien cultures in the world around us."

The practical effect of such conclusion gradually shifts the understanding of God and of human life in relationship to God from the corporate sense of being a channel of blessing to all the nations of the world, toward an extremely individual emphasis upon personal morality and cultic purity. A relationship with a merciful God expressed in social compassion gave way to obedience to codified laws of God and religious fidelity to ritual practice. This pure life not only required the exclusion of outsiders who did not embrace the God of Law but also censure of fellow Israelites whose lives or beliefs did not conform to purity laws that were prescribed by religious authorities whose influence permeated every aspect of private life. The prophetic passion for social justice and the expression of hospitality as illustrations of the justice and mercy God had shown to the ancient Hebrews were displaced by a sterile orthodoxy and a rigidly proscribed daily life governed by the casuistic application of dietary and ceremonial rules.[95]

The centuries over which this shift occurred were concurrently the centuries when the rise of Hellenism, Greek culture, came to dominate the world militarily and culturally. A major school of Greek philosophy known as Stoicism, with its associated ethical principles, became the most influential intellectual force in the Greco-Roman world. The Jews consistently refused to embrace foreign philosophies because they saw them as incompatible with the growing importance of renouncing any contamination from pagan cultures. Nevertheless, the spread of asceticism, a radical offshoot of Stoicism that disavowed sensual pleasure and promoted withdrawal from the world, resonated among Jews with their growing concern for personal holiness and ritual purity. A spirit, common to both Stoicism and Judaism, imbued ethical principle with extreme stringency against the disordered feelings and passions of human experience, particularly sexual feelings.

Many of the pious Jews took extreme precautions not to defile themselves in matters of sex. Sexual intercourse on the Sabbath was forbidden, fornicators were to be burned, women were blamed for seducing men, and Jewish Essene groups encouraged

---

[95] Marti, *The Religion of the Old Testament*, 187–88. "For its most characteristic feature is the law, more especially the written law, the Torah. The will of God is stereotyped in a law reduced to writing, and regarded as strictly regulative . . . When a religion has become a book-religion, and its followers are bound to a sacred book, which is conceived as a law, then all further evolution is excluded; all that can be done is the exposition and application of the material already to hand; the holy book must be explained, and its principles adapted to special circumstances as they arise. In place of the prophets and priests who, in earlier times, handed down the will of God to the people, we have teachers of the law and scribes. Religion, which was before essentially a matter of life, comes to be more and more an object of doctrine; almost more important than religion is theology."

celibacy. Although the majority of the religious leaders and ordinary individuals avoided the extremes, nevertheless an elaborate system of purity laws evolved that extended to every aspect of individual life.

Especially the religion of the Pharisees, with strict adherence to the Law, allowed no relaxation of the Leviticus prohibitions:

> Sexual codes were made to bear a heavy weight of meaning. The prohibition of marriage to non-Jews; the condemnation of close-kin marriages; the insistence of the careful observance of the codes of purity that governed the woman's menstrual cycle and the man's emission of seed; a carefully nurtured disgust for the promiscuity, public nudity, and same-sex love allowed to the young male in pagan cities: all these points of difference heightened the sense of Israel's separation from the pagan world.[96]

In this climate, same-sex behavior would not be viewed favorably even if the denunciation in Leviticus did not exist. Even so, same-sex practice was not singled out for moral diatribe in the religion of the Pharisees, probably because the general hostility of Pharisaism toward sexual pleasure focused on the more commonly identified instances of sexual vice among heterosexual couples. To some extent, militancy against same-sex behavior relaxed due to the assumption that the vice of same-sex behaviors was unlikely to occur among the Jews.[97]

Saul of Tarsus, a Pharisee among Pharisees, and nurtured by these familiar intellectual strains, was notable in his zeal for strict adherence to religious morality and cultic purity. His conversion experience, after which he was named Paul, moderated his disposition profoundly but did not erase significant aspects of his

---

[96] Brown, *The Body and Society*, 40.

[97] Greenberg, *The Construction of Homosexuality*, 202. "Maimonides held that Jewish men were so unlikely to engage in homosexuality that they could be permitted to sleep together."

previous convictions. Under the surface of his theology, the influence of his upbringing still lingered, exemplified in his attitude toward women—revolutionary in one way, but traditionally patriarchal in another, and also in his negative view of sex—realistic about its emotional power, but repressive in recommending celibacy as the preferable way to serve God without the distractions of marriage. He embraced the notion that sexual behavior spawned from lust and therefore required stringent self-discipline with a restricted expression only in marriage. Little suggests that Paul regarded sex positively as an expression of pleasure for its own sake even for heterosexual conjugal relationships, and certainly not least for same-sex relationships. Even where he encourages husbands and wives to share conjugal rights (see 1 Cor 7:3–5), Paul frames his advice with a warning that it is well for a man not to touch a woman, and with his wish that everyone would be like himself: celibate (see 1 Cor 7:1, 7).

Paul's exposure to Greek Stoicism furthered his ascetic negativity toward many aspects of heterosexual sexuality, and correspondingly made him even more negative toward homosexual behavior. Having been born in Tarsus, a major Stoic center, he would be familiar with the Stoic management of lust, or of any extreme emotions or behaviors. Adding to this his upbringing in Hellenistic Judaism that embraced significant aspects of asceticism emerging from the dualistic nature of Greek Stoicism, the result becomes an ultimately negative view of sex (see 1 Thess 4:3–5).[98]

Paul used the terms 'natural' and 'unnatural' (see Rom 1:26–27) to refer to the boundaries of legitimate sexual relations. The terms express an understanding of sex founded on both his Hebrew and Stoic background. From his Hebrew background he drew from the Biblical bias that the divine order for sex is male

---

[98] Greenberg, *The Construction of Homosexuality*, 215–16. "Sexuality was not something Paul valued for itself, or for the contribution it could make to an interpersonal relationship. He saw sex as lust therefore as something that was best suppressed or, if that was impossible, permitted only the most restricted outlet."

and female complementariness for marriage and procreation. What is 'natural' is that God created human beings male and female and designed them to enter a union from which children would be born. Male sexual relation with a male, or female sexual relation with a female, is therefore by definition 'unnatural.' Consequently, he not only viewed various idolatrous sexual excess with disgust, but he also considered same-sex behavior as evidence of an idolatrous people's rejection of God's design for men and women.

From Paul's stoic background, he employs terminology typical of Stoicism's censure of sexual behaviors. For censuring same-sex behavior, he uses the abstract words 'natural' and 'unnatural' as well as the concentration in just four verses of the morally loaded, affective words 'desire,' 'passion,' 'inflame,' 'appetite,' and 'error'—all borne from Stoicism's view that unruly passion proves unnatural because it opposes the naturalness of reason. Some suggest the Stoic source for Paul's censure of homosexual behavior is the sole basis for his attack on homosexual behavior.[99] This view seems an oversimplification, implying that Paul would not have infused the language of Stoicism with the moral content of his Jewish tradition. Suffice it to say that Stoicism very definitely lies behind Paul's censure of male or female same-sex behavior, but so also does his Jewish tradition.

1 Cor 6:9–10 — General Censure

The Biblical texts referring to homosexual behavior that we have looked at so far make clear that the context of these passages applies to specific sexual behaviors. All of the behaviors refer to pagan practices and are condemned in the context of apostasy as

---

[99] Frederickson, "Natural and Unnatural Use in Romans 1:24–27," 208. Frederickson categorically states: "Romans 1:24–27 is not an attack on homosexuality as a violation of divine law but a description of the human condition informed by the philosophic rejection of passionate love."

either outright abandonment of the faith, or as syncretistic blending of faith with the prevailing culture, or as admonition against the defiling influence of alien cultures. One Biblical text appears to be more general in context, however. In his letter to the Corinthian church Paul writes that the unrighteous "will not inherit the kingdom of God" (1 Cor 6:10). This verse occurs in a larger section of Paul's letter concerning instructions about incest, standards of behavior, prostitution, marriage, and a brief segment on lawsuits.

An immediate question that arises about this section is whether apostasy is at issue here. Because of the social environment in which the Corinthian Christians lived, apostasy certainly would be of concern to Paul in his letters to Corinth. As noted earlier, Corinth was a large urban center with a notorious reputation for immorality. When one considers that much of this immorality was institutionalized by social and religious sanction, the added pressure of social conformity encouraged the ordinary person to participate in the dominant social practices. The insidious pressure of social convention in that time was possibly more intense than we can imagine, because although we face an erotically charged social atmosphere, we do not confront *institutionalized* sensuousness that forces us to conform out of social and economic necessity.

In addition to the pressure upon Christians trying to maintain their faith in a powerful, pagan culture, Paul provides clues to his own concern about apostasy, as in the greeting of his letter where he addresses believers as *"sanctified* in Christ Jesus, *called to be saints* together with all those who in every place call on the name of our Lord Jesus Christ" (1 Cor 1:2) The emphasis upon Corinthian Christian identity as *sanctified* people, as people *called to be saints,* echoes the appeal of Leviticus for Israel to be holy as the Lord their God is holy (see Lev 19:2). Twice in the section on sexual morality, Paul refers to the crucifixion of Jesus and urges Christians to remember they "were bought with a price" (see 1 Cor 6:20, 7:23). He implores Christians in Corinth to remember that they are a unique people who must understand that their sanctified status at the expense of Jesus' death precludes falling back into cultic immorality whether by visiting temple prostitutes (see 1 Cor 6:13–18) or by reentering the cultural economic struggle regarding indentureship (see 1 Cor 7:20–22).

The most telling evidence of Paul's concern about apostasy appears when he refines his intentions regarding the temptation to adopt pagan behaviors. Paul refers to an earlier letter[100] in which he admonished Christians not to associate with immoral men. He emphasizes that his first admonition to shun association with immoral men did not at all mean "the immoral of this world, or the greedy and robbers, or idolaters" (1 Cor 5:9). Rather, his admonishment was about associating with anyone "who bore the name of *brother* if he is guilty of immorality or greed, or is an idolater, reviler, drunkard, or robber—not even to eat with such a one" (1 Cor 5:11). Paul declares that God will judge those outside the Church, but Christians are to judge those within the Church. Quoting Deut 13:5, Paul commands, "Drive out the wicked person from among you" (1 Cor 5:13).

Paul seems to convey that the most serious problem facing the Corinthian church is the threat of culture when it infiltrates and resides *within* the Church, not the threat of culture that exists *outside* the Church. This form of apostasy is like a communicable disease that must be quarantined to prevent spreading to other believers. Paul's severe recommendation for handling apostate believers is used today by some Christian colleges, universities, and churches with homonegative policies to justify expulsion of gay or lesbian students, firing gay or lesbian music leaders, education leaders, etc., and shunning, if not banishing entirely, many gay or lesbian Christians from families, churches, and private organizations.

Apostasy indeed provides an important context for Paul's condemnation of homosexuals. The next question, however, is what specific behavior Paul has in mind when he states that homo-

---

[100] 1 Cor is the first extant letter of Paul to Corinthian Christians in which he refers to a previous, non-extant letter.

sexuals will not inherit the kingdom of God. The term translated as 'homosexuals' in the Revised Standard Version of the Bible (RSV) is not original. In the RSV, a footnote clarifies that "two Greek words are rendered by this expression": *malakoi* and *arseno-koitai*. In other Bible translations, the two words are translated very differently:

- ▼ The New Revised Standard Version, separates the words and translates *malakoi* as "male prostitutes" and *arsenokoitai* as "sodomites."

- ▼ The American Standard Version translates them respectively "effeminate" and "abusers of themselves with men."

- ▼ The International Standard Version translates them "male prostitutes" and "homosexuals."

- ▼ The King James Version translates them "effeminate" and "abusers of themselves with mankind."

- ▼ The New King James Version translates them "homosexuals" and "sodomites."

Obviously, translators disagree as to the exact meaning of these two terms. Among theologians, general consensus surrounds only the literal meaning of the Greek words: *malakoi* literally means "males who are soft," and *arsenokoitai* is a compound word that combines the literal words "male" and "lying with, or sleeping with." Beyond that, opinions conflict as to their meaning, though less so with *malakoi* than with *arsenokoitai*. *Malakoi* is variously understood to suggest some kind of masculine weakness, as in the case of someone considered effeminate, or the passive, penetrated participant in male-with-male sexual intercourse, or any male whose moral behavior is less than respectable, or even a man who remarries his former wife.

Arsenokoitai is far more problematic and widely argued. Consensus exists that the *second* part of the compound word, *koitai* (from which we derive the word "coitus" or sexual intercourse) implies something coarse, if not vulgar. The compound word appears to be derived from the Septuagint, the name given to the

Greek version of the Jewish Scriptures translated into Greek between 300–200 BCE. The Septuagint was the Old Testament source for early Gentile Christians during the first few centuries CE, as well as New Testament writers who relied heavily on the Septuagint for quotation sources. The connection between Paul's use of the word *arsenokoitai* (Paul may even have coined the word) and the Greek translation of Leviticus seems quite clear. Quoting from the Septuagint, Lev 18:22: *meta **arsenos** ou koimethese **koiten** gynakois* literally means "with a man do not lie [as one] lies [with a] woman." The more striking derivation of the compound word is the parallel reference in Leviticus 20:13: *hos an koimethe meta **arsenos koiten** gynaikos* that literally means "whoever lies with a man [as one] lies with a woman."

Because of this seemingly obvious derivation, scholars who condemn 'homosexuality' with the claim that Lev 18:22 applies to all and any form of same-sex behavior, extend their claim as well to the Apostle Paul's use of *arsenokoitai* in 1 Cor 6:9. Namely, that the "prohibition of same sex relations was consciously carried over from Leviticus, perhaps originally by Paul himself, although in his case not on the ground of ritual impurity but on the ground of immorality."[101] On the other side of the issue, scholars who regard homosexual persons favorably claim that Leviticus applies only to *specific* kinds of same-sex behavior and that Paul, notwithstanding the relationship between his use of *arsenokoitai* and the Greek version of Leviticus, does not refer to anything more than the specific kinds of homosexual behavior manifest in Pagan cults and Greco-Roman pederasty.

Such conflicting opinions raise interesting hypothetical questions: Which side of the issue would Paul take were he alive today? Would he approve or censure couples of same-sex gender connectivity that seek to live with the same authentic love, commitment, and fidelity idealized among couples of other-sex gender connectivity? From the perspective of Romans and 1 Corinthians, Paul's condemnation of same-sex behavior, his dis-

---

[101] Schmidt, *Straight & Narrow*, 95–96.

gust toward pagan sexual practice, his ascetic negativity toward sexuality in general, and his full embrace of the procreative bias might suggest that he would side with those who censure homosexuality, no matter what form it takes. But against the background of Paul's seminal book of theology, the Letter to the Galatians, where Paul defends his ministry on behalf of the outcast 'uncircumcised,' where he claims people should not live under the weight of condemnatory laws but by God's grace through faith, and where he cautions believers to be gentle with one another when sin occurs while being mindful of one's own weakness and need for spiritual strength—then even if he might not bestow full approval, Paul at least might *include* people of same-sex gender connectivity within the community of faith.

Obviously such hypothetical questions cannot be resolved because we simply cannot know what Paul would think about what we today call 'homosexuality.' Therefore, claiming Paul as an advocate for *either* side of the modern homosexuality debate proves risky. We *do* know, however, that Paul's condemnation of same-sex behavior referred to specific kinds of same-sex practices commonly known within the cultures outside the community of Hebrew and Christian faith. He condemns these behaviors within the scope of his concern to keep the faithful from slipping back into the seductive environment of these pagan cultures.

Theological Debate on the Homosexuality Issue

Theologian Robert Gagnon asks the rhetorical question, "Did Paul only [sic] oppose exploitative instances of adultery, fornication, and sex with prostitutes or did he oppose every instance?"[102] Quite obviously, the answer to the rhetorical question is that Paul opposed every instance of adultery, fornication, and sex with prostitutes. Gagnon intends to counter a claim occasionally made by homopositive advocates that the Bible condemns only ex-

---

[102] Gagnon, *The Bible and Homosexual Practice*, 325.

ploitative same-sex behavior, whereas the same-sex behavior defended today is *non*-exploitive. Gagnon maintains the distinction makes no difference.

His rhetorical question, however, proves disturbing in its assumption that 'homosexuality' *inherently* belongs among immoral heterosexual behaviors such as adultery, fornication, and prostitution. Defining 'homosexuality' as a behavior suggests that it represents yet another form of the perverted heterosexual norm of conjugal sex—along with adultery, fornication, prostitution, rape, sexual child abuse, and bestiality. Following this line of reasoning, however, when heterosexual perversions are identified as behaviors, then heterosexuality *itself* must be a behavior. That is, heterosexuality therefore consists of a range of sexual behaviors of which only *one* is legitimate: conjugal sex between a man and a woman. Every other behavior represents a perverted deviation from the heterosexual norm that allows sex only between a husband and wife. If the only legitimate erotic expression is sexual intercourse in the connubial bed of one man and one woman, the distinction between 'heterosexual' and 'homosexual' is essentially erased. Thus, following Gagnon's reasoning, same-sex behavior, by nature non-conjugal, becomes a perverted form of heterosexual sexual intercourse restricted to the married, and belongs legitimately among the other deviant behaviors listed.

By implication, the institution of marriage represents a legal permission slip to behave sexually. Should it be the marriage license that legitimizes the sexual boudoir? Should we not, instead, focus upon something fundamental to the nature of our humanity rather than our sexual behavior? The fundamental nature of our humanity is to develop close interpersonal relationships encompassing emotional, social, intellectual and spiritual needs, not merely physical sex and procreation. It is not good for humans to be alone (Gen. 2:18). Many kinds of deep human connections form within these relationships, of which marriage offers the most potential for creating intimacy across every one of the emotional, social, intellectual, spiritual, and physical needs. It is a flask into which may be poured the life stuff of two people wherein, hopefully, the stirring and heating of all their individual elements will transform the molecular essence of feelings, thoughts, skills, history, sensations, convictions, aspirations, and activities into an environment of love, fidelity, kindness, faith, integrity forgiveness, and mutuality.

In other words, human sexuality is not merely a sexual behavior but a commonwealth of attributes that contribute to the formation of authentic human relationships. No more or less than other-sex gender connectivity, same-sex gender connectivity also represents more than a sexual behavior. It also is a commonwealth of attributes. A couple with same-sex gender connectivity is linked by a desire for durable and fulfilling relationships in no way different from that of couples with other-sex gender connectivity.

Because of this broader meaning of other-sex and same-sex gender connectivity, the Biblical texts condemning homosexual behavior must be delimited within the specific context of apostasy and of specific behaviors associated with pagan culture. A two-dimensional point of view frames this assertion. One dimension holds that *any* behavior that diminishes or deprecates the human capacity or opportunity for close interpersonal relationship is therefore immoral, whether that behavior be heterosexual adultery (e.g., the Biblical story of David and Bathsheba), pornographic excess (e.g., homosexual or heterosexual lasciviousness conspicuous in world urban centers), or cheapened sexuality (e.g., those who divest themselves from the emotional needs of a spouse, whom they still expect to be willing partners in sex). The second dimension holds that same-sex relationships deserve the same effort to encourage faith, love, integrity, fidelity, and wholesomeness of relationship applied to other-sex relationships.

A profound risk is taken by those who insist that homosexual behavior is *de facto* sinful behavior, and who also insist that the root of the behavior stems from wrong choices resulting from lack of moral resolve. The risk lies in consigning *every* homosexual person to condemnation and ascribing to all a laxity of moral will, while dismissing the abundant evidence that homosexual identity is an immutable attribute of a person's sexuality inherent by nature. Concluding that an innately homosexual person is abhorrent to God is deeply problematic and raises the serious question: "Should we list just, faithful, and loving homosexual unions among activities judged vicious by God?"[103]

To be sure, 1 Cor 6:9–10, taken as a whole, clearly warns against moral laxity in general, and libertine sexual practices in particular. This warning proves as relevant today, given our cultural environment, as in the days of Paul. However, to extend this indictment upon *all people* of same-sex gender connectivity is as unwarranted and dangerous as to condemn all heterosexual persons by equating them with the sexually violent men of Sodom and with the practitioners of the Aphrodite and Cybelle cult rituals. It is indefensible on Biblical grounds to generalize about the immorality of a group of people based on Biblical condemnation that specifically addresses sexual behavior identified with abusive and/or lascivious idolatrous practices. The Bible does claim that "all have sinned and fallen short of the glory of God" (Rom 3:23), but a general indictment upon human failure to attain ethical perfection is a far cry from imputing condemnation upon a class of people based upon specific, time-conditioned, ancient depravities.

Certainly individual homosexual persons practice immoral and lascivious behaviors just as egregious as those condemned in the Bible. *Equally* true, however, certain heterosexual persons engage in sexual behaviors no less appalling than the sexual immoralities between heterosexual men and women that the Bible condemns. Pious folk are misguided when they ascribe to straight people the righteous virtues of deep, religious conviction, of love, integrity, and fidelity, and of exemplary moral character, but imply by their anathemas against homosexual persons that these virtues may not be ascribed to gays and lesbians. One risks judging those whom God has cleansed (see Acts 10:15,) and thereby risks judgment upon oneself for mistakenly judging others.

I deeply believe that Christians in particular should conscientiously reflect the same grace toward same-sex gender connected

---

[103] Jung and Smith, *Heterosexism: An Ethical Challenge*, 76f.

individuals that Jesus Christ demonstrated when he came to dwell in the midst of ordinary people and embraced *all* humanity. This attitude and practice seems to lie at the heart of what it means to fulfill the unique character of Jewish and Christian religion—to demonstrate that we know and experience the grace and mercy of God *by being gracious and merciful to others*. To do so means, at the very least, that heterosexual Christians must draw near enough to gay and lesbian persons to understand them before condemning them outright. Jesus emphatically denounced the Pharisees and Scribes for putting principle before people and censure before compassion. He said that even the people of Sodom and Gomorrah would have repented sooner than the Pharisees and Sadducees. He likened their censorial behavior to leaven that permeates bread dough, and warned his disciples to "beware of the leaven of the Pharisees and Sadducees" (Matt 16:6).

Therefore, heterosexual Christians also should place people before principle by making certain they do not equate gay and lesbian persons with the pagan apostates of the ancient world. And heterosexual Christians also should put compassion before censure by being certain not to equate gay and lesbian persons with the promiscuous and bizarre behaviors whose lewdness the homonegative groups claim reflects the attitudes and behaviors of all gay and lesbian people. And finally, heterosexual Christian people should respectfully listen to the life experience, the heart and faith of gay and lesbian persons, in order to experience the privilege and pleasure of sharing faith, service, and ministry together within their communities of faith.

CHAPTER SIX

Ethical Principles

Personal Prologue: Talking about Sex

"What are you thinking about, Dad?"

Our youngest son and his boyfriend sat across the table from me in a restaurant. We sipped ice water while waiting for a server to take our order for Sunday lunch. Several weeks before, the two sat across our kitchen table from Beth and me, and our son haltingly told us he was gay, and that his friend was more than a school acquaintance.

Between these two occasions, we had many conversations with our son, including a discussion about his hesitancy to come out to his mother and me. Although he was only seventeen, we assumed he knew that he did not need to fear judgment and reprisal from us based on our acceptance of his older brother, who came out to us eight years earlier. He was not concerned about our response in that way, however. He was concerned about how two siblings in the same family could possibly be gay. When he later learned that having multiple gay siblings in one family is a fairly common occurrence, he then felt more assured to talk with us.

Another of these conversations was a father–son talk that I initiated in order to inquire considerately about the self-discovery process of his sexual identity. I dared ask him about this process of self-awareness to allow him to verbalize his inner experiences and to give me an opportunity to learn and to better understand him. The insights I gained were fascinating. He shared memories of early childhood experiences in which he was drawn to males rather than females. He corrected my assumption that his early adolescent collection of "girlfriends" reflected heterosexual interest. He engaged in frequent contact with the other sex not out of interest in *them*, but because of his delight in chattering about the same cute boys in whom he and the girls shared a common interest. Even when he semi-seriously dated a girl in high school, his attraction for her proved far different than I assumed. As a boy probing his sexual identity in a heterosexual environment, he was drawn to the girl, a good-looking, athletic cheerleader, for her *masculine* traits rather than her feminine characteristics. In reference to another of his "girlfriends," he asked whether I remembered the occasion when I came home to find several teens together in his bedroom. In his arms nestled a petite and very attractive girl. He told me that in spite of what I might have thought at the time, he was terribly uncomfortable having a girl cuddling up to him. At the end of this conversation, I had no doubt but that this son, too, was gay.

"I can always tell when you're thinking about something, Dad. Come on. What is it?"

Yes, I did a lot of thinking while we drove from the church where we had just worshipped and while we waited for the server to take our order. During the church service I looked across the congregation of mostly gay and lesbian worshippers, and with my son as a backdrop to my thoughts, reflected on those I saw.

I saw the young worshippers, not much older than my son, and I thought that they, like so many late-adolescent youth I knew in boy/girl relationships, were most certainly struggling with powerful sexual feelings vis-à-vis the standard of chaste behavior to which their church subscribed.

I recognized the "widowers" singing the hymns and anthems of faith, men whose partners died of AIDS and who themselves were taking HIV drugs. They were like those I knew who lost loved ones to heavy smoking that brought on lung cancer, or to negligence about healthful eating and disciplined exercise that contributed to a fatal heart condition.

I saw men sitting alone in church for the first time since their partner left them for someone else. They sought forgiveness, solace, hope, renewal—just like the men and women I knew in other congregations who were recovering from failed marriages into which they first stumbled because of unplanned pregnancy or out of which they exited to relieve the bitterness of infidelity or the oppressiveness of incompatibility.

I saw men and women I admired, whose towering personal integrity, profound articulation of faith, and enthusiasm for the church's mission, were just like respected men and women who provided leadership in congregations I once served as a pastor.

I saw many, many older gay or lesbian couples, some of whom had lived together with compassion, integrity, and fidelity for more than thirty or forty years. They were inspiring models of durable human relationship that were similar in kind to those of husbands and wives whose diamond, silver, or golden wedding anniversaries were celebrated with family and friends in a church fellowship hall of my former congregations.

Against the background of these reflections, I looked at my son and his boyfriend seated across from me. They both were in the vigor and robustness of youth: adventurous, indestructible, ambitious, bright, inexperienced, naïve—and loaded with male hormones. Indeed, I was doing some serious thinking! I was thinking like any concerned parent whose late-adolescent child is falling in love in total free fall. I desperately wished for some kind of pull cord to open his parachute in time to soften the crash into hard reality. I wished I had road signs to place at strategic places in his mad rush on life's journey, to guide him safely around and through the hazards. I wanted to speak the uniquely effective words that would impress upon his mind those discretions that would direct him away from risky, quick pleasure and into be- haviors that ensured mature character.

"I'm not thinking about anything," I calmly fibbed as the waiter approached.

My son laughed mockingly and insisted, "No, you've got *something* on your mind!"

While the waiter took our order, I thought, "I can't tell him what I'm really thinking: not here; not with another person present." But I was perplexed by his doggedness. He didn't usually press me this hard. What was behind his insistence? My inclination shifted back and forth: should I, shouldn't I? The waiter left, a server refilled our water glasses, and I decided to go for it.

"So you really want to know what I'm thinking about?"

"Yes!" he responded. Both boys raised their glasses, sipped ice water and waited.

"All right!" I breathed deeply. "I was thinking about sex."

Their glasses of ice water froze to their lips. Their eyes grew round as fish eyes.

"I was thinking that sex is a good and wonderful idea of God," I continued. "Yet we are so reticent to talk about it and candidly discuss how its energy can be directed to constructive purposes rather than destructive. Perhaps we have some psychic, libidinal disgust associated with sex because we relate genital organs capable of intense pleasure to their function to eliminate waste."

A spray of water splattered the napkin and tableware in front of my son's boyfriend. With an involuntary gasp he had sucked water into his windpipe and erupted with a paroxysm of coughing. The water in my glass sloshed from side to side when his abrupt exit from the booth bounced the table as he headed for the men's restroom. Stunned for a moment, my son jumped up and followed him.

I sat alone mulling the reaction to my shot at opening a window of dialogue about an issue so fundamental to every serious couple's relationship. In time, the waiter came, and with a perplexed look at the empty places, set down the plates of hot food.

Moments later, the boys returned, sat down, and began eating. We talked intermittently about inane topics for the rest of the meal.

Since that restaurant incident, family members have razzed me fervidly about my imprudent, Sunday-lunch sex talk. Perhaps I have not always been circumspect about the time and place to talk about sex, but I have always been concerned about the ethics of human relationship, including its sexual aspect. Particularly after my journey toward understanding homosexuality, I have been acutely interested in the ethics of human relationship as it relates to the relationships of same-sex gender connectivity.

Grounding Our Ethics

I propose that ethical/moral decisions should be grounded in the question "Why?" Why do we decide this way and not another? "Why" asks not merely the reason for an ethical/moral imperative, but also asks whether the imperative is grounded in valid, fundamental ethical principles that warrant obedience. For example, an ethical principle might generalize that human life is inherently valuable in and of itself. An imperative based upon this principle might be the Decalogue command, "You shall not kill."

An old sermon illustration offers insight into this "Why?" After attentively watching her mother prepare dinner for a family gathering, a child asked, "Why did you cut a piece off the end of the roast?" "I've always done it that way," answered Mother. "I guess I learned it from my mother. She always cut off a piece of the roast before putting it in the oven. Go ask Grandma."

Asking Grandma the same question, she received the same response and the same suggestion, "Your great-grandma is coming for dinner: ask her when she comes."

Before dinner the child approached her great-grandmother and asked, "Why did you always cut a piece off the end of the roast before you put it in the oven?" Great-Grandma answered, "Well you see, I didn't have a long enough pan. I always had to cut off the end of the roast to make it fit the pan."

From this little anecdote, we deduce two ethically unsound ways to respond to moral imperatives. First, we can *rebel* against an imperative without understanding the reason for it (that baking an oversize roast in Great-Grandma's undersized pan would be foolish and dangerous). Second, we can *obey* the imperative without understanding the reason for it (continuing to cut the end off the roast in deference to custom after replacing Great-Grandmother's pan with a larger pan). In both cases, the "I don't give a damn!" refusal to obey and the unquestioning submission to "Do as I say and don't ask questions" prove foolish responses to an untested imperative.

The assertion that ethical principle should be foundational to ethical living does not imply that moral law is dispensable. Ethical principle does not *substitute* for Law but should authentically establish and validate Law, whether Law means the codified laws and legislations established by the state, the generally accepted mores that evolve out of a culture's history, or the commandments rooted in religious moral conviction. We would be in an impossible moral dither if for every moral situation we encounter, we had to "start from scratch," to extrapolate from foundational ethical principles the laws or commandments that apply.

On the other hand, foundational ethical principles cannot be archived on a shelf like ethical molds that, having served their purpose to shape law, can be set aside while imperatives derived from them continue to serve as inviolable standards for moral living. The definition of laws, legislation, or commandments is indeed necessary; but valid ethical principle is essential for an imperative's continued application, not just for its initial formation.

Problems with legal, legislative, or moral imperatives emerge when they are made to stand on their own without adequate or accurate reference to the ethical principle that formed them. Problems also emanate from the application of law, legislation, or commandment to personal or societal conditions, when the ethical principle from which laws are formed is ill defined or invalid at the outset.

▼ *Laws may be time conditioned.* Most people agree that drunkenness and its dangerous and unfortunate consequences require laws, mores, and commandments to manage the problems associated with alcohol abuse. What those laws should be, however, differs greatly between our generation and that at the turn of the twentieth century. Throughout the 1800s, prohibition movements, promoted largely by religious groups, cropped up across the growing United States. Sprawling across newly populated areas of the great frontier, towns and cities were dotted with saloons that became increasingly violent in the era of the "Wild, Wild West." The Women's Christian Temperance Union and the Anti-Saloon League gained such influence that, early in the last century, their endorsement of political candidates and relentless lobbying for anti-saloon legislation ultimately galvanized support to prohibit the manufacture of alcoholic beverages in almost half the 48 states. Finally, in 1918, prohibition legislation, codified as the Eighteenth Amendment to the United States Constitution, was enacted to ban the manufacture, sales, transportation, or importation of intoxicating liquors, and was ratified into law by a majority of state legislatures. Supporters of prohibition, influenced by cultural and economic factors distinctive to the late nineteenth and early twentieth centuries in the United States, considered the law to be the right policy at the time. But society soon learned that the stringency of the law created more lawlessness than it suppressed. The law lasted for only a short time before it was repealed by enactment of the Twenty-First Amendment to the US Constitution. Thus, a valid fundamental ethical *principle* led to the Eighteenth Amendment, but resulted in an ill-defined and poorly applied law.

▼ *Laws may be unjust.* In nineteenth-century America many citizens believed that the red man and the black man represented a species inferior to the white man: Native Americans were widely regarded to be wild savages, and African slaves to be ignorant, amoral primitives. Many European immigrants, contrasting their godly, moral and civilized culture to the "inferior," religious, and primitive culture of the red man and black man, considered them a not-fully-human species just a step above animals. On the basis of such beliefs, they devised laws to affirm or at least justify slavery, and passed legislation mandating the forced deportation of all Native American tribes to lands west of the Mississippi. From the vantage point of history, we know the laws and mores were unjust because they were based upon an invalid ethical principle.

▾ *Laws may be impossible to apply universally.* Laws exist banning public nudity and against depicting human beings, particularly women and children, in nude poses or engaging in explicit sexual acts. However, these laws prove far from universally consistent. In some cultures, women's bodies must be covered completely, even the eyes veiled. In others, women's bodies may be completely naked except for a "g-string." While an art gallery legitimately displays paintings and sculptures of nudes, sometimes in provocative poses, Internet sites are worrisome avenues to offensive visual content containing explicit adult and child sex. Our laws must discriminate between cases when nudity and explicit sexuality are offensive and when they are not; but such laws are not consistently and universally applied. To facilitate judgment between offensive and non-offensive situations, an ethical principle must be defined clearly (a task that proves daunting due to varying and conflicting understandings of morality and offensiveness).

▾ *Laws may reverse what was previously acceptable.* Polygamy is now against the law in many countries where Christian or Jewish majorities claim the Old Testament as a moral authority. Yet the Bible never condemns polygamy, which, according to Biblical accounts, was practiced widely among patriarchs and prophets. Billboards in the state of Utah boldly demand the repeal of polygamy laws in order to return to the previously acceptable privilege among Mormon men to marry more than one wife. A valid ethical principle must be determined from which to decide the justification for establishing laws that make polygamy, lawful in previous times, *un*lawful today.

In the current controversy about homosexuality, the importance of ethical principle becomes particularly vital. At this point in time, the weight of cultural tradition and majority opinion lies heavily with those who censure homosexuality. These groups and individuals enjoy a power base from which to preemptively legislate their moral reproach, *despite* the swelling support of public opinion and legal judgment favorable to homosexual persons. But new opposition to censure continues to grow, thereby challenging us to reexamine traditional values and to reconsider the validity of old ethical principles.

Some may argue that in the battle to recognize and uphold same-sex gender connectivity, invalid ethical principles may be invoked. True. Certain principles may be valid for other reasons but not acceptable by some for ethical determination about homosexuality. For example, in the dispute over whether same-sex gender connectivity is mutable or immutable, the predominance of evidence supports the conclusion that unchangeable same-sex gender connectivity exists; that is, individuals may possess an inherent nature of same-sex *gender connectivity*, fully integrated in the three aspects of *attraction, arousal,* and *attachment.* Yet even while conceding this innate quality of same-sex gender connectivity, some will still argue that what one *is* does not necessarily justify *approval* of same-sex gender connectivity in and of itself. A maxim in the field of ethics states, "Is-ness does not make ought-ness." In other words, because something *is,* for example, the human instinct of self-defense, does not make physical assaults morally *right*. On the other hand, "Is-ness" does not auto-matically *preclude* 'ought-ness.' Because same-sex gender connectivity "Is" may not in and of itself make it right, but *neither* does it force the corollary that it is *wrong*.

The assertion "It is moral because it is natural" provides another example of a principle some consider invalid in over-ruling the religious censure of same-sex gender connectivity. Even the copious evidence that homosexuality, existing in nature across a broad spectrum of non-human species, is *natural* does not persuade some people to approve same-sex relations among *humans*. Though the numerous instances of 'homosexuality' in nature provide an appreciation for nature's broad diversity, there-by challenging the argument that homosexuality is something "unnatural," nevertheless religious dogma trumps the evidence of natural science as the legitimate basis for evaluating same-sex gender connectivity.

Neither the argument that something "is" nor the argument that something is 'natural' will dispel the religious censure against homosexuality. For those entrenched in religious dogma, "I was born this way" does not offer an adequate defense. Neither does the fact that a male pair of gay zoo penguins refuses to mate with female penguins. These concepts often prove useful to homo-sexual individuals for dispelling negative self-images of abnormality and for contesting the religious stigma of being a supposedly loathsome creature hated by God, but they do not adequately lift religious censure. But then, these principles do not need to serve that purpose. Other Biblical and valid ethical prin-ciples exist with which to address the religious issue regarding same-sex gender connectivity.

The contemporary face-off over 'homosexuality' arises because we live within a distinctive period of history in Western civili-zation. Unprecedented scientific study offers growing information about the nature of human sexuality in our era, both heterosexual and homosexual. The most recent research into the nature of same-sex gender connectivity provides an understanding of its essence and its causes that refutes the assumptions upon which previous eras based their censures.

Concurrent to these scientific insights, the uniqueness of today's cultural climate, a climate virtually non-existent through the largest part of Western human history, should compel us to revisit our moral injunctions against people with same-sex gender connectivity. Within little more than a generation, an unprecedented number of gay and lesbian persons have renounced societal pressure to hide in closets of secrecy and clandestine relationships. They no longer tolerate the stereotyping that defames them as sinister perversions. They insist that society consider their humanity fairly, and acknowledge that character and integrity mark their lives and relationships as much as they do persons of opposite-sex gender connectivity.

Taken together, these scientific and cultural understandings should cause us to evaluate seriously our current ethical stance regarding same-sex gender connectivity (instead of appealing to "thousand year" traditions) and lead us to challenge the universalized and absolute censure against 'homosexuality' present in many quarters of our society. Failure to show them sincere and just consideration proves nothing less than a travesty.

In forming ethical principles regarding same-sex gender connectivity in this cultural period, I personally look to religious faith for inspiration and insight, but I do *not* bind reason to religious dogma. I therefore derive valid and reasonable ethical principles with confidence, but do not claim that they are or should be absolute and universal. I recognize that many people prove extremely wary of any ethics grounded in religious faith—and often for good reason. But I hope that the ethical principles I identify, though grounded in religious faith, reflect essentially *human* principles, and consequently may resonate with those who are not religious or who belong to religious cultures different from my own. With that caveat, I turn to the first of several ethical principles upon which I base my consideration of same-sex gender connectivity.

The Knowledge of Good and Evil

As popularly assumed, the essential ethical task lies in distinguishing Good from Evil. Parents see their primary responsibility as teaching their children right from wrong. Law enforcement presumably protects the "Good Guys" from the "Bad Guys." These assumptions rest on a simple view of morality: do good and avoid evil. If only everyone would abide by the Ten Commandments, people lament, then we would all live in a just, peaceable, and orderly world. Sentimentally expressed, pop culture rhapsodizes that what the world needs now is love, sweet love. Good is love, and evil is whatever is *not* love.

Somewhat surprisingly then, the Bible warns to avoid the knowledge of both good and evil. Note the curious incident in the creation story of Gen 2: "The Lord God took the man and put him in the Garden of Eden to till it and keep it. And the Lord God commanded the man, saying, 'You may freely eat of every tree of the garden; but of the tree of the knowledge of *good and evil you shall not eat*, for in the day that you eat of it *you shall die*'" (Gen 2:15–17).

One might think we *should* eat freely from a tree whose fruit provides knowledge of good and evil. But on the contrary, the admonition warns: *"Don't*—it will kill you." How strange: should we not learn to know the good that is desirable at least, and remain innocent of evil entirely? Or, perhaps the story should have two trees: the tree of the knowledge of good from which we could eat freely, and the tree of the knowledge of evil from which we should never eat. Some have intimated that God was rather naïve to think he could command humans to leave the tree of the Knowledge of Good and Evil alone. God should have realized what adults quickly learn about children: tell children *not* to touch something, and they are all the more likely to do so. Human nature seems to possess an innate impudence to do what we are told not to do. In spite of potential consequences, human beings repeatedly transgress ethical limits.

'Good' is more than moral excellence. It includes quality, genuineness, reliability, benefit, freedom from distress or pain, etc. And 'Evil' is more than immorality. It includes injury, misfortune, disease, suffering, etc.[104] One can simply enough ascribe a variety of attributes to good and evil, but to establish absolute definitions proves highly problematic. Not all that might be called good or evil is universally agreed upon. A life-threatening illness may seem evil, but some have found that the experience brought positive, life-changing benefits. Winning a million dollars may seem good, but for some the instant wealth disastrously corrupted their lives. The Manifest Destiny was *good* for European pioneers, but *evil* for displaced Native Americans. Clearly, good and evil remain a bit more complex than the simple task of distinguishing right from wrong.

What seems God's intent to keep human beings naïve about good and evil actually points to this ambiguity concerning the way different people perceive good and evil differently. In the story in which the tree of Knowledge of Good and Evil appears, the writers may have been focusing on human society's capacity to *create cultures*, like those of their Canaanite neighbors. As the Hebrew writers perceived it, the Canaanite culture fostered cultic sex rituals and sexual abuse against strangers, practices that the Hebrew culture condemned. The syncretism within the Hebrew community, literally the attempt to practice both Canaanite and Hebrew religion, demonstrated that not all Hebrews were of a common mind about the morality or immorality of these practices. The Hebrew writers argued, therefore, that the right to determine good and evil ultimately belongs to an authority that transcends the egocentric vagaries of human culture. The knowledge of good and evil belongs to God, *not* human beings.

A fundamental human dilemma remains at stake regarding the question whether the basic authority for determining good and evil should rest with human beings themselves, or with some

---

[104] See definitions of 'good' and 'evil' on http://dictionary.reference.com/ (accessed on June 10, 2008).

transcendent entity. When human beings usurp the prerogative of deciding good and evil for themselves, two results may occur. First, God (or 'god' metaphorically as a transcending authority) is essentially eliminated from ethical deliberation. A transcending authority, or 'god,' becomes incidental when an individual or group of individuals need no higher authority to justify their actions than their own intentions.

This situation creates a great moral and psychological dilemma. Among all the mammals and other creatures on earth, human beings appear to be the only species that profoundly senses its own mortality and fears it. Resisting mortality reflects a human striving for immortality, even if to ensure only that our tombstone epitaph forever validates our existence as a "good person."

The endeavor to resist mortality necessitates managing one's personal world to ensure that one's life is successful, or to ensure one's basic worth by making the right decisions about what is ultimately good or evil for one's self. In effect one makes oneself a 'god,' which can be a fearsome thing because one thereby becomes solely responsible for one's own destiny—whether it turns out well or not. As the sole cause of one's ultimate success or failure in life, some people develop a fear of living that corresponds to the fear of dying. The fear of living grows out of the self-doubt over the reliability of one's own skill, courage, or stamina to create success: failure is a terrifying possibility, the dread of which causes stress that leads to withdrawal into internalized fantasies of success. On a national scale, the Myanmar military dictatorship's paranoid refusal to allow entry of foreign aid workers to help with the May 2008 cyclone recovery efforts reflects an anxiety about the ability to retain absolute authority over the nation. On the personal scale, being a 'god' frustrated with failure, or obsessed with fantasies of success, provokes some people to brutal violence as a means of managing their destiny, sometimes culminating with suicide at the end of a killing rampage.

Second, the human community becomes vulnerable to reigns of terror and death created by those who hold ultimate rule-making power, and who use power that causes dehumanizing oppression upon other human beings. The theological concern of Genesis, that a transcending authority should form the basis of ethical deliberation, points to a fundamental and critical human fallacy. Human society faces a dangerous threat when individuals, rulers, or political parties appoint themselves the highest authority in making ethical decisions and immunize themselves against any challenge to the self-justified legitimacy of their own standards. Whether or not a God exists, real human tragedy frequently results when human beings make themselves the highest standard of ethical deliberation and are accountable to no higher standard. Historically, human beings who justify themselves and their self-defined values (as for instance, the Nazis of mid-twentieth-century Germany) also prove capable of committing, rationalizing, and justifying horrendous evil.

Constitutional government based upon the transcending authority of just law seeks to minimize, if not eliminate, the hazard of unrestrained human power to define good or evil. Constitutional law lessens human aggrandizement of ultimate moral and legal authority by making rulers accountable to a standard higher than their own ethical inclinations. They should not change law, adopt contrary law, or rescind laws sustained by the constitution when their personal or their party ambitions conflicts with the constitution. The United States Constitution guarantees that its citizenry shall be a people governed by law, not by rulers—a condition strengthened by the checks and balances of the nation's three branches of government.

Therefore, my first ethical principle is that no human being or arbitrary group of human beings should presume to be the ultimate arbiter of what is good and evil. Not one of us has the right to justify ourselves without at minimum measuring our life by values codified to ensure the humanity, the integrity, the freedom, and the justice entitled to all other individuals around us. No group or nation has the right to justify its own sovereignty with laws and orders that protect its own self-interest while jeopardizing the well-being of its own citizens or the citizens of neighboring nations.

When I say that God should be the sole arbiter of good and evil, or if not God, then some other source of ethical principle that transcends any one person's vision of good and evil framed in law and order, I recognize a risk exists. Someone, or some group must interpret what God, or some other source of ethical principle, determines to be good or evil. Too much human misery has arisen and still arises from individuals or groups who presume to know exactly what God determines to be good and evil and who stand more than ready to mediate this knowledge absolutely. We also have concerns about our ability to understand fairly the legal documents by which we govern ourselves. Such concerns prove evident when the appointment of new US Supreme Court justices enjoins opposing sides in protracted hearings to determine how a candidate for US Supreme Court justice might interpret and apply the Constitution to cases brought before the Supreme Court. What does the candidate believe are appropriate sources of authority to guide interpretation of the Constitution in cases that require application of the Constitution to new or changed conditions, and what relative weight should be assigned to the various sources?

Proper understanding of good and evil becomes a critical issue when applied to gay, lesbian, and transgender persons at this particular moment in history. Some religious groups unequivocally condemn homosexual persons as abominations in the sight of God. Yet other religious groups unequivocally accept homosexual persons as God's children, many of whom were consecrated in childhood by some practice of ritual incorporation into the religious faith community. Both groups claim understanding of God's determination of good and evil.

Similarly, State Supreme Courts have ruled or are on the verge of ruling that denying civil marriage to same-sex couples is unconstitutional. Conversely, federal and state legislatures have passed or are on the verge of passing legislation to define marriage as a union between one man and one woman. In these opposing actions, *both* groups claim to uphold the principle that constitutional law preserves public order and civic well-being for all citizens.

The debate over these issues at all levels of civil discourse proves intense and frequently overheated. The least we can do with the ancient Hebrew story that warns against arrogating the knowledge of good and evil to oneself or one's group is to acknowledge that the higher we stand upon holy ground, the more *humbly* we must stand. Therefore, the first ethical principle (that no human being or arbitrary group of human beings is the absolute or ultimate measure of what is good and evil) requires additional principles.

The Image of God

Western notions of God, as expressed in popular piety, derive to some extent from the Biblical concept of the "Image of God": Then God said, "Let us make man in our image, after our likeness" (Gen 1:26). As the simple rationale goes, if *we* have been made in the likeness of *God*, then inversely, *God* must be something like *us*, just a great deal bigger. This widely held anthropomorphic image of God presents him as a stern, grandfatherly figure, someone who reclines in the ether of space watching the human tragi-comedy for occasions to strike us with wrath or stroke us with compassion at his whim. Numerous portrayals solidify this popular image, such as Michelangelo's Creation of Adam painting on the ceiling of the Sistine Chapel, which depicts a white-bearded God languidly stretching his finger toward the recumbent Adam. Without a doubt, this image of God is also supported by traditional systems of patriarchy that respectfully venerate and accede to the will and authority of elders.

The distinctive Hebrew way of thinking about God or the Divine does not support the notion of a resemblance in appearance between human beings and God: quite the contrary. On the one hand, God cannot be conceived of at all. God's essence or Being surpasses all human comprehension. We have no intelligent means of grasping who or what God really is. On the other hand, despite God's inscrutability, Hebrew writers claim that many individuals experienced God as an immanent, but indescribable reality in human affairs. The reality of God's immanence becomes accessible only through metaphorical portraits, likening God to an eagle who bears up her young on her wings, a hen gathering her chicks under her wings, a king who rules his subjects fairly with mercy and justice, a husband who patiently loves an adulterous wife, a father who longs for reconciliation with rebellious children, a fortress, a rock, water, light, a shepherd, etc.

While we cannot derive conclusions about God's essential nature, Hebrew writers claim we nonetheless can derive certain ideas about divine characteristics. Namely, some personal characteristics about God's nature may be detectable in the events of human history, particularly in the lives of those persons whose character demonstrates their understanding of the authentic significance of those events. For example, the Hebrew concept of hospitality toward strangers provides a genuine reflection of the character of God as demonstrated in the lives of a particular culture. If the faithful Hebrew genuinely appropriates the experience of divine compassion, particularized in the Exodus event that imprinted the passion for freedom and independence upon Hebrew culture for generations, he or she will demonstrate this compassion and justice toward others no matter who they may be.

At the heart of the idea of the "Image of God" lies the concept that human beings are first and foremost *expressions* of Divine *intent*. The primary dictionary definition of 'image' is an "actual or mental picture." For example, a statue is the actual image of what was first in the mind of the sculptor; a landscape painting is the actual image of a scene in the mind of a painter, regardless of whether the scene painted is a real geographical place or a construct of the artist's imagination; a novel is an actual image of the story formed in the creative mind of an author. In many ways, these actual images reflect something of the creative artist. For example, the techniques of Rembrandt, Renoir, or Cezanne possess telltale qualities belonging specifically to each artist. In this sense, the stamp of the creator is intrinsically reflected in the actual image created. Even so, the primary idea of the image is that it expresses the *intent* of the creator. Only derivatively may it reflect something of the creative artist behind the image.

We better understand the intention of the Hebrew writer, therefore, if we think of the creation story's reference to the "Image of God" as a faith statement of believers who declare that human beings are unique among the creatures of nature because they are a distinctive expression of God's intent. The translation of the Hebrew *tzelem*—image, literally means "how we are to be." Whatever else we may be—mortal like animals, made out of the stuff of matter like everything else, existing within the same boundaries of natural limitation as every other creature—the Hebrew writer believed humans are unique beings who live in communities of compassion and justice because *that* is what God intended.

The idea that we are created in the "Image of God" embodies the second ethical principle: every human being possesses intrinsic and unique dignity and worth that is to be shared in human community. This belief does not reflect exclusively religious belief, but is encoded in many secular dogmas meant to defend human dignity. Society affirms the dignity of human life by establishing laws that ensure fair trials even for the most heinous criminal. The world community establishes international standards regarding the treatment of prisoners of war in order to protect human dignity. We struggle over the ethical quandaries in which the human dignity of one person conflicts with the human dignity of another. For example, although every child deserves a quality education, class divisions between educational districts severely challenge urban and suburban school districts to provide all children an equal education, whether a child lives in property-tax rich districts or property-tax poor districts. Also, we express our belief in the dignity of every human being when, setting aside debate about individual responsibility for poverty or homelessness, we remember that by virtue of their humanity, we owe the poor and homeless basic respect. Both the doctrine of the "Image of God" and the democratic ideal that "all men are created equal" affirm that every human being has unique dignity and is a person of worth in society.

This ethical principle also means that persons of same -sex gender connectivity, no less than persons of opposite-sex gender connectivity, deserve respect for his or her human dignity. At minimum this principle requires addressing public policy, whether in the form of legislation or the lack thereof, that enables discrimination or declines to prohibit discrimination against gays, lesbians, and transgender persons.

Following this principle also requires that fair-minded people challenge the use of obsolete data and skewed perceptions to ascribe a negative cause of 'homosexuality' (i.e., a first childhood sexual experience was homosexual; family abnormality; unusual childhood exposure to pornography, group sex, bestiality; adopting 'homosexuality' due to its approval and normalization by society, adult authority figures, or implications within sex education materials). The principle also means that those who demean the character and integrity of homosexuals through generalized pronouncements—cataloguing homosexuals within pathologies including bestiality, necrophilia, and sexual predators of children—must responsibly enter into dialogue with those they disparage, so that knowledge learned from persons of dignity supplants prejudice derived from bias. Those who steadfastly reduce 'homosexuality' to immoral behavior, and accordingly condemn homosexual persons by equating them with the same-sex behaviors condemned in the Bible, should, in respect for the human dignity of those they condemn, revisit their Biblical interpretations in light of the substantial scientific evidence for the immutability of same-sex gender connectivity.

To the ethical principle that no human being or arbitrary group of human beings is the absolute or ultimate measure of what is good and evil, we thus add the second ethical principle: respect for human dignity and worth is due every person in society, gay or straight, created in the image of God. The third ethical principle relating to these considerations of same-sex gender connectivity is embodied in the Biblical assertion: "It is not good for the man to be alone."

It Is Not Good to be Alone

Two creation stories occur in Genesis, the Bible book of beginnings. The first merely chronicles progressive events of creation, which culminate in the final act of creating humankind: "male and female he created them" (Gen 1:27).

The second story, however, reports God's creating not a male/female pair as the grand finale, but instead creating a solitary human being. After creating this individual, God then fashioned a primeval garden in which to cloister the human. But he seems to sense something amiss. The story portrays God as a craftsman who needs to revisit his creative effort to achieve the right effect. The Garden of Eden has a glitch: the human is alone, and aloneness is not good. "Then the LORD God said, 'It is not good that the man should be alone; I will make him a helper fit for him'" (Gen 2:18).

The man (literally "earth creature") is alone, lonely, and incomplete—he needs companionship. The Hebrew *ezer* (helper, translated "a helper fit for him") literally means "opposite him," not in the sense that "opposite" inherently designates woman (opposite sex), but rather can imply a like person who stands opposite the earth creature as one capable of mutual interaction. In the sense of mutual interaction, therefore, 'helper' is best understood *not* as someone subordinate, but as someone who is *distinct* from the earth creature (man) and who provides *completeness* for that which the earth creature lacks. According to this connotation, a parent (certainly not a subordinate) proves a helper fit for the child with incomplete maturity; a master craftsman (also not a subordinate) becomes a helper fit for the novice with undeveloped skills. Within this framework, a human being is neither complete nor competent to move through life as a solitary unit. In order to achieve completeness, a human being *needs* a fit 'helper'—another human being distinct from and standing across from him or her. Until another person of the same essence came into existence, the first person in the Garden of Eden was only partially a person. Until interpersonal engagement occurs with someone across a delimited space from oneself, most of us are functionally limited.

The One and the Helper are transposing positions. The Helper is also One who needs the Other to be the Helper. Loneliness is amended, therefore, not by a subordinate though companionable sidekick, but by a helper who is the same in essence but differentiated in person. Both One and the Helper provide a requisite mutuality that makes both persons authentically human.

In the story that describes the creation of the first two human beings, God tries to amend the deficiency experienced by Adam alone. First, he provides the human with the companionship of animals. But the effort fails because not one creature among the beasts of the field and birds of the air prove fitting to be the Helper that can complete the human's lack of relationship. The man is still lonely. And so after deliberation, God decides upon another plan.

> So the Lord God caused a deep sleep to fall upon the man, and while he slept took one of his ribs and closed up its place with flesh. [22]And the rib which the Lord God had taken from the man he made into a woman and brought her to the man. [23]Then the man said,
>
> "This at last is bone of my bones and flesh of my flesh; she shall be called Woman, because she was taken out of Man."
>
> [24]Therefore a man leaves his father and his mother and cleaves to his wife, and they become one flesh. (Gen 2:21–24)

The Gen 2 creation story follows a somewhat strange sequence. On the day God created the heavens and the earth, nothing grew because God had not yet caused rain *and there was no man to till the ground*. Then God creates Adam (the earth creature) after the heavens and earth, but before the plants or herbs of the field (see Gen 2:5) or beasts of the field or birds of the air (see Gen 2:19). God forms Adam, the first man, from *the dust of the ground* (Gen 2:7), and then God plants a garden that grows *out of the ground.*(Gen 2:9) After noting that Adam is lonely, God creates the beasts of the field and the birds of the air *out of the ground* (Gen 2:19). Significantly, God creates Adam, the plants, herbs, beasts and birds all from the same stuff, that is, from the *ground* of the earth. Finally, after creating all living things from the ground, then, like a closing parenthesis, God creates a woman. But God does not create her from the ground like everything else, but from Adam's rib.

As one looks at the Gen 2 story more closely, one has to question the purpose for underscoring that the man, plants, herbs, beasts, and birds all derived from the ground of the earth, but not the woman. A long history of Biblical interpretation and a distressingly long tradition of male dominance exists among many cultures deriving their religious heritage from the Bible, that takes the creation of the woman from the rib of the man to mean that women are inferior to and subservient to men. I believe this interpretation derives from the patriarchal social structure that evolved from primitive human civilizations. If we dispense with this patriarchal bias, the concept that a woman is made of material extracted from the man suggests a far more egalitarian relationship between men and women. The woman is created not from the stuff of the earth, but from the very essence, the raw materials of the earth creature himself. The essential substance of the man and woman, therefore, are the same. In essence, the woman cannot be inferior to the man because their substance is identical.

Of course, scientifically and historically, the Gen 2 creation story makes no sense at all as an explanation of cosmic and human origins. Thus, we must ask, "What is the purpose of this creation story?" I argue that the primary purpose of the Gen 2 creation story is to make a theologically significant statement about the nature of humanity. Because the story tells us that God created the first human being before any other living thing, clearly it conveys the idea that God intended to make human beings pre-eminently unique. But just as clearly, the story conveys the notion that the first two human beings, both of whom are made of exactly the same *stuff*, are uniquely designed to form mutual, inter-personal relationships.

First of all, note the twice-mentioned isolation of this first creature of the earth: God observes that Adam is alone, decides this is not good, and twice attempts to rectify the problem (see Gen 2:18, 21). The first attempt to resolve Adam's aloneness—providing him with beasts of the field and birds of the air—fails. Among the creatures made out of the ground like Adam, not one proves fit to be a helper. Adam remains alone. Only the second attempt—providing someone of Adam's own substance, bone of bone, and flesh of flesh—succeeds. Distinguishing the woman's substance from that of all other creatures indicates that in order for the human being to be complete, the man requires another human being like himself with whom to relate: "I will make a helper fit for him." Made from the earth creature's rib, identical in substance, yet a differentiated person, the woman, the helper ('ezer'), provides the mutuality of interpersonal relationship the man requires. Conversely, Adam, from whose substance the woman is made, is now also the helper ('ezer'), who provides the mutuality of interpersonal relationship the woman needs.

If an interpreter looks at Gen 2 from the perspective of a hetero-sexual, patriarchal culture, ordinary logic assumes that because the first earth creature must propagate to survive, the first person created after him naturally must be a woman. If we allow the Gen 2 story to be interpreted from this perspective only, it raises the serious question for every person who reads it, "What does this story mean to me?" Does the story have contemporary relevance to anyone other than male/female couples who plan to have chil-dren? It probably does not if the story primarily addresses gender and procreative marriage. It excludes those who choose to remain single, those who become widowed, and, of course, those who are gay and lesbian. Conversely, if the primary issue of the story is *not* gender and procreative marriage, but rather is the basic human need for interpersonal relationships, then the story becomes relevant to every human being. It is not good for any man to be alone. Each woman needs a helper fit for her.

One must differentiate, therefore, between the ultimate and penultimate issues of the story. An "ultimate" issue identifies the main point of an argument. A "penultimate" issue consists of one or more sub-issues that extend or illustrate the meaning of the ultimate issue and have importance in reference to the main point only. Therefore, in the Gen 2 story, the *ultimate* issue is that human beings are created for interpersonal relationship; it is not good for the man to be alone. The *penultimate* issues are gender—*so* human beings are created male and female—and marriage—*therefore* a man leaves his father and mother and cleaves to his wife.

The ultimate and penultimate values are intrinsically defined by the logical structure of the sentence. Because of this, so that, and therefore the other. Both "so" and "therefore" are conjunctives that join subsequent phrases that illustrate or elaborate upon the consequence or result of the main point stated in the primary phrase. The logic inherent in sentences containing phrases joined by these conjunctives is clear from the sequential order of each phrase. Each penultimate phrase either answers the ultimate phrase's implicit "why" or states the ultimate phrase's inferred corollary introduced by "because." God created human beings to be in relationship, *so* God made them male and female to continue the species, *therefore* God established marriage within which human relationships may be nurtured.

We cannot, therefore, reverse the ultimate and penultimate issues of Gen 2:18–24 and make marriage the ultimate principle. We cannot say that the primary human principle is that God wanted all men to leave father and mother and cleave to a wife, *and so* human beings were created male and female; *therefore* all men and women are unfortunately alone until they marry. One can say that most men characteristically leave father and mother and cleave to a wife, but only because both men and women are created for mutual interpersonal relationships, marriage being only one such relationship.

To assert that marriage is the ultimate purpose of humanity makes little sense because such an assertion is neither conceptually correct, nor does it apply factually to human experience. Not everyone marries, yet everyone has a primary need for interpersonal relationships. Death and divorce terminate marriages, but they do not end the need for interpersonal relationships. Interpersonal relationships also form within the community, the workplace, and the school; and they form in the various shapes of friendships, teams, collaborators, partners, and colleagues.

In effect, the creation story answers the question, "What is the will of God?" God's will is that human beings should not be alone but should live in mutual interpersonal relationship with other human beings. Interpersonal relationship proves, in effect, the *sine qua non* of humanity. Without interpersonal relationship, human civilization would not be possible as a distinct culture differentiated from the groupings among other natural species. The Hebrew writers do not view the capacity for this relationship as merely another aspect of the natural order, but as a unique quality that emerges from God. This capacity makes human beings the very image of God, the expression of God's will and purpose. Personal relationship is God's will. Because personal relationship is God's will, relationship with God and with others is righteousness, but alienation from God and from others is sin.

The Gen 2 story implies that being part of nature, even an ideal nature of perfect primeval gardens and companionable creatures, does not prove sufficient in itself for satisfactory human existence. No matter how successfully people create their own ideal "garden" in this world, no matter how productive they are or how much they achieve, those who experience no communion with others face an empty world, a lonely world where there is no one to know and by whom to be known.

To be sure, *some* individuals prove exceptions to the need for close, interpersonal relationships. Loners, recluses, hermits, and some monastic individuals may avoid personal relationships because of psychological, ascetic, or personal reasons. But there is a great difference between *voluntarily* embracing life without personal relationships and being *involuntarily* forced to forsake such relationships, or to be so psychologically or emotionally disfigured by family or societal pressures that one is incapable of forming such relationships.

Many examples found in literature illustrate the adverse effect upon society from individuals who face an empty world in loneliness. Stories abound of "Scrooge"-like people who, isolated from and hostile toward those around them, live a miserable existence and cause misery to others.

Parents who are unloving, uncaring, and emotionally absent during their son's or daughter's childhood can destroy that child's adult capacity to create healthy, interpersonal relationships.

Occasionally (and fortunately rarely) "loners," who actually or subjectively experience profound isolation from a community of friends and family, substantiate their unappreciated worth by fatally depreciating the worth of others, such as the incomprehensibly tragic massacres at Columbine High School in 1999 or Virginia Tech University in 2007.

A social majority can render a minority group culturally invisible when it inflicts upon them economic and political injustice, and it socially marginalizes them through neglect, indifference, and insensitivity to the minority's needs.

This discussion raises ethical questions regarding persons with innately same-sex gender connectivity, as well as the authentic relationships they seek to establish. Persons with innately *other*-sex gender connectivity may establish—are *encouraged* to establish—a close, primary interpersonal relationship (associations we call 'marriage' or perhaps 'soul mates') with someone of the other sex that brings mutual fulfillment and joy for many years. Yet people whose gender connectivity is innately *same*-sex are expected to remain chastely celibate, forbidden from establishing a close, primary interpersonal relationship that brings mutual fulfillment and joy to their lives—merely because their relationship

happens to involve someone of the same sex? What do these constraints actually say to these individuals? That in the closest and
most personally intimate of interpersonal relationships they must
remain alone? What about their humanity? Does society have the
right to revoke their essential humanity by coercing them to
remain celibate? Does this censure of primary relationship not
repudiate God's dictum that it is not good to be alone? Is it not un-
ethical to deny persons of same-sex gender connectivity access to
a fundamental characteristic of humanity—a primary interpersonal relationship that has the same civil protections granted in
marriage to heterosexuals?

In summary, three ethical principles form the basis of these ethical
deliberations regarding same-sex gender connectivity:

- ▼ No human being or arbitrary group of human beings is
  the absolute or ultimate measure of what is good and evil
  because we all must humble ourselves before the awe-
  some responsibility of balancing often competing and
  contradictory values of human classes and cultures.
- ▼ Respect for human dignity is due every person created in
  God's image.
- ▼ Human beings are created for interpersonal relationship,
  including a fulfilling primary, close interpersonal relationship.

I combine these three principles to comprise a comprehensive
ethical principle that I call *'Intimacy.'*

Intimacy

"Intimacy ('ɪn tə mə si) – *noun.* 1) the state of being intimate, 2) a
close, familiar, and affectionate personal relationship."[105] In this
definition, the phrase "personal relationship" clearly suggests that

---

[105] "intimacy." http://www.dictionary.com (accessed June 3, 2008).

intimacy involves more deep-seated connections between two or more persons rather than toward more casual contacts between strangers, or even mere acquaintances. In ordinary conversation *intimacy* often connotes close sexual relations. In order to avoid an oversimplified association with physical intimacy, I offer a revised definition of intimacy from the one above:

Intimacy is to know and to be known.

This definition obviously involves two major dimensions. First, intimacy requires that one endeavors to know another person. Secondly, intimacy requires that one allows oneself to *be* known, to possess the will and trust to open oneself to allow others knowledge. But this acquired knowledge represents far more than simple information gathering, far more than cerebral knowledge alone. 'Knowledge' in this sense also involves intuitive, empathetic, and appreciative regard between the persons interacting together. Because a person is comprised of more than a mind or body or both, the cerebral and affective knowledge accumulates based on interaction with another person across the *entire range* of human experience: emotional, mental, spiritual, social, as well as physical. In both knowing and being known, the attributes just listed demand risk, trust, patience, honesty, care, integrity, fidelity, and earnest effort within a relationship. Intimacy is not merely a physical closeness involving bodily, carnal knowledge. Neither is it a spiritual abstraction of esoteric, platonic ideals. Intimacy involves knowing and being known as whole persons, as individuals possessing all of the following attributes:

▼ *Physical* – anatomy, senses, and appetites

▼ *Emotional* – feelings and affections, including the ability to love as well as to hate, to feel confidence as well as fear

▼ *Mental* – thought processes with which to reason, decide, imagine, dream, remember

▼ *Social* – the capacity to build families, friendships, institutions and culture

▼ *Spiritual* – consciousness of 'me' as a distinct self with a sense of purpose and worth, and also consciousness of others as distinct selves with the same sense of their purpose and worth

When I say that intimacy involves knowing and being known as whole persons, I mean that I view an individual as a unity of attributes as opposed to the notion that a person is a duality having a body within which dwells a separate soul. Furthermore, I do not view the five attributes as distinct elements joined in one person, as though a person is modular with each component capable of being unplugged and replaced like the components of a home theatre system. And I do not mean to imply that each of these attributes is a separate ingredient in a person like the precisely measured ingredients in a cake recipe. I mean that each person is one personality whose attributes are describable from these differing points of view.

When speaking of intimacy, therefore, one must consider that a close, familiar, affectionate relationship includes the whole range of human attributes listed above. A relationship intended to be very close, a marital relationship, for example, is *not* intimate when attention is focused on only one or two of these human attributes. A personal relationship limited to one or two attributes either expresses a casual, even superficial relationship, or distorts and may even destroy a relationship expected to be close.

A disclaimer of sorts must accompany this emphasis on the whole-person quality of intimacy. Intimacy is not one-dimensional, but multi-dimensional. By that, I mean that intimacy possesses many degrees of intensity and appears in many different social forms. A distinct dimension of intimacy exists between lovers that differs from that between close friends, or acquaintances, or colleagues. A distinct dimension of intimacy exists within a family, as well as within the neighborhood, or in a workplace, or city or nation. For each dimension of intimacy, the depth of what persons know of each other or allow to be known of themselves varies across the range of human attributes.

For example, the intimacy of a close friendship between individuals in significantly different careers does not require in-depth knowledge of one another's *mental* efforts or *social* inter-actions in their jobs (although personal interest in one another often elicits some knowledge). On the other hand, the friendship may involve in-depth knowledge of *emotional* struggles in the workplace if they opt to support and encourage each another—to "be there" for one another. The friendship may involve intense *spiritual* intimacy, as each friend gives to the other a profound sense of being valued. Yet the depth of the *physical* relationship may extend only to shared physical tasks, occasional hugs, or pats on the back.

Obviously, the form and depth of intimacy between lovers who aspire to entwine their lives for life, for better or for worse, differs greatly from the intimacy between the hypothetical friends above. Lovers want to know and be known by one another as deeply as possible across the full range of human attributes, from spiritual to physical. Unfortunately, for some lovers, the relation-ship becomes boring, superficial, and commonplace, and finally dies because somewhere along the line, one or both of the lovers abandoned the pursuit of intimacy across the entire range of human attributes. One of the lovers might be interested primarily in physical intimacy but not emotional. A lover in another rela-tionship might be interested chiefly in social intimacy, perhaps even using the other as a means of getting ahead, but not interested in the spiritual intimacy of upholding and respecting the other person's sense of innate worth and value. In each in-stance, one or both lovers abort the work of knowing the other person more deeply, or hesitate to risk being known across the entire range of human attributes. Sometimes lovers who have just "fallen in love" get caught up in physical or emotional excitement, and make knowing each other beyond this initial excitement incidental to the relationship. Their relationship grows dull when the excitement fades and no close familiarity exists in the other aspects of the relationship to rekindle their enthusiasm.

Revisiting the discussion of marriage proves useful within the interpersonal context of defining intimacy as "knowing and being known" across the range of human attributes. In the Gen 2 creation story, interpersonal relationship, not gender and marriage, is the fundamental and primary issue from which everything else follows. The story culminates with God's decision to complete the earth creature with someone like him and of the same essence, but distinct enough to serve as enabler and partner in life, someone to know and someone by whom to be known. To be sure, within Genesis this culminating relationship unfolds in the form of gender relationship and the social arrangement we identify as marriage. Nevertheless, the story addresses primarily the issue of the human capacity for relationship.

When we consider the "leaving" and "joining" of Gen 2, this implicit 'marriage' is often viewed through a contemporary cultural lens that concludes that marriage is a monogamous, cohabitation of a man and woman united by civil licensure commonly sanctified by some form of sectarian ritual (and that some period of romantic courtship precedes this union). But in the actual Gen 2 story, 'marriage' is simply a man and woman whom God creates, blesses, and commissions to be fruitful and multiply. In truth, one can say little more about this pair than about a pair of cattle in a breeding pen. The Genesis story provides no descriptions, conditions, or instructions about marriage; it prescribes no ritual or licensure; and it offers no guidelines about how to love or to be faithful. Between that simple union and our unions today, a long and varied history of 'marriage' has evolved throughout various times and various cultures.

Given this historical and cultural plasticity of marriage, we should recall that the 'marriage' implied at the end of the Gen 2 creation story remains a *penultimate* issue that cannot be elevated over the *ultimate* issue: emphasizing the primary importance of human relationship itself. The story proves far too brief and simple a sketch of marriage to raise the importance of marriage above the importance of overcoming aloneness through ordinary human relationship. When individuals proclaim the story's support of 'marriage' over its primary message of relationship, they therefore devalue those who, for various reasons, cannot marry, or for whom, because of a life situation, marriage can never be an option. The Biblical story may end with 'marriage,' but the issue remains secondary to the primary issue of the human capacity for relationship. Thus, *intimacy* (to know and to be known) not necessarily *marriage* proves essential and fundamental to the human integrity of each person.

Truly, marriage can powerfully illustrate the basic nature of human relationships, and potentially demonstrates that the fundamental nature of human intimacy can apply to all kinds of human relationships. Any two persons who live together in a publicly recognized relationship throughout a lifetime of love, commitment, mutuality, respect, candor, and fidelity speak volumes about the human capacity for intimacy.

Most individuals agree that respectful, caring relationship between human beings, whether spouses or friends, neighbors, acquaintances, etc., prove a worthy ideal. Regardless of marital status, most people affirm qualities in any relationship such as love, commitment, and respect; and most generally approve relationships in which these qualities deepen the mental, emotional, social, and spiritual attributes of our human relationships.

The one attribute that seriously troubles many people when expressed outside the institution of marriage is physical intimacy. Conventional social mores indicate that although emotional, mental, social, and spiritual intimacy may be shared between non-married individuals, the degree of physical intimacy considered appropriate outside of marriage ought to be limited. The issue of physical intimacy, therefore, particularly sexual intimacy, requires separate discussion.

Some Biblical views on human sexuality, such as expressed in the Song of Solomon and even in the Gen 2 creation account, offer a positive disposition toward those attributes of *gender connectivity* we consider more erotic—arousal and attraction. Gen 2 affirms the nakedness and intercourse of the man and his wife as something positive: "Therefore a man leaves his father and his mother and cleaves to his wife, and they become one flesh. And the man and his wife *were both naked, and were not ashamed"* (Gen 2:24–25). Within this positive eroticism, nudity is not and should not be something shameful. Apparently some ancient Hebrew writers, at least, did not believe sexual pleasure alone, or at least eroticism per se, evoked only lustful, self-gratifying passion. They seem to have recognized an honor in human eroticism's capacity to bind lovers together in mutual intimacy.

Later, due to moral law and prudery, guilt and eroticism became conjoined, particularly in the notion that lust is a passion to tame, and should be released only for procreation. But if conjugal sex is virtuous *only* when a couple seeks to procreate, then how can marital sex be justified if a man or woman is infertile, or when couples engage in intercourse outside the week or so of fertility in the menstrual cycle? Presumably under the conditions of procreative sex, a couple in which the woman has already experienced menopause cannot justify sex by claiming that they were *previously* open to procreation during childbearing years. Clearly, this kind of moralizing justification proves artificial, unnecessary, and emotionally debilitating. Surely most marriage partners in the very throes of sexual passion do not pause to sanction their non-procreative acts by claiming, "It's okay, we *could* be procreating!"

Sex was made for pleasure, regardless of procreation. If one truly believes God created human beings male and female, one should not overlook the biological reality that females can experience and enjoy orgasm independently of issues of procreation. Whereas male orgasm is functionally associated with procreation because of the ejaculated sperm, procreation is only incidentally associated with female orgasm. The procreative element for women exists only within a limited window of an ovulatory cycle generally independent of orgasm. Thus, a woman can have erotic pleasure from orgasm without procreative risk when copulation occurs outside the limited ovulatory window. In contrast, in male orgasm a man can rarely separate erotic pleasure from the procreative ejaculation of sperm. For the woman, erotic experience and procreation can be very distinct.

This distinction between erotic experience and procreation points to two related but independent functions of conjugal male/female sex: to procreate and to share sexual pleasure. In contrast to the expectations of nineteenth-century church ethics, spouses today are not required to restrict conjugal pleasure to those times when the possibility of conception exists. The sheer pleasure of physical intimacy remains crucial to the health of a loving relationship between spouses during incidental times of romantic adventure, as well as during the post-menopausal time of irreversible infertility for women.

Physical intimacy, expressed through the maximum intensity of sexual pleasure, should not be repressed because it is erotic, nor justified only by some other, supposedly higher purpose such as procreation. This human attribute demands the same consistent condition of knowing and being known that is part of all other aspects of human intimacy. Each person within a couple must learn how to receive and how to give sexual pleasure to one another.

Perhaps because physical sexuality relates so fully to the significance of the whole person, to the integration of human attributes—mental, emotional, spiritual, and social—into the physical act, that many individuals hardly disassociate sexual physicality from the broader aspects of a relationship. Notably, therefore, the Biblical euphemism for such physical intimacy, sexual intercourse, is "to know." Adam "knew" Eve. The expression refers not only to procreation but also to the importance of involving the whole person in the experience. In a profound sense, one reveals one's whole self—with all the attributes—at least symbolically, by the giving and receiving involved in foreplay and coitus. During this activity, lovers should accept the risk of exposing oneself, and in turn be careful and respectful of the self that the other person reveals. Each partner should strive to prove worthy of the trust implied when the other reveals the whole self in this manner.

We can be emotionally detached, mentally aloof, spiritually indifferent, or socially tolerant of people with whom the workplace or community requires involvement. But somehow physicality, particularly sex, draws into the physical connection the personal aspects of one another's feelings, thoughts, worth, and presence. That expectation, at least, lies so very close at hand for most individuals, that one or both persons in a couple may feel violated or guilty about physical sex partitioned from the other human attributes.

In a sense, therefore, the nature of "having sex" symbolizes all other aspects of intimacy. Just as one often "gets naked" to have sex, so also a kind of "nakedness" occurs in revealing the other human attributes of our personal relationship. We can and must risk emotional, mental, spiritual, and social nakedness in order to allow the closest and most committed human relationships to mature and develop. Covering up and repressing our identity will stifle any relationship meant to be close. When this occurs, intimacy may die.

Sexual intimacy for mutual pleasure between married couples (without forcing a connection with procreation) remains crucial for the health of the relationship. Far from being something lustful to be repressed, physical intimacy offers an occasion to be reminded of the importance of intimacy in the other attributes as well. Sexual pleasure is a natural expression of love that must be encouraged to grow along with the emotional, mental, spiritual, and social aspects of a loving relationship.

The Apostle Paul knew that enforcing ascetic abstinence from sex upon Christian couples in the church of Corinth was wrong: "it is well for a man not to touch a woman. But because of the temptation to immorality, each man should have his own wife and each woman her own husband. The husband should give to his wife her conjugal rights, and likewise the wife to her husband" (1 Cor. 7:1–3).

During the Protestant reformation of the sixteenth century, Lutheran theologians argued that priests should be allowed to marry because mandated celibacy repressed the Godly gift of desire they called "natural love." Instead of causing purity, repression of this 'gift' caused sinful lust to break out in rampant scandal and sexual immorality among priests in the Roman Catholic Church at the time. The Reformers advised that marriage would remedy sinful lust, and that natural love within marriage should be given appropriate expression. They even quoted Paul's dictum that "it is better to marry than be aflame with passion."

A similar issue applies to those with same-sex gender connectivity. A natural love exists between persons of the same sex that is no different from the natural love between persons of another sex. Granted, selfish desire and lust can inflame natural love into something immoral and destructive for persons of same-sex *and* other-sex gender connectivity. But just as surely, natural love cradled within a selfless and caring embrace of authentic love between persons of either same-sex or other-sex gender connectivity can glow with mutually expressed sexual pleasure. Why should we enforce celibacy and sexual abstinence upon same-sex couples who find a healthy and satisfying primary interpersonal relationship with one another? Is it not cruel to deny same-sex couples the full dimension of intimacy and the full rights and privileges of marriage with which to grow in a loving relationship of knowing and being known? As in the days of Paul or the Protestant Reformers, a primary interpersonal relationship of mature intimacy helps remedy the flagrant abuse of sex. For other-sex couples, marriage often provides such a remedy. But what about for same-sex couples?

First, however, let us shift from the negative and puritanical notion that marriage provides a "remedy" for "sinful lust." Instead, let us frame marriage as a positive gift that channels the growth of intimacy. In civil marriage, the state gives to couples more than a thousand rights and privileges to protect the legal recognition of their joined lives. In religious marriage, the faith community believes that God offers a blessing to couples in front of the community of friends and family who witness and support their union.

Marriage, more than simply a remedy for lust, offers a state of primary interpersonal relationship in which sexual pleasure may be a mutual experience of knowing and being known, together with knowing the wholeness of each person mentally, emotionally, socially, and spiritually. Marriage provides a venue in which persons who have committed themselves to one another can be open to the intimacy of knowing fully and being fully known in a life-long journey of discovery . . . a journey that *includes* the intimacy of sexual pleasure.

In conclusion, intimacy proves just as ethically validating for same-sex relationships as for other-sex relationships. *"To know and to be known"* offers a valid principle upon which to base ethical deliberation about human relationships in any form of gender connectivity; a principle from which we effectively may derive laws, rules, and mores to guide and direct the intricacies of those relationships.

CHAPTER SEVEN

Conclusion

When one social group possesses and exerts dominance over another, decisions and judgments often reflect the following attributes: privilege assumed without thought, truth presumed without question, life and society perceived against the normative consensus of the majority, power administered by the advantaged, and influence brokered by the elite. Although American society has made great strides in combating racism, the dominance of the white majority still impacts our race relations and permits a shadowy haze of stereotype, suppression, neglect, and insensitivity that depersonalizes the real humanity of others.

Similarly, heterosexual privilege, heterosexual definitions of sexual identity, the predominance of heterosexual images in the media, advertising, and everyday life, heterosexual values controlled by legislatures and courts—all manifest the heterosexism permeating our society. Fortunately, the last thirty years have offered a challenge to heterosexism unlike ever before in Western history. One contributing factor is the increasing and publicly available scientific information about the complexities of determining the exact origins of an individual's sexual identity. Maintaining a binary understanding of sex or insisting upon the traditional mores of sexual relations without considering the complex factors that shape individual sexual identity simply proves unreasonable.

Disturbingly, a subtle bias of blatant heterosexism continues to confront the emerging appreciation and respect for homosexual persons. The same shadowy haze of stereotype, suppression, neglect, and insensitivity characteristic of white privilege in our culture's racism manifest themselves in the same way in the form of heterosexual privilege that continues to dominate Western culture. Many heterosexuals, who otherwise may be tolerant of gays and lesbians, deny the principle of intimacy for people of same-sex gender connectivity out of sheer frustration. Tired of the ensuing debate about the origins of homosexuality or the rights gays and lesbians seek to claim, these individuals want merely for the issue to go away, regardless of the injustices gays and lesbians endure. But heterosexual people can no longer passively avoid the current sexual controversies and by their inaction perpetuate prejudice and injustice against those whose sexuality does not reflect the heterosexual norm. Heterosexual people must acknowledge and end their silent participation in this sexual bias not merely to "tolerate" gay, lesbian, bisexual, and transgender people, but actively to recognize and counter the heterosexism that diminishes the full humanity of sexual minorities.

Until recent decades the heterosexual community forced gay and lesbian persons into closets in which, even now, many homosexual individuals feel obligated to remain. But more and more gay and lesbian people refuse to stay closeted, despite the continuing pressure to do so, particularly apparent in small towns and rural areas. They lift their voices against emotional and spiritual violence perpetrated against them—violence that obstructs their freedom to experience the entire range of human intimacy. Heterosexual individuals should also protest the constrictiveness of a society that deprives homosexual individuals of the normal experiences of intimacy that heterosexuals take for granted. Following are some of the ways gays and lesbians have experienced emotional and spiritual violence from the heterosexual community across the entire spectrum of human attributes. Though not as prevalent or severe today as they were a decade or so ago, emotional and spiritual violence still occurs.

▾ In the *mental* dimension of intimacy, many gay or lesbian couples felt they could not openly display their intellectual interests together; i.e., discussing together their common interest in concerts, lectures, museums, literature, art, etc. Perceived as a *couple,* whose conversation, banter, and humor betrays a more than common likeness of mind and thought, the intellectual interests they shared might raise suspicion that "something is going on" between them.

▾ In *social* situations, gay or lesbian couples felt a need to be cautious about being seen together too much, or felt obligated to meet out of town, lest they risk losing their jobs or social respect if someone observes by their frequent association in public that they may be "that kind."

▾ Many homosexual persons carefully ensured that the *spiritual* aspect of intimacy, valuing and being valued, should not be too conspicuous to the casual observer, especially in church, lest the admiration for and encouragement they gave to each other aroused suspicion that they were a little "too close."

▾ *Emotional* repression particularly damaged many homosexual persons when they hid their same-sex feelings and emotions, and adopted pseudo-heterosexual appearances in order to "fit in" with the dominant sexual culture. Investing so much energy in camouflaging their feelings or attractions also proved psychologically detrimental. Straight people can freely indicate interest in someone of the other sex through innumerable means in almost any situation. But for someone with same-sex gender connectivity, meeting and connecting emotionally with someone who is also gay or lesbian, given that they are a comparatively small percentage of the total population, proves highly challenging and potentially discouraging. Given the past and even current social climate, initiating an emotional connection with someone of the same sex is fraught with risk and danger, as seen in cases where gay-baiting ended in beatings and occasionally murder.

▼ Perhaps most severely, many homosexual persons felt inhibited to display *physical* intimacy. Gays and lesbians often gave up even casual hand-holding in public in order to avoid embarrassment and attacks from others who may shout, "Perverts! Fags!" Times may be changing, but they still have far to go. Although straight couples hold hands on the street, during movies, at school dances, and in church, many gay or lesbian couples still do not feel safe expressing the same affection in most public places.

A number of religious groups within the heterosexual majority endeavor to abridge the rights of gays and lesbians and force them to submerge their identity (so as not to affront heterosexual moral sensibilities). The effort violates the ethical principle that no human being or arbitrary group of human beings is the absolute or ultimate measure of what is good and evil for all other people. Numerous heterosexual religious communities tell homosexual individuals that engaging in homosexual practice condemns them to Hell, thereby leading some who have been condemned as such to decide that they might as well live like Hell! Others testify that, having suffered such enormous guilt for failing over and over again to measure up to religious mores and laws against homosexuality, the oppressive condemnation led them into severe depression and to dysfunctional behaviors such as drug and alcohol addiction. Still others simply left the church, taking a "screw you" attitude toward those who censured them religiously and socially.

Fundamentally, the heterosexual condemnation of homosexuals violates the ethical principle of respect for human dignity because it presumes to define homosexuals without consideration for how they define themselves. Just like the white race once negatively defined the identity of African- and Native Americans, so also many heterosexuals define homosexuals as immoral individuals who "choose" to engage in sexual behaviors for lack of control over lustful, sinful, homoerotic desire.

The heterosexual community also violates the ethical principle of interpersonal relationship by insisting that gay and lesbian persons should be denied primary intimacy altogether. Some in the heterosexual community declare a willingness to tolerate homosexuals, but *only* if they remain celibate. Like every other human person, the gay, lesbian, or transgender person has been created with the fundamental capacity for intimate, mutual, interpersonal relationship, including the gender connectivity attributes of arousal, attraction, and attachment—basic human needs and gifts. The heterosexual imposition of celibacy upon homosexual individuals as a condition of acceptance is an unjust and self-righteous constraint.

Religious people need to recognize that homosexual men and women live lives of character, faith, love, constancy, service, and caring that fulfill the highest purpose and ideal of the Bible—that they love God, and love and honor one another as God loves them. The religious person should remember that many gay, lesbian, bisexual, or transgender individuals were baptized or blessed in religious rites of purification and of affirmation of divine acceptance as children. They were confirmed and initiated into the adult community of faith that nurtured them. As adults, many continue to live in the certainty of God's love, and they hunger for the spiritual nourishment their faith tradition provides. Yet many devoutly religious believers perceive homosexuals to be unclean untouchables with three options: change their "lifestyle" and become heterosexual; seclude themselves "in the closet"; or leave the community of faith. Rather than *knowing* them as devoted fellow believers, too many *brothers and sisters* in the faith isolate or exclude them from their fellowship.[106]

Religious groups should stop focusing on homosexual behavior and instead encourage the expression of physical sexuality within the whole dimension of intimacy. They should treat same-sex couples just as other-sex couples by providing information, counsel, and encouragement to express healthy sexual practices. Religious communities should help gay or lesbian couples, together with couples of which one or both is bisexual, or one of which is transgender, to experience understanding, care, sharing, love, character, fidelity, and integrity rather than discouraging these important relational aspects. Rather than opposing gay rights, religious communities should stand beside activists to shape the same kind of legal/social protections that heterosexuals enjoy. They should be just as concerned about preserving and protecting gay and lesbian families as heterosexual families; the goal should be to *strengthen* not divide families—whether straight or gay.

Religiously motivated efforts to "protect" marriage from the social decay that "gay marriage" supposedly embodies has no bearing on the health and strength of heterosexual marriages, nor does it prevent gays and lesbians from forming committed relationships. Perhaps denying gay marriage in "protection" of marriage in actuality cloaks the fear that if homosexual persons receive this basic civil right, homosexuality itself will never again be declared illegal? Of course, such regression, albeit unlikely, would be a profound violation of the principle of intimacy.

The civil right of marriage belongs fully to homosexual couples as much as to heterosexual couples. The sexuality of homosexual persons—as *one* aspect of their whole humanity: emotional, spiritual, social, intellectual, and physical—must be valued. Society must grant the privilege of marriage equally to persons of same-sex gender connectivity as to persons of other-sex

---

[106] For the testimonies of gay and lesbian Christians spurned by the churches of which they longed to be a part, see Alexander, *We Were Baptized Too: Claiming God's Grace for Lesbians and Gays*.

gender connectivity so that *all* couples may experience the expression of intimacy and be able to honor that intimacy across every human aspect.

It is not good to be alone. Gay men and women have the same need to know and to be known as those who experience life heterosexually. Abuse sometimes occurs in the fulfillment of this need regardless of one's gender connectivity. Both homosexuals and heterosexuals occasionally try to replace intimacy with complex distortions of spiritual, emotional, social, physical, and mental needs that prove destructive to themselves and those with whom they try to establish intimacy. Likewise, both heterosexual persons and homosexual persons successfully establish intimacy that is noble, wholesome, and authentic.

"To know" (and to be known) is a Biblical euphemism for sexual intercourse. As a euphemism, however, "to know" points beyond physical sexual behavior to all the dimensions of human relationship of equal importance. Same-sex gender connectivity, like other-sex gender connectivity, encompasses these dimensions of human relationship in which a person's multifaceted being is open to be known, understood, and appreciated by another person who opens his or her multifaceted self to the other.

▼   †   ▼

It is not good to be alone. For each of us, straight or gay, may there be someone in our lives to know deeply, and by whom to be known as deeply.

References

Alexander, Marilyn Bennett, and James Preston. *We Were Baptized Too: Claiming God's Grace for Lesbians and Gays*. Louisville: Westminster John Knox Press, 1996.

American Lutheran Publicity Bureau. *Can Homosexual Love Be Blesssed?* 2000. CM06.

Bagemihl, Bruce. *Biological Exuberance: Animal Homosexuality and Natural Diversity*. New York: St. Martin's Press, 2000.

Bem, Sandra Lipsitz. "Dismantling Gender Polarization and Compulsory Heterosexuality: Should We Turn the Volume Up or Down?" *The Journal of Sex Research* 32 (1995): 329–34.

Biale, David. *Eros and the Jews: From Biblical Israel to Contemporary America*. New York: Basic Books, 1992.

Blackwell, Richard J. *Science, Religion and Authority: Lessons from the Galileo Affair*. Milwaukee: Marquette University Press, 1998.

Booker, A. Keith. "Cultural Crisis Then and Now: Science, Literature, and Religion in John Banville's Doctor Copernicus and Kepler" *Critique* 39. 2 (1998): 176-192.

Brizendine, Louann. *The Female Brain*. New York: Morgan Road Books, 2006.

Brown, Peter. *The Body and Society: Men, Women and Sexual Renunciation in Early Christianity*. New York: Columbia University Press, 1988.

Buss, David M. "Sexual Strategies Theory: Historical Origins and Current Status." *The Journal of Sex Research* 35 (1998): 19–31.

Carter, D. Bruce, ed. *Current Conceptions of Sex Roles and Sex Typing: Theory and Research.* New York: Praeger Publishers, 1987.

Chandler, Kurt. *Passages of Pride: Lesbian and Gay Youth Come of Age.* New York: Times Books, 1995.

Chapman, Patrick M. *Thou Shalt Not Love:What Evangelicals Really Say to Gays.* New York: Haiduk Press, 2008.

Chilstrom, Herbert W., and Lowell O. Erdahl. *Sexual Fulfillment: for Single and Married, Straight and Gay, Young and Old.* Minneapolis: Augsburg Fortress, 2001.

Coontz, Stephanie. *Marriage, a History: from Obedience to Intimacy or How Love Conquered Marriage.* New York: Viking, 2005

Davis, Mark. "Is 'Gay Marriage' an oxymoron?" *Fort Worth Star–Telegram*, November 19, 2003, sec. B.

Elkind, Daniel. "The Moral Code and the Trials That Test Our Adherence to It" *The Humanist* 62.4 (July/August 2002): 34–5.

Fausto-Sterling, Anne. *Sexing the Body: Gender Politics and the Construction of Sexuality.* New York: Basic Books, 2000.

Frederickson, David E. "Natural and Unnatural Use in Romans 1:24–27: Paul and the Philosophic Critique of Eros." In *Homosexuality, Science, and the "Plain Sense of Scripture,"* edited by David L. Balch. Grand Rapids: William. B. Eerdmans Publishing Co., 2000.

Gagnon, Robert A. J. *The Bible and Homosexual Practice: Texts and Hermeneutics.* Nashville: Abingdon Press, 2001.

———. *The Bible and Homosexual Practice: Theology, Analogies, and Genes.* Theology Matters: A Publication of Presbyterians for Faith, Family and Ministry.

Greenberg, David E. *The Construction of Homosexuality.* Chicago: The University of Chicago Press, 1988.

Herdt, Gilbert. *Same Sex, Different Cultures: Exploring Gay & Lesbian Lives.* Boulder, Colorado: Westview Press, 1997.

The Holy Bible, Revised Standard Version. Philadelphia: Westminster, 1952.

"Intimacy." *Dictionary.com Unabridged (v 1.1)*. Random House, Inc. <http://dictionary.reference.com/browse/intimacy> (accessed: June 3, 2008).

Jenkins, William Sumner. *Pro-Slavery Thought in the Old South*. Chapel Hill: The University of North Carolina Press, 1935.

Judson, Olivia. *Dr. Tatiana's Sex Advice to All Creation: The Definitive Guide to the Evolutionary Biology of Sex*. New York: Henry Holt and Company, 2002.

Jung, Patricia Beattie, and Ralph F. Smith. *Heterosexism: An Ethical Challenge*. Albany: State University of New York Press, 1993.

Edward O. Lauman et al. *The Social Organization of Sexuality: Sexual Practices in the United States*. Chicago: The University of Chicago Press, 1994.

Marti, Karl. *The Religion of the Old Testament: Its Place among the Religions of the Nearer East*, translated by G. A. Bienemann, edited by W. D. Morrison. New York: G.P. Putnam's Sons, 1907.

Milgrom, Jacob. *Leviticus 17–22: A New Translation with Introduction and Commentary*. *The Anchor Bible*. New York: Doubleday, 2000.

Miller, Patrick D. *The Religion of Ancient Israel*. Louisville: SPCK, 2000.

Mondimore, Francis Mark. *A Natural History of Homosexuality*. Baltimore: The Johns Hopkins University Press, 1996.

Massachusetts Department of Elementary and Secondary Education, *2005 Youth Risk Behavior Survey*, <http://www.doe.mass.edu/cnp/hprograms/yrbs/05/> (accessed: January 2007).

Motts, Lloyd and Jefferson Hane Weaver. *The Story of Astronomy*. Cambridge: Perseus Publishing, 1995.

O'Connor, J.J., and E. F. Robertson, <u>Galileo Galilei</u>. School of Mathematics and Statistics, University of St. Andrews, Scotland. November 2002, <http://www-history.mcs.st-andrews.ac.uk/Mathematicians/Galileo.html >

Olyan, Saul M. "And with a Male You Shall Not Lie the Lying Down of a Woman: On the Meaning and Significance of Leviticus 18:22 and 20:13" *Journal of the History of Sexuality* 5 (1994): 179–206.

Rosen, Peg. "The Gender Divide." *Americanbaby.com*. Aug. 2003. 82–86.

Schmidt, Thomas E. *Straight & Narrow: Compassion & Clarity in the Homsosexuality Debate.* Downers Grove, Illinois: InterVarsity Press, 1995.

Sherer, Lester B. *Slavery and the Churches in Early America 1619 – 1819*. Grand Rapids, Michigan: William B. Eerdmans Publishing Company, 1975.

Stein, Edward, ed. *The Mismeasure of Desire: The Science, Theory, and Ethics of Sexual Orientation*. New York: Oxford University Press, 1999.

Worthington, Roger L., et al. "Heterosexual Identity Development: A Multidimensional Model of Individual and Social Identity" *The Counseling Psychologist* 30 (2002): 496–561.

For Further Reading

"About the Project." *National Marriage Project.* 21 Nov. 2003.
    <http://marriage.rutgers.edu/about.htm>.

"Articles and Essays." *One By One.*
    <http://www.oneby1.org/articles.htm>.
    <http://www.churchmoraldebate.com/intro.htm>.

Anderson, G.W. "Hebrew Religion." *The Old Testament and Modern
    Study: A Generation of Discovery and Research Essays,* edited by
    H.H. Rowley. Oxford: Clarendon Press, 1951.

Blumer, Robyn. "Military Opposition to Gays is Unhelpful." *Fort
    Worth Star–Telegram,* May 12, 2003.

Brooks, David. "Genes, Hormones play key role in behavior." *The
    Olympian,* September 21, 2006, sec. A7.

Burke, Phyllis. *Family Values: Two Moms and Their Son.* New York:
    Random House, 1993.

Carlson, Betsy, ed. "Church History, Early and Recent, is
    Background for Homsexuality Talks" *Network News* 5.3 (May–
    June 2004): 3.

———. "Theologians disagree on Bible's outloook on
    homoseuxality" *Network News* 5.3 (May–June 2004): 4.

D'Angelli, Anthony R., and Charlotte Paltow. *Lesbian, Gay and
    Bisexual Identities in Families: Psychological Perspectives.* Oxford
    University Press, 1998.

Davis, David Brion. *The Problem of Slavery in Western Culture.*
    Ithaca, New York: Cornell University Press, 1966.

"Debating the Moral Issue of Homosexuality". *The Committee on Marriage and Family of the WordAlone Network.* November 21, 2003. <http://www.churchmoraldebate.com/intro.htm>.

Dobson, James D. *Family News From Dr. James Dobson.* 9. September, 2003.

"First Things." *Journal of Religion and Public Life.* November 21, 2003 <http://www.firstthings.com/index.html>.

Fisher, Helen E., Arthur Aron, Debra Mashek, Haifang Li, and Lucy L. Brown. "Defining the Brain Systems of Lust, Romantic Attraction, and Attachment." *Archives of Sexual Behavior* 31.5 (October 2002): 413–19.

Flamm, Fay. "Pheromone-driven sex lives? Reptile shemales? Snakes Alive!" *The Seattle Times,* September 24, 2006 <http://community.seattletimes.nwsource.com/archive/?date=2 0060924&slug=carnalknowledge24>.

Flunder, Yvette. *Cross Purposes? A Perspective on Gays' and Lesbians' Uneasy Relationship with the Church.* New York: Pride, 2003.

Hart, Albert Bushnell."Try This Again." *Slavery and Abolition, 1831–1841.* New York: Harper & Brothers, Publishers, 1906.

Helminiak, Daniel A. *What the Bible Really Says about Homosexuality.* New Mexico: Alamo Square Press, 2000.

Jech, Carl L. *Will the Gay Issue Go Away?: Questioning Heterosexual Myths – Toward a New Theological Consensus On Sexual Oriientation.* PublishAmerica, 2002.

Jordan, Winthrop. *White over Black: American Attitudes toward the Negro.* Baltimore: Penguin Books, 1969.

Jost, John T, Jack Glaser, Arie W. Krugllanski, and Frank J. Sulloway. "Political Conservatism as Motivated Social Cognition." *Psychological Bulletin* 129.3 (2003): 339–75.

Katz, Jonathan N. *Gay Amercian History: Lesbians and Gay Men in the U.S.A.* New York: Thomas Y. Crowell, 1976.

Kozhamthadam, Job. *The Discovery of Kepler's Laws: the Interaction of Science, Philosophy, and Religion*. Notre Dame: University of Notre Dame Press, 1994.

Kraus, Clifford. "Gay Canadians' Quest for Marriage Seems Near Victory." *The New York Times* International. June 15. 2003. 3.

Lamb, Michael E. *Parenting and Child Development in "Non Traditional" Families*. Mahwah, New Jersey: Laurence Erlbaum Associates, 1998.

Miller, Mitch. "Something Fishy." *Fort Worth Star–Telegram*, May 19, 2003, sec. A.

Murphy, Goerge L. "Science and Sexuality." *Lutheran Partners* 20.1 (2004): 32–33.

Myers, David G., and Letha Dawson Scanzoni. *What God has Joined Together: A Christian Case for Gay Marriage*. San Francisco: HarperCollins, 2005.

"NARTH." National Association for Research and Therapy of Homosexuality. November 22, 2003. <http://www.narth.com/>.

Nessan, Craig L. *Many Members yet One Body: Committed Same Gender Relationships and the Mission of the Church*. Minneapolis: Augsburg Fortress, 2004.

Nouwen, Henri J.M. *Intimacy: Essays in Pastoral Counseling*. San Francisco: Harper & Row, 1969.

Piazza, Michael S. *Holy Homosexuals: The Truth about being Gay or Lesbian and Christian*. Dallas: Sources of Hope Publishing House, 1994.

———. *Queeries: Questions Lesbians and Gays have for God*. Dallas: Sources of Hope Publishing House, 2003.

Rudy, Kathy. *Sex and the Church: Gender, Homosexuality, and the Transformation of Christian Ethics*. Boston: Beacon Press, 1997.

Sinfield, Alan. *Gay and After: Gender, Culture, and Consumption*. London: Serpent's Tail, 1998.

Smith, Mark S. *The Origins of Biblical Monotheism: Israel's Polytheistic Background and the Ugaritic Texts.* New York: Oxford University Press, 2003.

Smith, W. Robertson. *Lectures on the Religion of the Semites the Fundamental Institutions.* London: Adam and Charles Black, 1901.

Stommen, Merton P. *The Church and Homosexuality.* Minneapolis: Kirk House Publishers, 2002.

Switzer, David K., and Shirley Switzer. *Parents of the Homosexual.* Edited by Wayne E. Oates. Philadelphia: The Westminster Press, 1980.

Szymanski, Zak. "Snips and Snails and Puppy Dog Tails: Transgender Boys, Guys, Men, Butches, and others are changing the world, one Identity at a Time." New York: Pride, 2003.

Taylor, Curtis L. Newday. "Study: Fathers' chemical signals could delay onset of puberty in girls." *The Olympian*, September 26, 2006.

Tilley, Reade. *Holy Reckoning.* New York: Pride, 2003.

Trible, Phyllis. *God and the Rhetoric of Sexuality.* Philadelphia: Fortress Press, 1978.

Tripp, C. A. *The Homosexual Matrix.* New York: McGraw Hill, 1975.

Van Binsbergen, Wim. *Rupture and Fusion in the Approach to Myth.* <http://www.shikanda.net/ancient_models/myth%20mineke%20defdefdef.pdf>, 2004.

Wallner, Mary Lou. *The Slow Miracle of Transformation.* Denver: Teach Ministries, 2003.

Wright, G. Ernest. *Biblical Archeology.* Philadelphia: Westminster Press, 1957.

Index

Aquinas, Thomas, 115
Abram, 147–48
Ambiguity, 91–97
American Lutheran Publicity
    Bureau, 83
Analogy, 91, 97–99
Aphrodite, 161, 163
Apocalyptic, 116
Apostasy, 137–140, 143–44,
    149, 151–52, 156, 158, 160–
    62, 168–170, 175, 177
Arousal, 50, 53–56, 66, 72, 77,
    124, 212
Asceticism, 115, 118, 158, 165,
    167, 172, 205, 214
Asherah, 145, 152
Assyrians, 164
Astarte, 152, 158
Attachment, 50, 52, 58–60, 65,
    72
Attis, 162
Attraction, 51–53, 56-58, 61,
    72, 129, 212
Augustine, 90, 100, 109, 115
Babylonians, 143, 164
Bagemihl, Bruce, 60, 74, 95,
    120

Behaviorist, 20–21
Bellarmine, Cardinal Robert,
    108–09
Bem, Sandra Lipsitz , 19
Benjaminites, 152
Bethlehem, 151
Bible References,
    1 and 2 Kings, 152
    1 Corinthians, 115, 117, 167,
        172, 214
    1 Thessalonian, 167
    2 Peter, 138
    3 John, 136
    Amos, 143
    Deuteronomy, 138, 142
    Exodus, 140–41
    Ezekiel, 144, 160–61
    Genesis, 23, 29, 97, 110, 112,
        121, 126, 138, 144, 147–
        151, 154, 190, 195, 199–
        204, 210–12
    Isaiah, 144
    Jude, 135–39
    Judges, 151–54
    Leviticus, 154–59, 166
    Mark, 110
    Revelation, 136

Bible References,
    Romans, 5, 137, 161, 167,
        172
Binary view of sexuality, 14–
    16, 23, 39–40, 68, 110–11,
    120, 217
Biological/environmental
    determinants, 15, 17–20
Bipolar view of sexuality, 31,
    69–70
Brahe, Tycho, 106
Brizendine, Louanne, 20
Brown, Peter, 118
Buss, David, 20
Canaan, 141–45, 147, 152, 157,
    159, 164, 191
Cezanne, 196
Chedorlaomer of Elam, 147
Closet, 2, 13, 30, 78, 105, 132,
    189, 218, 221
Complentary, 110, 119, 123–27,
    167
Connectivity, 49-50, 65, 70–71,
    154, 172–73, 175, 187–88,
    205
Constructionist, 15, 19
Copernicus, 106, 109
Corinth, 161, 169–70, 214
Corpus callosum, 36
Cosmology
    Geocentric, 106, 109, 110
    Heliocentric, 103, 107, 109,
        110
Council of Trent, 108, 109

Culture war, 1, 3, 12, 18, 21, 67,
    96
Cybele, 158, 162–63
Damascus, 147
Diaspora, 164
Divine order, 111, 119, 121, 123,
    126, 128, 167
Domestic partner, 2–3, 38
Egypt, 138, 140, 142, 155, 157,
    159
Elitism, 103–05
Ellis, Henry Havelock, 75
Essene , 165
Essentialist, 15, 20
Estrus, 51–53
Euphrates, 140
Fausto-Sterling, Anne, 19, 29
Fellatio, 62–63
Fertility cults, 144, 145, 152,
    158–60
Gagnon, Robert, 121
Galilei, Galileo, 108
Gay Pride, 12
Gender stereotypes, 31–33
Gender variant, 2, 90, 92
Gibeah, 151–54
Greek, 106, 118, 141–43, 161,
    163–65, 167, 171–72
Hebrews, 113–14, 138–44, 147,
    151–52, 155–57, 164, 167, 173,
    191, 194–97, 199, 204, 212
Hegemony, 104–05, 128
Hellenism, 165
Heterosexism, 47–48, 217–18

Bible References,
Romans, 5, 137, 161, 167,
172
Binary view of sexuality, 14–
16, 23, 39–40, 68, 110–11,
120, 217
Biological/environmental
determinants, 15, 17–20
Bipolar view of sexuality, 31,
69–70
Brahe, Tycho, 106
Brizendine, Louanne, 20
Brown, Peter, 118
Buss, David, 20
Canaan, 141–45, 147, 152, 157,
159, 164, 191
Cezanne, 196
Chedorlaomer of Elam, 147
Closet, 2, 13, 30, 78, 105, 132,
189, 218, 221
Complentary, 110, 119, 123–27,
167
Connectivity, 49-50, 65, 70–71,
154, 172–73, 175, 187–88,
205
Constructionist, 15, 19
Copernicus, 106, 109
Corinth, 161, 169–70, 214
Corpus callosum, 36
Cosmology
Geocentric, 106, 109, 110
Heliocentric, 103, 107, 109,
110
Council of Trent, 108, 109

Culture war, 1, 3, 12, 18, 21, 67,
96
Cybele, 158, 162–63
Damascus, 147
Diaspora, 164
Divine order, 111, 119, 121, 123,
126, 128, 167
Domestic partner, 2–3, 38
Egypt, 138, 140, 142, 155, 157,
159
Elitism, 103–05
Ellis, Henry Havelock, 75
Essene , 165
Essentialist, 15, 20
Estrus, 51–53
Euphrates, 140
Fausto-Sterling, Anne, 19, 29
Fellatio, 62–63
Fertility cults, 144, 145, 152,
158–60
Gagnon, Robert, 121
Galilei, Galileo, 108
Gay Pride, 12
Gender stereotypes, 31–33
Gender variant, 2, 90, 92
Gibeah, 151–54
Greek, 106, 118, 141–43, 161,
163–65, 167, 171–72
Hebrews, 113–14, 138–44, 147,
151–52, 155–57, 164, 167, 173,
191, 194–97, 199, 204, 212
Hegemony, 104–05, 128
Hellenism, 165
Heterosexism, 47–48, 217–18

Hierarchism, 100–03

Hobah, 147

Holy Roman Empire, 109

Homonegative, 14, 61, 73, 77–83, 110, 127, 133, 170, 177

Hospitality, 146

Hypothalamus, 8, 20, 25, 26, 53–55, 88

Inter-sex, 23–27, 30, 93, 120

Israel, 103, 113, 114, 138–44, 146, 150–53, 157, 159–60, 164, 166, 169

Jebus, 151

Johnson, Justice James M., 40

Judah, 114, 164

Kepler, Johannes, 107

Kinsey, Alfred, 68–69

Krafft-Ebing, Richard, 75–76, 116

Levite, 151–54

Lifestyle, 14, 49–50, 63, 127, 135–36, 221

Lot, 145, 147, 150, 153

Luther, Martin, 109

Medes, 142

Melanchthon, Philipp, 110

Melchizedek, 148

Mendel, Gregor, 111

Mesopotamia, 140

Michelangelo, 195

Mondimore, Francis, 70, 71, 76, 79

Moses, 138, 140–41

National Coalition of Anti-Violence Programs, 1

Nazis, 193

New Guinea, 62–63

Paul, Apostle, 88, 100, 116–18, 137, 161–63, 166–73, 176, 214–15

Persians, 142

Pharisees, 166

Pheromones, 51, 53

Philo, 114–15

Procreation, 110–20

Promiscuity, 53, 77, 166

Psychopathia Sexualis, 75

Ramus, Peter, 106

Reformation, 109

Rembrandt, 196

Renaissance humanism, 109

Renoir, 196

Roman Catholic Church, 106, 109, 116, 215

Romans, 54, 117–18, 142–43, 158, 162–63, 165, 172

Rome, 162

Schmidt, Thomas, 129–30

Sex chromosome, 14, 22–23, 25, 91, 111

Sexual Inversion, 75

Sexual Orientation, 70–71

Sexual Orientation Identity, 71

Sidim, 147

Sistine Chapel, 195

Sodom, 135–39, 143–44, 147–50, 161, 176–77

Solomon, 152

Southern Presbyterian Review, 101

Stein, Edward, 24, 69

Stoicism, 114, 116, 158, 163, 165, 168

Supreme Court
  California State, 1
  United States, 194
  Washington State, 40

Symonds, John Addington, 75

Syncretism, 142, 168, 191

The Fall, 29–30, 101

The Music Man, 94

Thornwell, Rev. Dr., 101

Toevah, 156

Transgender, 39, 45, 74, 79, 194, 198, 218, 221–22

United States Constitution, 193–94

University of Padua, 108

Ur cause, 23

Venus, 158

Violence, 1, 59, 78, 82, 84, 150, 192, 218, 219

Whitefield, George, 104

Worthington, Roger L., 70

Zimah, 156

Zygote, 22